eKNOW 2021

The Thirteenth International Conference on Information, Process, and Knowledge Management

July 18 – 22, 2021

Nice, France

eKNOW 2021 Editors

Takao Terano, Chiba University of Commerce, Japan
Susan Gauch, University of Arkansas, USA

Printed from e-media with permission by:

Curran Associates, Inc.
57 Morehouse Lane
Red Hook, NY 12571

Some format issues inherent in the e-media version may also appear in this print version.

Printed with permission by Curran Associates, Inc. (2023)

International Academy, Research, and Industry Association (IARIA)
412 Derby Way
Wilmington, DE 19810

Phone: (408) 893-6407
Fax: (408) 527-6351

petre@iaria.org

Additional copies of this publication are available from:

Curran Associates, Inc.
57 Morehouse Lane
Red Hook, NY 12571 USA
Phone: 845-758-0400
Fax: 845-758-2633
Email: curran@proceedings.com
Web: www.proceedings.com

Table of Contents

eKNOW 2021

Forward

The Thirteenth International Conference on Information, Process, and Knowledge Management (eKNOW 2021) was held in Nice, France, July 18 - 22, 2021. The event was driven by the complexity of the current systems, the diversity of the data, and the challenges for mental representation and understanding of environmental structure and behavior.

Capturing, representing, and manipulating knowledge was and still is a fascinating and extremely useful challenge from both theoretical and practical perspective. Using validated knowledge for information and process management and for decision support mechanisms raised a series of questions the eKNOW 2021 conference was aimed at.

eKNOW 2021 provided a forum where researchers were able to present recent research results and new research problems and directions related to them. The topics covered aspects from knowledge fundamentals to more specialized topics such as process analysis and modeling, management systems, semantics processing and ontology.

We take this opportunity to thank all the members of the eKNOW 2021 Technical Program Committee as well as the numerous reviewers. The creation of such a broad and high-quality conference program would not have been possible without their involvement. We also kindly thank all the authors who dedicated much of their time and efforts to contribute to the eKNOW 2021. We truly believe that, thanks to all these efforts, the final conference program consists of top quality contributions.

This event could also not have been a reality without the support of many individuals, organizations, and sponsors. We are grateful to the members of the eKNOW 2021 organizing committee for their help in handling the logistics and for their work to make this professional meeting a success.

We hope that eKNOW 2021 was a successful international forum for the exchange of ideas and results between academia and industry and for the promotion of progress in knowledge management research.

eKNOW 2021 Chairs

eKNOW Steering Committee

Susan Gauch, University of Arkansas, USA

Martijn Zoet, Zuyd University of Applied Science, The Nederland

Samia Aitouche, Laboratory of Automation and Manufacturing (LAP), University Batna 2, Algeria

Eric J.H.J. Mantelaers, Zuyd University of Applied Sciences, Sittard, the Netherlands

eKNOW 2021 Advisory Committee
Roy Oberhauser, Aalen University, Germany
Nitin Agarwal, University of Arkansas at Little Rock, USA

eKNOW 2021 Publicity Chair
Alvaro Liebana, Universitat Politecnica de Valencia, Spain
Mar Parra, Universitat Politecnica de Valencia, Spain

eKNOW 2021

COMMITTEE

eKNOW Steering Committee

Susan Gauch, University of Arkansas, USA
Martijn Zoet, Zuyd University of Applied Science, The Nederland
Samia Aitouche, Laboratory of Automation and Manufacturing (LAP), University Batna 2, Algeria
Eric J.H.J. Mantelaers, Zuyd University of Applied Sciences, Sittard, the Netherlands

eKNOW 2021 Advisory Committee

Roy Oberhauser, Aalen University, Germany
Nitin Agarwal, University of Arkansas at Little Rock, USA

eKNOW 2021 Publicity Chair

Alvaro Liebana, Universitat Politecnica de Valencia, Spain
Mar Parra, Universitat Politecnica de Valencia, Spain

eKNOW 2021 Technical Program Committee

Giuseppe A. Di Lucca, University of Sannio | RCOST (Research Center on Software Technology), Italy
Rocío Abascal Mena, Universidad Autónoma Metropolitana - Cuajimalpa, Mexico City, Mexico
Raoua Abdelkhalek, LARODEC | Institut Supérieur de Gestion de Tunis | Université de Tunis, Tunisia
Marie-Hélène Abel, Sorbonne universités - Université de technologie de Compiègne, France
Awais Adnan, Institute of Management Sciences Peshawar, Pakistan
Nitin Agarwal, University of Arkansas at Little Rock, USA
Maroi Agrebi, Université Polytechnique Hauts-de-France, France
Joyce Aguiar, Center for Psychology at University of Porto (CPUP), Portugal
Abdullah Fathi Ahmed, University Paderborn, Germany
Samia Aitouche, University Batna 2, Algeria
Arnulfo Alanis, Instituto Tecnológico de Tijuana | Tecnológico Nacional de México, Mexico
Abdulwahab Alazeb, University of Arkansas, USA
Mohammed Alqahtani, University of Arkansas, USA
Mohammad T. Alshammari, University of Hail, Saudi Arabia
Bráulio Alturas, Instituto Universitário de Lisboa (ISCTE-IUL) | ISTAR-Iscte (University Institute of Lisbon), Portugal
Gil Ad Ariely, Lauder School of Government, Diplomacy and Strategy - Interdisciplinary Center Herzliya (IDC), Israel
Mohamed Anis Bach Tobji, ESEN – University of Manouba | LARODEC Laboratory – ISG of Tunis, Tunisia
Mário Antunes, Polytechnic of Leiria, Portugal
Michal Baczynski, University of Silesia in Katowice, Poland
Zbigniew Banaszak, Koszalin University of Technology, Poland
Basel Bani-Ismail, Oman College of Management and Technology, Oman
Peter Bellström, Karlstad University, Sweden
Asmaa Benghabrit, Moulay Ismaïl University, Meknès, Morocco

José Alberto Benítez Andrades, University of León, Spain
Julita Bermejo-Alonso, Universidad Isabel I, Spain
Carlos Bobed, University of Zaragoza, Spain
Zorica Bogdanovic, University of Belgrade, Serbia
Gregory Bourguin, LISIC | Université Littoral Côte d'Opale(ULCO), France
Loris Bozzato, FBK-Irst | Fondazione Bruno Kessler, Trento, Italy
Bénédicte Bucher, University Gustave Eiffel | ENS | IGN | LaSTIG, France
Ozgu Can, Ege University, Turkey
Qiushi Cao, Swansea University, UK
Massimiliano Caramia, University of Rome "Tor Vergata", Italy
Vítor Carvalho, 2Ai-EST-IPCA / Algoritmi Research Center - Minho University, Portugal
Dickson K.W. Chiu, The University of Hong Kong, Hong Kong
Ritesh Chugh, Central Queensland University, Australia
Anacleto Correia, Naval Academy, Portugal
Miguel Couceiro, University of Lorraine | CNRS | Inria Nancy G.E. | Loria, France
Juan Pablo D'Amato, Universidad Nacional del Centro de la PRov (UNCPBA) / CONICET, Argentina
Anca Daniela Ionita, University Politehnica of Bucharest, Romania
Gustavo de Assis Costa, Federal Institute of Education, Science and Technology of Goiás, Brazil / LIAAD - INESC TEC, Portugal
Joaquim De Moura, University of A Coruña, Spain
Andrea De Salve, University of Palermo, Italy
Cláudio de Souza Baptista, University of Campina Grande, Brazil
Sylvie Despres, Université Sorbonne Paris Nord, France
Vasiliki Diamantopoulou, University of the Aegean, Greece
Mihaela Dinsoreanu, Technical University of Cluj-Napoca, Romania
Tomasz Dudek, Maritime University of Szczecin, Poland
Tygran Dzhuguryan, Maritime University of Szczecin, Poland
Tome Eftimov, Jožef Stefan Institute, Ljubljana, Slovenia / Stanford University, Palo Alto, USA
Kemele M. Endris, L3S Research Center, Hannover, Germany
Amélia Ferreira da Silva, Centre for Organizational and Social Studies of Porto Polytechnic, Portugal
Joan Francesc Fondevila, Universitat de Girona / Universitat Pompeu Fabra, Spain
Igor Garcia Ballhausen Sampaio, Instituto de Computação (UFF), Brazil
Susan Gauch, University of Arkansas, USA
Dipesh Gautam, Institute for Intelligent Systems (IIS) | The University of Memphis, USA
James Geller, New Jersey Institute of Technology, USA
Alfonso González Briones, University of Salamanca, Spain
Malika Grim-Yefsah, University Gustave Eiffel | ENSG (Ecole Nationale des sciences géographique - Géomatique), France
Markus Grube, VOQUZ IT Solutions GmbH, Germany
Teresa Guarda, Universidad Estatal Peninsula Santa Elena - UPSE / Universidad de las Fuerzas Armadas – ESPE / ALGORITMI Research Centre | ESPE | UPSE, Ecuador
Michael Guckert, Technische Hochschule Mittelhessen, Germany
Carolina Guerini, Cattaneo University Castellanza (Varese) / Sda Bocconi, Milan, Italy
Barbara Guidi, University of Pisa, Italy
Gunadi Gunadi, Gajayana University, Malang, Indonesia
Juncal Gutiérrez-Artacho, Universidad de Granada, Spain
Mounira Harzallah, LS2N | University of Nantes, France
Stijn Hoppenbrouwers, HAN University of Applied Sciences, Arnhem / Radboud University, Nijmegen,

Rúben Pereira, ISCTE, Portugal
Adriano Peron, University of Napoli "Federico II", Italy
Salviano Pinto Soares, University of Trás-os-Montes and Alto Douro (UTAD), Portugal
Rodica Potolea, Technical University of Cluj-Napoca, Romania
Adam Przybylek, Gdansk University of Technology, Poland
Saqib Qamar, Huazhong University of Science and Technology (HUST), China
Paulo Quaresma, University of Évora, Portugal
Lukasz Radlinski, West Pomeranian University of Technology in Szczecin, Poland
Arsénio Reis, Universidade de Trás-os-Montes e Alto Douro, Portugal
Simona Riurean, University of Petrosani, Romania
Irene Rivera-Trigueros, University of Granada, Spain
Mário Rodrigues, University of Aveiro, Portugal
Polina Rozenshtein, Aalto University, Helsinki, Finland
Inès Saad, Amiens Business School & University Picardie Jules Verne, France
Tanik Saikh, Indian Institute of Technology Patna, India
Omar Salman, University of Arkansas, USA
Virginie Sans, INRISA/IRISA Université of Rennes 1, France
Lalia Saoudi, Msila University, Algeria
Antonio Sarasa Cabezuelo, Universidad Complutense de Madrid, Spain
Domenico Fabio Savo, Università degli Studi di Bergamo, Italy
Erwin Schaumlechner, DS Development GmbH (part of the HRS group), Astria
Hartmut Schweizer, Institute for Applied Computer Science - TU Dresden, Germany
Filippo Sciarrone, ROMA TRE University, Italy
Houcine Senoussi, Quartz laboratory - EISTI, Cergy, France
Luciano Serafini, FBK - Fondazione Bruno Kessler, Italy
Nuno Silva, ISEP - IPP (School of Engineering - Polytechnic of Porto), Portugal
Andrzej M.J. Skulimowski, AGH University of Science and Technology, Krakow, Poland
Koen Smit, Hogeschool Utrecht -Institute for ICT, Netherlands
Christophe Soares, Universidade Fernando Pessoa, Portugal
Darielson Souza, Federal University of Ceará (UFC), Brazil
Gautam Srivastava, Brandon University, Canada
Deborah Stacey, University of Guelph, Canada
Efstathios Stamatatos, University of the Aegean, Greece
Abel Suing, Universidad Técnica Particular de Loja, Ecuador
Marta Silvia Tabares, Universidad EAFIT, Medellín, Colombia
Nelson Tenório, UniCesumar, Brazil
Takao Terano, Chiba University of Commerce / Tokyo Institute of Technology / University of Tsukuba, Japan
Giorgio Terracina, University of Calabria, Italy
Michele Tomaiuolo, Università di Parma, Italy
Christos Troussas, Department of Informatics - University of Piraeus, Greece
Esteban Vázquez Cano, Universidad Nacional de Educación a Distancia (UNED), Spain
Marco Viviani, University of Milano-Bicocca, Italy
Hans Weigand, Tilburg University, Netherlands
Rihito Yaegashi, Kagawa University, Japan
Zurinahni Zainol, Universiti Sains Malaysia, Malaysia
Brahmi Zaki, Taibah University, KSA
Cecilia Zanni-Merk, INSA Rouen Normandie, France

Copyright Information

Myoko Model for Balancing Infectious Disease Control and Local Economy

Hideyuki Nagai
Kyoto Arts and Crafts University
Kyoto, Japan
email: nagai-h@g.kyobi.ac.jp

Setsuya Kurahashi
University of Tsukuba
Tokyo, Japan
email: kurahashi.setsuya.gf@u.tsukuba.ac.jp

***Abstract*—Under the situation where the resolution of 2019 novel coronavirus diseases (COVID-19) cannot be foreseen, tourism locations have continued to be exposed to the risk that receive intermittent influxes of people from other regions. Therefore, it is an urgent issue to establish countermeasures for accepting tourists. Based on this background, this study designed an agent-based model that can simulates a spreading infection process, brought by a continuous influx of tourists, among regional residents. This study compared the COVID-19 control measures in tourism locations by simulation experiments. As a result, it was found that certain effects can be expected from active epidemiological investigation. Greater effects can also be expected from the regular testing of tourism business employees, but large-scale testing is currently a major barrier. While the introduction of contact tracing apps is effective as a countermeasure therefore, there is a need for further improvement.**

Index Terms*—*COVID-19, agent-based simulation, epidemic model, tourism, policy science

I. Introduction

On October 1, 2020, in view of the governmental update that the situation of COVID-19 infections in Japan was under control, the "Go To Travel" campaign was executed in full with the aim of economic stimulation in tourism areas by promoting consumption [1]. After that, it was not until the arrival of the worst third wave ever is clarified at the end of December that the tourism promotion established by the directive to "make Japan better through travel" had been not completely canceled. Elsewhere, preliminary calculations were announced stating that the gross domestic product (GDP) for the full year of 2020 had decreased by 4.8% because of COVID-19 and that economic losses were expected to reach 30 trillion yen [2]. The impact on the tourism industry, in particular, is far-reaching, including not only travel agencies and accommodation businesses but also land, sea, and air transport; the restaurant industry; and consumer goods businesses, which are crucial to the economies of many regions. For example, a preliminary calculation of economic losses in Okinawa due to the reduction in tourists was 186.7 billion yen for the February-May period [3]. Total domestic travel and tourism expenditure in 2019 including inbound tourism was 27.9 trillion yen [4], so there were serious concerns that the "evaporation" of the tourism demand supporting regional economies would cause critical disruption thereof. Therefore, this study models the spread of COVID-19 infection in tourism locations and compares the effects of hypothetical prevention and control measures to find feasible, effective, astute infection prevention and control measures with consideration for the effects both on those directly involved in the target regions and on others. The purpose of this study is not to discuss the superiority or inferiority between a bottom-up approach in terms of personal behavior, such as avoiding the three Cs (closed spaces, crowded places, and close-contact settings) and voluntarily restricting movement, and a top-down approach in terms of strong government restrictions, such as the declaration of a state of emergency. Rather, this study examines the idea of infection prevention and control measures that enable the continuous growth of the entire region, without bound by such categories.

A. COVID-19 agent-based simulations

Even with the negative impacts of COVID-19 infections around the world, we have acquired greater expertise. Accordingly, several researchers are working on modeling social systems that include non-linear interaction to create simulations for policy-making support toward the prediction of infection expansion in the future, which is almost impossible by intuition alone, to resolve the situation. Agent-based models excel at the manifestation of effects through micro-level behavioral changes among individual citizens as specific intervention measures against infection, as well as at operability based on intervention scenario finding. Therefore, they are used with existing infectious diseases, such as smallpox [5] [6] [7], measles [8] [9], Zika fever [10], Ebola hemorrhagic fever [10] [11], and rubella [12]. As for the proposed COVID-19 simulations, most are based on macro-scale mathematical models including the studies, but there are also some interesting agent-based models. Ferguson et al. [13] reports that non-medical intervention, such as wider social distancing, home isolation, and home quarantine throughout the UK and the United States may mitigate the spread of the infection to some degree, but as long as there is no prevention system, such as a vaccine or antiviral drug, pressure on medical resources is unavoidable, and large numbers of fatalities are likely. Based on this report, the UK government shifted immediately from its initial mass immunization strategy to strict intervention measures to ensure social distancing. Silva et al. [14] simulated not only the epidemiological dynamics but also an estimation of the economic effect of various intervention scenarios with regard to ensuring social distancing and demonstrated that where a lockdown is unfeasible because of the scale of economic impact, a combination of the use of face masks and partial isolation is more realistic. Aleta et al. [15] constructed an agent-based model based on census research and movement data in the greater Boston area and demonstrated that by means of testing, contact tracing, and home quarantine after a period of strict social distancing, it was possible to resume economic activity while protecting the health system. D'Orazio et al. [16] suggested that a reduction of virus spreading in public buildings "emerges" from individuals' protection measures, such as facial masking, by using an agent-based model which can jointly simulate people's movement and virus transmission . Then, D'Orazio et al. [17] suggested that such individuals' protection measures are also keys to sustainable economic activities in touristic urban areas, by a similar approach.

B. *Summary of related studies and positioning of this study*

These studies demonstrate that the use of an agent-based model is possible but do not sufficiently verify the effects of non-medical interventions with attention to the heterogeneity of residents' daily lives and their close relations to these interventions when a vaccine or antiviral drug is not available. Further, there are also not adequate spatial or temporal estimates of regional characteristics with regard to countermeasures and their effects on parts of tourism locations, for instance, that receive intermittent influxes of people from other regions. Therefore, this study explores feasible, effective non-medical infection prevention and control measures using a COVID-19 agent-based model with the assumption of specific tourism locations. The remainder of this paper is organized as follows. Section 2 describes the COVID-19 agent-based experimental model which can evaluate various non-medical infection prevention and control measures. Section 3 explains the experimental scenarios assuming the implementation of the measures to prevent and control infection. Section 4 discusses the experimental results. Section 5 concludes this paper by describing the research achievements.

II. COVID-19 INFECTION MODEL FOR TOURISM LOCATIONS

As an expansion of existing infectious disease studies in which validity evaluations have been conducted for the transition of infection—namely an Ebola hemorrhagic fever model [11] and a rubella model [12] —a COVID-19 model [18] was constructed for Myoko City in Niigata Prefecture. The model uses restored population data created with the household composition restoration method [19], a method of restoring population data so that it conforms to various published statistics (e.g., national census, demographics, business/industry statistics, etc.), which is optimized using simulated annealing with the errors in the recreated data (restored data) collation after calculation as the objective function. This restored population data includes the longitude and latitude of the location of the household and its members' gender, age, employment status, type of industry, scale of business, etc. Using this data, FIG. 1 shows the population distribution of the target city. With attention to place names, terrain, road connections, school district divisions, etc., the town is divided into nine zones as shown in the figure. The valley-shaped terrain is traversed by a local railroad, with residential areas distributed next to the line. Most of the population is concentrated in the north, forming an urban area integrated with the center of Joetsu City, where the terminal station is located. In addition, there are many ski and hot spring resort areas at the foot of the mountains in the southeast and southwest.

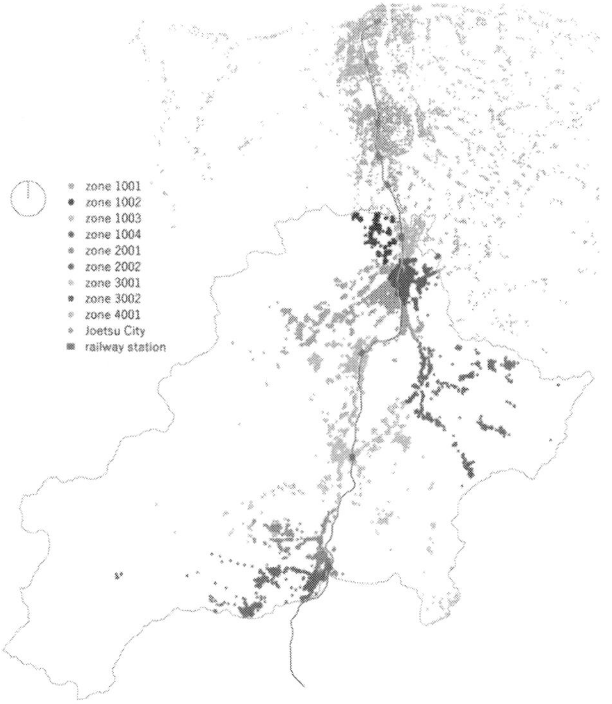

FIG. 1. POPULATION DISTRIBUTION OF MYOKO CITY

The total population based on the restored population data is approximately 31,500 people, but for ease of calculation, it was rounded down to approximately 1/5 in the model. However, the ratios of household composition, number of households, population per zone, etc. were set according to the actual population composition (see TABLE I).

TABLE I. POPUPATION COMPOSITION

	actual city	model
population	31,560	6,000
number of households	11,854	2,295
average household size	2.66	2.61
0-29 years old (young)	25.3%	25.0%
29-64 years old (adults)	44.6%	45.7%
65- years old (elderly)	30.3%	29.3%
average age	50.4	-

TABLE II shows the model household composition. Actually, infection spreads through diverse and complex routes, based on people's heterogeneity, such as age and lifestyle. Therefore, by implementing such demographic information in the model, it is possible to simulate the complex behavior of infection.

TABLE II. MODEL HOUSEHOLD COMPOSITION

househould composition	households	population
single (adult)	200	200
single (elderly)	300	300
couple (adults)	125	250
couple (elderly)	400	800
couple + one child	300	900
couple + two children	250	1,000
one parent + one child	250	500
couple + parents	50	200
couple + onw parent	100	300
couple + one child + parents	40	200
couple + two children + parents	100	600
couple + one child + one parent	150	600
couple + two children + one parent	30	150
total	2,295	6,000

A. Behavior of citizen

Resident agents in the model who commuted to work or school were set based on restored population data, municipal public information regarding public facilities, tourism guides, etc. 66% of young people—that is, 17% of the total population—attended childcare facilities or school. There were 10 childcare facilities, nine elementary schools, and four junior high schools in the city, as well as one senior high school in the city and four outside. 70% of the remaining young people, 80% of adults, and 20% of the elderly—that is, 48% of the total population—were workers. This corresponds to a 48.3% total employment ratio in the restored population data. TABLE III shows the employment locations of workers.

TABLE III. EMPLOYMENT LOCATIONS OF WORKERS

employment locations	ratio
hospitality industry	**15%**
local shop of 11	
tourism spot of 5	
large hotel of 4	
small hotel of 10	
night spot of 3	
education	**3%**
childcare facility of 10	
elementary school of 9	
junior high school of 4	
senior high school of 5 (1 in the city and 4 outside)	
medical and welfare	**3%**
large hospital of 2	
nursing home of 8	
other employment location (in the city)	**39%**
other employment location (outside city)	**39%**

The area has many popular tourist locations, and the ratio of employees at wholesale or retail businesses, accommodation, or food service businesses and daily life-related services and entertainment businesses was 26%. Reflecting this, the ratio of workers in actual customer-facing roles was set at 15%, just over half. These employees in the hospitality industry are considered to have contact with tourists, the main topic of this study. In the hospitality industry, local shops are established near local railway stations in the model area, with their employees set as residents of nearby zones. These local shops refer to retail stores, such as supermarkets and restaurants that are mainly served to local residents. However, tourists also use the two in the south, near the resort areas in the southeast and southwest. Tourism spots, hotels, and night spots are located in the southeastern and southwestern resort areas, with the majority of their employees living in nearby zones. Some of the resident agents other than workers at local shops and residents of nursing homes go shopping at local stores neighboring to their residential zones after work or school. Finally, all resident agents other than hospital inpatients go home.

FIG. 2 shows the household and facility distribution in the model space.

B. Progress of infection and symptoms

In each round of simulations, infection was modeled on localized interaction among resident agents. Resident agents were activated sequentially in random order; in the case of contact with other resident agents who were infected on the model plane, the contact ratio cr was generated probabilistically because of interaction, with infection occurring in line with the transmission ratio tr. The infection ratio ir, the probability of the occurrence of infection, was defined as follows.

$$ir = cr * tr \tag{1}$$

This infection probability defines how much a nearby infected person infects each agent. This probability was set so that the expected value would be the same based on the basic reproduction number R0 (2.5) of COVID-19 and the estimated contact time of the inhabitants per day at each contact scene such as workplace, school, home, and so on.

Based on reports of detailed analyses of the infection prevalence of COVID-19 [20] [21], the following process of the progress of symptoms was defined. The incubation period is 5 days following infection, but the person can infect others by the third day even during this period. On the sixth day, when the incubation period has ended, symptoms, such as fever, coughing, and diarrhea occur in most infected people. After the fever, the basic scenario included a 50% probability of home isolation after visiting a doctor. The remaining 50% of infected people are either essentially asymptomatic or have minor symptoms, so they continue to go to work or school while self-medicating with febrifuges, etc. After the symptoms have continued for 4 days or more, infected people see a doctor and undergo a polymerase chain reaction (PCR) test with the results confirmed the following day, leading to hospitalization if the results are positive. Regarding the actual number of fatalities, because the estimated number of infected people has been drastically reduced, the test supplementary ratio was set at half (50%). Further, 20 days after infection, 20% of infected people become seriously ill and are hospitalized even without having seen a doctor in advance. Also, by 41 days

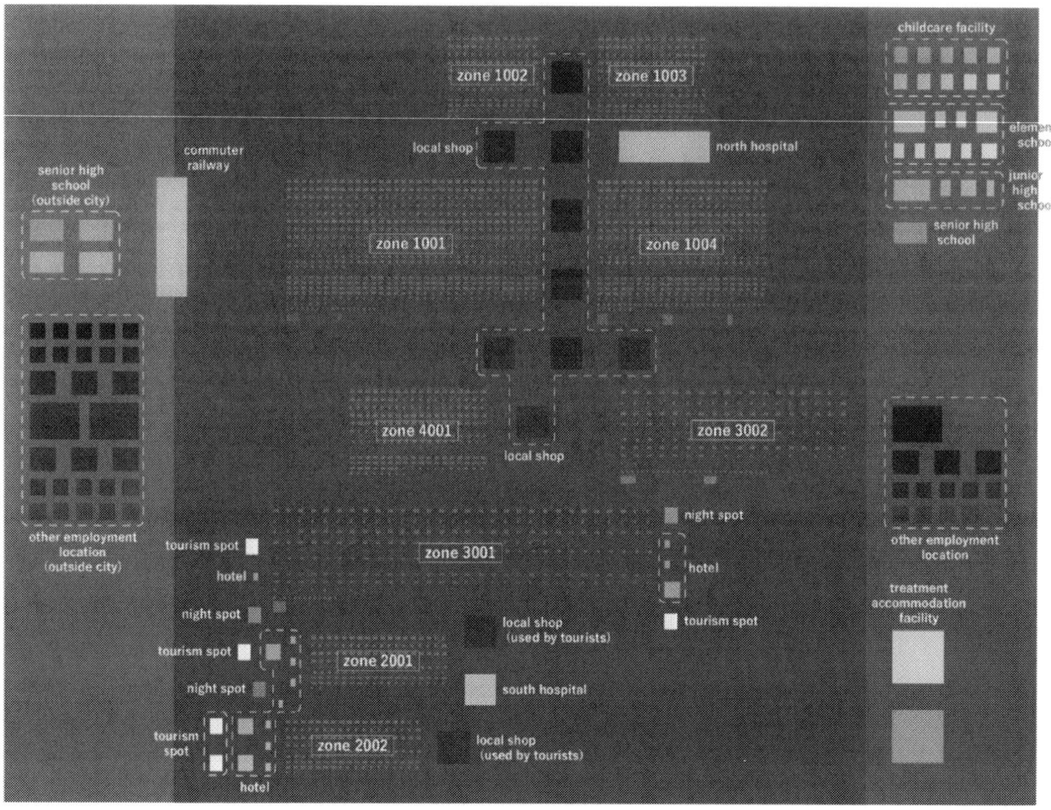

FIG. 2. HOUSEHOLD AND FACILITY DISTRIBUTION

after infection of those hospitalized with serious symptoms, fatalities comprise 0.06% of young people, 0.21% of adults, and 1.79% of the elderly. The mildly ill recover by 27 days after infection and the surviving seriously ill by 49 days after infection, achieving temporary immunity.

III. ESTIMATING EFFECTS OF INFECTION PREVENTION AND CONTROL MEASURES

For this model, simulation scenarios for infection prevention and control measures for the entire region were set, including the hospitality industries that may be used by infected tourists. Table IV shows the settings of the scenarios. There are a total of 12 scenarios, defined by whether to accept tourists, infection control at shops, nightspots, tourist spots, quarantine facilities for infected people, degree of tracking close contacts, frequency of PCR tests, and so on.

These infection prevention and control scenarios are roughly divided into four; social distancing (scenarios S1-S2), contact tracing (scenarios S3-S4), regular testing for high-risk workers (scenarios S5-S7), and combination of contact tracing and regular testing (scenarios S8-S11). In Scenario B0, tourists are not accepted by the hospitality industry overall, and there is no influx of infections, but one resident is infected at the initial point. In Scenario B1, tourists are accepted by the hospitality industry overall, and one infectious tourist per week enters. In Scenario S1, local residents' visit to local shops is reduced by 75%; in Scenario S2 local residents' visit to local shops is reduced by 75% and contact between hospitality industry workers and tourists is reduced by 75%. In scenarios S3 and S4, local residents' visit to local shops is reduced by 75%, contact between hospitality industry workers and tourists is reduced by 75%, forward tracking (once) of persons in close contact and PCR tests are implemented, and those testing positive are isolated at a treatment accommodation facility. Here, a forward tracking of persons in close contact with the objective of preventing further infection expansion is implemented by tracking tests, e.g., via interviews and the contact app COCOA, [22], etc. for persons in post-infection close contact with people who have tested positive for infection. The tracking ratio is defined as the discovery ratio of persons in close contact and the infection source. In scenarios S5-S7, local residents' visit to local shops is reduced by 75%, contact between hospitality industry workers and tourists is reduced by 75%, workers undergo regular PCR testing, and those testing positive are isolated at a treatment accommodation facility. In scenarios S8-S11, local residents' visit to local shops is reduced by 75%, contact between hospitality industry workers and tourists is reduced by 75%, forward tracking of persons in close contact and PCR tests are implemented, workers undergo regular PCR testing, and those testing positive are isolated at a treatment accommodation facility.

TABLE IV. SIMULATION SCENARIOS FOR INFECTION PREVENTION AND CONTROL MEASURES

scenario	tourists	influx of infections	local shop	hotels	night spots	tourism spots	isolation	tracking	regular testing
B0	not accepted	one resident	100%	-	-	-	-	-	-
B1	accepted	one per week	100%	100%	100%	100%	-	-	-
S1	accepted	one per week	25%	100%	100%	100%	-	-	-
S2	accepted	one per week	25%	25%	25%	25%	-	-	-
S3	accepted	one per week	25%	25%	25%	25%	Yes	forward 50%	-
S4	accepted	one per week	25%	25%	25%	25%	Yes	forward 80%	-
S5	accepted	one per week	25%	25%	25%	25%	Yes	-	every 2 wks 50%
S6	accepted	one per week	25%	25%	25%	25%	Yes	-	every 2 wks 75%
S7	accepted	one per week	25%	25%	25%	25%	Yes	-	every 2 wks 100%
S8	accepted	one per week	25%	25%	25%	25%	Yes	forward 50%	every 2 wks 50%
S9	accepted	one per week	25%	25%	25%	25%	Yes	forward 50%	every 2 wks 75%
S10	accepted	one per week	25%	25%	25%	25%	Yes	forward 80%	every 2 wks 50%
S11	accepted	one per week	25%	25%	25%	25%	Yes	forward 80%	every 2 wks 75%

IV. EXPERIMENT RESULTS

Each simulation scenario was implemented 100 times. The infection prevention and control measures were evaluated by the average of the peak number of people hospitalized with serious symptoms, which is the major serious impact on medical resources. The results are shown in FIG. 3.

The average number of mildly infected persons was 14.3 (B1) at the maximum and 2.4 (B0) at the minimum. The infection process has an incubation period of 5 days and a recovery time of 27 days, so the number of new positive cases per day ranges from 0.65 to 0.11, which is 11 to 2 per 100,000. In Tokyo, where the infection was spreading at that time, the number was 14 to 2 per 100,000. Therefore, the average results of the simulation are almost the same as the actual values of Tokyo.

The effects of the voluntary infection prevention and control measures (Scenarios S1 and S2) endorsed as the new normal and new travel etiquettes were, in comparison with the peak number of patients hospitalized with serious symptoms with canceling tourism (Scenario B0), 738% if tourists are accepted without countermeasures (Scenario B1), 385% with reduction in residents' visit to local shops (Scenario S1), and 148% with thorough reduction in contact between workers and tourists (Scenario S2).

Scenarios S3 and S4 were 114% with a forward one-time tracking ratio of 50% (Scenario S3) and 106% with a forward one-time tracking ratio of 80% (Scenario S4) in comparison with Scenario B0. These scenarios include reducing a visit to local shops, thorough reduction in contact, and the isolation of infected people, the effects of composite prevention and control measures also including the implementation of tracking tests for persons in close contact.

On the other hand, the combined spread prevention measures (scenarios S5 to S7), which carry out regular virus tests on hospitality employees who may come into contact with tourists, reduced the number of infected people. The results are 93% with a 50% test ratio every 2 weeks (Scenario S5), 71% with a 75% test ratio every 2 weeks (Scenario S6), and 63% with a 100% test ratio every 2 weeks (Scenario S7).

Furthermore, the combined spread prevention measures (scenarios S8 to S11), which carries out both follow-up inspections of close contacts and regular virus inspections of hospitality employees, effectively reduced the number of infected persons. In these scenarios, the results were 67% with a forward one-time tracking ratio of 50% and a 50% test ratio every 2 weeks (Scenario S8), 56% with a forward one-time tracking ratio of 50% and a 75% test ratio every 2 weeks (Scenario S9), 59% with a forward one-time tracking ratio of 80% and a 50% test ratio every 2 weeks (Scenario S9), and 53% with a forward one-time tracking ratio of 80% and a 75% test ratio every 2 weeks (Scenario S11).

V. DISCUSSION

The experiment results demonstrate that there are limited effects even when changes are made to local residents and tourist lifestyles or to hospitality business service methods in regions, such as tourism locations that are intermittently visited by infected people.

As a result of evaluating the effect of active epidemiological survey, for prospective surveys and tests in persons close contact with those testing positive, it was found that hospitalized patients can be kept at about the same as that of prohibiting tourism.

The discovery of infected people by means of substantial PCR testing at the regional level is expected to have an effect, but uniform testing for all regional residents is limited. So the effects of regular PCR tests were evaluated with regard to workers in contact with tourists in commercial stores, tourism spots, accommodation facilities, and entertainment districts. As a result, it was found that infection control effects were greater than that of prohibiting tourism. However, in Japan, the maximum testing capacity per day for PCR tests as of May 2021 is approximately 0.16% (203,477 tests [23] out of 126.5 million people), which is far below the testing standard of the scenarios where major effects were observed.

Regular PCR tests for just hospitality industry workers have an effect, but there are various barriers to realize it. So the effects of the combination of regular PCR tests and active epidemiological survey were evaluated. As a result, it was found that major effects on infection control were observed while reducing number of tests. However, such surveys also require the construction of systems that enable large-scale information collection and processing across large areas and over a long period of time. Therefore, the capacity is limited when relying only on the efforts of public health center workers, for example, and if infection expansion continues and

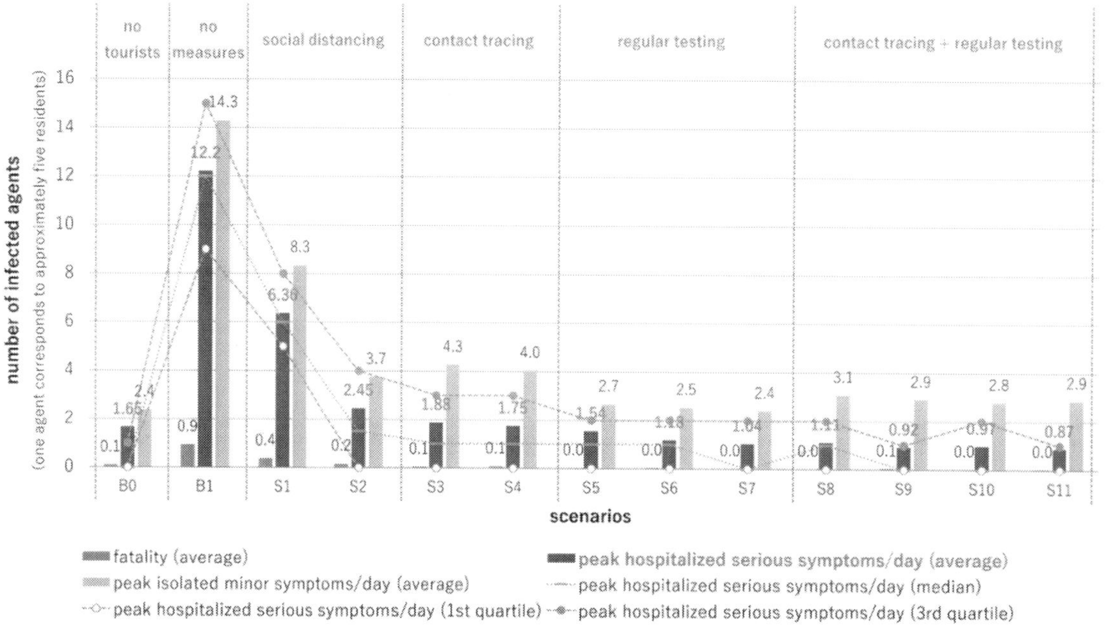

FIG. 3. COMPARISON OF THE EFFECTIVENESS OF PREVENTIVE MEASURES

the labor required for the survey expands likewise, the survey system and even the medical system are at risk of collapse. Therefore, the construction of comprehensive survey systems that utilize information technology, including tracking persons in close contact by means of mobile phones, etc., is expected to have a major effect on the prevention of increased infection. To this end, in addition to designing a top-down system, the key is to increase the users of COCOA and other contact tracing apps to contribute to a bottom-up system. As targets for infection prevention and control, from now on, the app usage ratio should be 80% both in the region and among visitors, and the delays between positive confirmation, app registration, and notifying persons in close contact should each be shortened as much as possible.

In Japan, in addition to the continuing low capacity for PCR testing, there are major barriers to access to tests for residents, namely decisions made by doctors and the fact that voluntary testing is not covered by insurance [24], so sufficient testing systems have not been constructed for the implementation of any of the infection prevention and control measures described above. Regardless of whether or not the region is a characteristic tourism location, for residents who want to be tested after becoming aware that they may have been infected or that they may infect others, testing is to be implemented without delay, allowing for subclinical cases, to identify infected people. Through the construction of a system with bottom-up aspects of this kind, for the first time, it will be possible to accurately grasp the infection situation, the highest priority for public health. This pandemic is still full of uncertainties regarding, e.g., the development and distribution schedule for a vaccine, the mutation of the virus, and the pathology of after-effects. Therefore, it is desirable to invest pertinent resources promptly to minimize the damage to citizens' health and to the economy to the extent possible.

VI. CONCLUSION

With the objective of evaluating the COVID-19 infection prevention and control measures in tourism locations, this study compared 11 types of infection prevention and control measures by constructing simulation models in imitation of specific tourism locations. As part of public health policy to prevent and control infection, analyses of tourist contact reduction measures, active epidemiological investigation—prospective tracking tests for people in close contact with those testing positive for infection, and regular PCR testing for tourism business employees were conducted. As a result of the simulated experiments, while there are certain effects from measures to reduce contact, it was found that the effects are limited in the case of a continuous influx of infected people to tourism locations. While certain effects can be expected from active epidemiological investigation; while greater effects can also be expected from the regular PCR testing of tourism business employees, this requires large-scale testing, which is currently a major barrier. While the introduction of contact tracing apps is effective as a countermeasure therefore, there is a need for further improvement in the registration delay time and the implementation systems for prompt testing after notification.

REFERENCES

[1] Japan Tourism Agency, *Change in the treatment of Tokyo in Go To Travel campaign (updated on September 18, 2020)*, 2020, Available at: https://biz.goto.jata-net.or.jp/info/2020091601.html. (retrieved: June 2021)

[2] Nihon Keizai Shimbun, *Real annual rate of GDP increase of 12.7% for the fourth quarter of fiscal 2020, decrease of 4.8% for the full year of 2020.* Nihon Keizai Shimbun February 15, 2021.

[3] Okinawa Times, *Economic loss of 186.7 billion yen in Okinawa.* Okinawa Times Plus April 4, 2020.

[4] Japan Tourism Agency Strategy Planning Division, *Travel/tourism consumption trend survey of 2019 annual*, 2020, Available at: https://www.mlit.go.jp/kankocho/siryou/toukei/content/001342441.pdf. (retrieved: June 2021)

[5] J. M. Epstein, D. A. Cummings, S. Chakravarty, R. M. Singha, and D. S. Burke, *Toward a Containment Strategy for Smallpox Bioterror: An Individual-Based Computational Approach.* Brookings Institution Press, 2004.

[6] J. M. Epstein, *Generative Social Science: Studies in Agent-based Computational Modeling.* Princeton University Press, 2006, vol. 13.

[7] Y. Ohkusa, "An evaluation of counter measures for smallpox outbreak using an individual based model and taking into consideration the limitation of human resources of public health workers," *Journal of health care, medicine and community*, vol. 16, no. 3, pp. 275–284, 2006.

[8] F. Liu *et al.*, "The role of vaccination coverage, individual behaviors, and the public health response in the control of measles epidemics: An agent-based simulation for California," *BMC public health*, vol. 15, no. 1, p. 447, 2015.

[9] E. Hunter, B. Mac Namee, and J. Kelleher, "An open-data-driven agent-based model to simulate infectious disease outbreaks," *PloS one*, vol. 13, no. 12, p. e0208775, 2018.

[10] S. Kurahashi, "A health policy simulation model of Ebola haemorrhagic fever and Zika fever," in *Agent and Multi-Agent Systems: Technology and Applications.* Springer, 2016, pp. 319–329.

[11] S. Kurahashi, "Agent-based health policy gaming and simulation for Ebola haemorrhagic fever," *Studies in Simulation and Gaming*, vol. 26, no. 2, pp. 52–63, 2017.

[12] S. Kurahashi, "An agent-based infectious disease model of rubella outbreaks," in *Agents and Multi-agent Systems: Technologies and Applications 2019.* Springer, 2020, pp. 237–247.

[13] N. Ferguson *et al.*, "Report 9: Impact of non-pharmaceutical interventions (NPIs) to reduce COVID19 mortality and healthcare demand," *Imperial College London*, 2020, DOI: https://doi.org/10.25561/77482.

[14] P. C. Silva *et al.*, "COVID-ABS: An agent-based model of COVID-19 epidemic to simulate health and economic effects of social distancing interventions," *Chaos, Solitons & Fractals*, vol. 139, p. 110088, 2020.

[15] A. Aleta, D. Martín-Corral, A. P. y Piontti, M. Ajelli, M. Litvinova, M. Chinazzi, N. E. Dean, M. E. Halloran, I. M. Longini Jr, S. Merler *et al.*, "Modelling the impact of testing, contact tracing and household quarantine on second waves of COVID-19," *Nature Human Behaviour*, vol. 4, no. 9, pp. 964–971, 2020.

[16] M. D'Orazio, G. Bernardini, and E. Quagliarini, "How to restart? an agent-based simulation model towards the definition of strategies for covid-19" second phase" in public buildings," *arXiv preprint arXiv:2004.12927*, 2020.

[17] M. D'Orazio, G. Bernardini, and E. Quagliarini, "Sustainable and resilient strategies for touristic cities against covid-19: an agent-based approach," *arXiv preprint arXiv:2005.12547*, 2020.

[18] S. Kurahashi, "Estimating effectiveness of preventing measures for 2019 novel coronavirus deseases (COVID-19)," *Transactions of the Japanese Society for Artificial Intelligence*, vol. 35, no. 3, pp. D-K28_1, 2020.

[19] T. Harada and T. Murata, "Reconstructing prefecture-level large-scale household composition using parallel computing," *Transactions of the Society of Instrument and Control Engineers*, vol. 54, no. 4, pp. 421–429, 2018.

[20] The Novel Coronavirus Pneumonia Emergency Response Epidemiology Team, "The epidemiological characteristics of an outbreak of 2019 novel coronavirus diseases (COVID-19) - China, 2020," *China CDC Weekly*, vol. 42, no. 2, pp. 145–151, 2020, DOI: https://doi.org/10.3760/cma.j.issn.0254-6450.2020.02.003.

[21] WHO-China Joint Mission Team, *Report of the WHO-China Joint Mission on Coronavirus Disease 2019 (COVID-19).* World Health Organization (WHO), 2020, Available at: https://www.who.int/docs/default-source/coronaviruse/who-china-joint-mission-on-covid-19-final-report.pdf. (retrieved: June 2021)

[22] Ministry of Health, Labour and Welfare, *COVID-19 Contact-Confirming Application (COCOA)*, 2020, Available at: https://www.mhlw.go.jp/stf/seisakunitsuite/bunya/cocoa_00138.html. (retrieved: June 2021)

[23] Ministry of Health, Labour and Welfare, *Novel coronavirus disease - situation in Japan*, 2021, Available at: https://www.mhlw.go.jp/stf/covid-19/kokunainohasseijoukyou.html. (retrieved: June 2021)

[24] Tokyo Metropolitan Government Bureau of Social Welfare and Public Health, *Information about novel coronavirus disease*, 2020, Available at: https://www.fukushihoken.metro.tokyo.lg.jp/smph/tthc/kansensho/singatakorona.html. (retrieved: June 2021)

An Agent-Based Model in Activity-Driven Network of COVID-19 Epidemic using Mobility and Infection Data in Tokyo 2020

Suggesting Practical Vaccine Strategies and Vaccine Passport

Kazumoto Takayanagi
Graduate School of Science and Technology
University of Tsukuba
Tokyo, Japan
e-mail: k.takayanagi1882@gmail.com

Setsuya Kurahashi
Graduate School of Science and Technology
University of Tsukuba
Tokyo, Japan
e-mail: kurahashi.setsuya.gf@u.tsukuba.ac.jp

Abstract—**In situations where the pandemic of Coronavirus Disease 2019 (COVID-19) has been destroying the daily lives of global human community, a model that reliably predicts the spread of infection within society would be extremely helpful for a variety of purposes. This paper presents an agent-based model over temporal networks that are fitted to real mobility data reported in Tokyo. The parameters of the model are inferred via approximate Bayesian computation to ensure that the model represents well the observed infection data. Through the simulations using this model, we demonstrate a comparison of the effectiveness of different vaccination strategies.**

Keywords-agent-based modeling; activity-driven network; approximate Bayesian computation; vaccination strategies; vaccine passport.

I. Introduction

Since early in 2020, the pandemic of COVID-19 has been devastating both the daily lives and the economic activities in human communities globally. For over a year, many governmental authorities have taken strong measures such as lockdowns of cities, to restrain the spread of infection of Severe Acute Respiratory Syndrome CoronaVirus 2 (SARS-CoV-2) within society. While these measures are effective in mitigating the epidemic of infection, their adverse impacts toward social and economic activities are significant. It is difficult to make political decisions that optimally balance reducing the number of infected people and maintaining social activity among individuals. Although vaccines can be a 'game-changer' in these circumstances, their supply is relatively abundant only in developed countries and has been extremely insufficient in developing nations until the middle of 2021. A social simulation model that may help predict the spread of virus infection under certain conditions would be remarkably helpful in this global context.

Agent-Based Modeling (ABM) is a method which is excellent at incorporating the heterogeneity of characteristics within agents as well as interactions and feedbacks among agents [1]. Because a well-designed ABM can serve as a tool to represent nonlinear dynamics emerging from the bottom of social system, it allows us to elucidate the mechanisms underlying complex macro phenomenon observed in society without reducing it to individual micro features. The spreading of infectious disease within society is one of the phenomena that have received a great deal of attention from researchers devoted to this modeling [2]. Many studies have already been performed on the COVID-19 pandemic using this method for a variety of purposes [3-10]. We have developed an agent-based model validated with observed infection data to help predict the courses of the COVID-19 epidemic under various conditions.

Temporal network is a modeling framework in which we explicitly consider the times when edges are active between nodes [11]. Because specifying who is connected to whom at each time is a significant determinant of how epidemic process behave within a society, temporal networks have frequently been utilized in models that aim at representing in detail the spreading process of infectious disease [12]. The present paper focuses on a particular kind of temporal network that is called *activity-driven network* where each node is characterized by an activity rate a [13][14]. In activity-driven networks, this activity rate a encodes the probability of the node to generate links with other nodes at each timestep. While the behavioral restrictions have been repeatedly imposed on individuals in the pandemic situation, this framework of activity-driven network allows us to represent the successive changes of people's real activities in the model. To the best of our knowledge, we are the first to have validated the modeling of activity-driven networks by fitting agents' activities to actual community mobility data provided by Google [15] in order to examine the epidemic of COVID-19 over temporal networks.

Since the ABM is an attempt to model complex phenomena with a high degree of freedom, it is crucial to validate the modeling using observed data so that the modeling is considered as reliable. Parameter inference that fits the parameters of a model to actual data allows us to exploit ABMs for trustworthy analysis. However, ABMs do not have explicit forms for their likelihood functions due to the intrinsic complexity of ABM [16]. *Approximate Bayesian Computation* (ABC) is a flexible Likelihood-Free Inference (LFI) method for posterior and is one of the widely accepted approaches to infer the parameters of ABM [17][18]. The parameter inference in ABC is to infer the values of parameters that yield a simulator's output that agrees with observed data. The ABC algorithm for parameter inference of ABM is typically as follows [16][19],

1. Sample parameter θ_i from prior $\pi(\theta)$.
2. Simulate $f(\theta_i)$ by running simulator f with θ_i.
3. Reject θ_i based on the metrics of comparison between $f(\theta_i)$ and the observed data X.
4. Repeat 1-3 until a sufficiently large number of samples are obtained.

We infer the parameters of our ABM by ABC using the observed infection data so that the model is sufficiently validated.

The contributions of this paper are threefold. Firstly, we have developed an ABM over activity-driven networks where agents' activities are fitted to actual mobility data, which enables us to investigate the effects of governmental restrictions imposed on people's behavior. We also incorporate the heterogeneity of immune response to viruses among agents, a key factor in the virus spreading process. Secondly, we have inferred the posterior distributions of the model parameters via approximate Bayesian computation using real infection data. Thus, our model with estimated parameter values represents the observed data accurately and can serve as a reliable tool to predict the spread of infection under various conditions. Finally, we have demonstrated several promising vaccination strategies through the 'would-be' simulations carried out under virtual conditions, which shows a comparison of the effectiveness between those strategies. In addition, we investigated the possibility of 'vaccine passport' scenario via simulations that focus on the association between social activity and vaccination as well as the effects of vaccination on the epidemic.

The remainder of this paper is constructed as follows. Section II describes related work. In Section III, we describe our agent-based model in detail. In Section IV, the results of simulations by our model are demonstrated using various graphs and some implications are derived from the results. In Section V, several vaccine strategies are presented and the comparison of effectiveness between those strategies is provided through simulations. Finally, in Section VI, conclusion of this paper and future work are described.

II. RELATED WORK

Significant efforts have already been devoted to modeling the spreading process of COVID-19 to forecast the epidemic of the viruses within community as well as to suggest effective measures to prevent the pandemic. Hoertel et al. [3] proposed an ABM of the epidemic of COVID-19 in France that is well fitted to observed data in order to predict the potential impact of certain post-lockdown measures on the spreading of the epidemic. Rossetti et al. [4] presented an agent-based framework that organizes the population in five statuses and incorporates activity-driven networks to simulate the effects of public interventions on the unfolding of epidemic. Silva et al. [5] developed an ABM of the COVID-19 epidemic to assess the social and economic effects of certain scenarios with several social-distancing interventions. Aleta et al. [6] built a detailed agent-based model of SARS-CoV-2 transmission in the Boston metropolitan area using mobility data to examine the impact of testing, contact tracing, and household quarantine on the epidemic. Nishi et al. [7] used agent-based simulations of a network-based infection model to investigate network intervention strategies for mitigating the spread of infection while maintaining economic activities. Kano et al. [8] proposed an agent-based model of COVID-19 that accounts for economic activities and examined the trade-off between health and economic damage through the simulations. Li et al. [9] used large-scale agent-based simulations to study the effectiveness of a nationwide vaccine campaign under different conditions related to vaccine efficacies and other factors. Moghadas et al. [10] developed an agent-based model of COVID-19 transmission to compare the impact of two different vaccination strategies, i.e., to vaccinate more individuals with the first dose and delay the second dose, or to continue with the recommended two-dose series.

To the best of our knowledge, few prior studies have provided an agent-based model integrated with activity-driven networks fitted to both mobility and infection data, which we propose in this paper.

III. MODEL

We generate an artificial society composed of N agents which represent individuals socially associated with others in temporal networks, which we describe in detail below.

A. Agent-based SEIR model

While the epidemic of virus infection in this society spreads over time, each agent belongs to one of four statuses, i.e., Susceptible, Exposed, Infectious, or Recovered (SEIR) at each timestep $t = 1, \ldots, T$.

A susceptible agent linked in a network with an infectious agent at timestep t gets infected according to the probability P that is obtained by multiplying the transmission rate Tr and the susceptibility s of the susceptible agent. P is calculated as,

$$P = Tr \cdot s. \tag{1}$$

An infected agent does not transmit the viruses to others during the incubation period and remains exposed. By the probability α, an exposed agent becomes an infectious one who may infect others with the viruses. An infectious agent recovers by the probability β and acquires continuous immunity to COVID-19. A recovered agent no longer transmits the viruses to others.

Since the strength of the immune response to viruses varies from person to person [20], our model presumes the heterogeneity of susceptibility to viral infection among agents. A susceptibility value s is assigned to each agent according to the Gaussian distribution, which is supposed plausible in this case [20].

B. Activity-driven networks fitted to real data

Activity-driven networks in which agents interact with others are created according to the algorithm as follows [14].

1. At each time step t, the network starts with N disconnected agents.

2. Each agent i becomes active with probability a_i and an active agent creates m links with m other randomly selected agents.
3. At the next time step $t + 1$, all the links in the network are deleted and the process returns to 1.

As observations in different real-world networks suggest [21], the activity value a is heterogeneous within agents and approximately follows a power law distribution described as

$$P(a)=Ba^{-\gamma}, \quad (2)$$

where B is a constant and γ denotes a scaling exponent.

In the present model, the values of activity a of all agents are fitted to real mobility data so that activity values change over time in accordance with the change of mobility observed in real data. The data report the *mobility* which indicates how visitors to or time spent in categorized places change within a specific region of a country. Categorized places include 'retail and recreation', 'grocery and pharmacy', 'parks', 'transit station', 'workplaces', and 'residential'. The reported mobility is shown as a positive or negative percentage since the mobility for the report date is compared with the baseline which indicates a normal value for that day of the week [15].

We have selected three categorized places that are likely to be affected by the 'state of emergency declaration', i.e., 'retail and recreation', 'transit station', and 'workplaces', because we focus on the period when the declaration was enacted. Figure 1 indicates the successive change of mobility values observed in the three selected places in Tokyo, Japan from February 15th until June 30th (137 days).

Using the mobility values reported from these three places, activity $a_{i,t}$ for agent i at timestep t is calculated as,

$$a_{i,t} = a_i \cdot M_t \quad (3)$$

where M_t denotes the average of the mobility values reported from the three categorized places at timestep t.

C. Settings and conditions of simulation

The number of agents N in our model is 100,000, which represents approximately one-hundredth of Tokyo's population. One timestep in the model corresponds to one day, so the simulation progresses for 137 timesteps, which represent the period from February 15th to June 30th. Figure 2 shows the course of the daily number of positive cases with SARS-CoV-2 during the same period in Tokyo [25]. Before running simulations, the values of both activity a and susceptibility s are allocated to all agents based on the distributions described before in this section. The values of the parameters to be estimated from the simulation results, i.e., Tr, α, and β are initially given by sampling from the prior distributions. Table I summarizes the hyperparameters of distributions from which the parameter values are sampled.

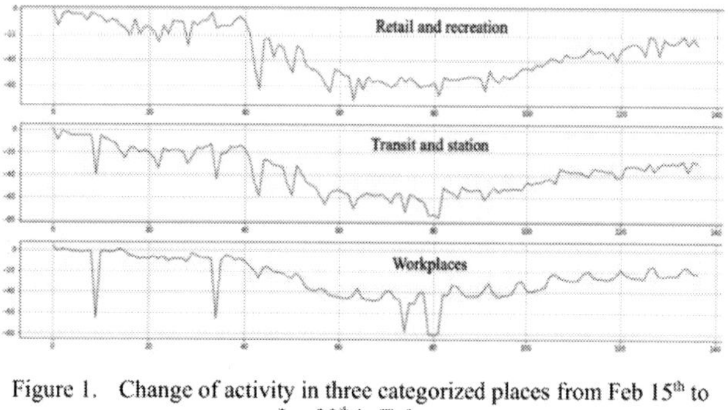

Figure 1. Change of activity in three categorized places from Feb 15th to Jun 30th in Tokyo.

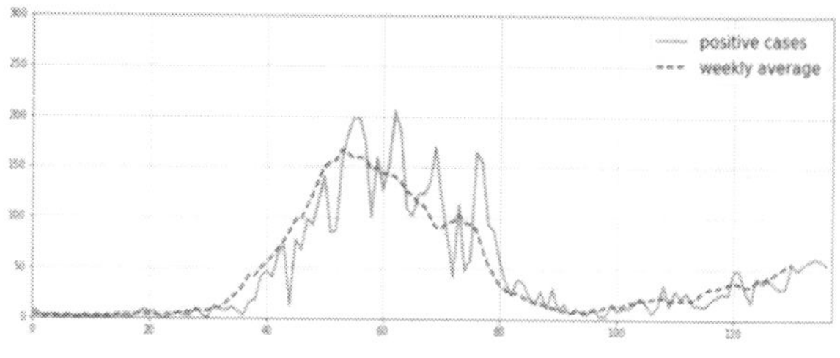

Figure 2. Course of number of daily positive cases from Feb 15th to Jun 30th in Tokyo.

A sequence of 137 edge-lists, each of which represents the links between agents in the activity-driven network at each timestep, is generated in advance following the algorithm presented in Section III *B*. The simulation starts with one infectious agent at the first timestep.

We have encoded all the models using Python Numpy, Scikit-learn, and other toolkits.

IV. RESULTS

Simulations were carried out 3,500 times in parallel on 30 CPUs yielding a total of 105,000 results over approximately 60 hours. A series of numbers showing the course of the number of newly infected agents at each timestep was obtained as the result of each simulation running with a particular set of parameter values.

We scored the result of each simulation based on the Mean Squared Error (MSE) calculated using the observed data in Tokyo described in Figure 2. With respect to the observed data, we assumed that only 10% of the actual number of daily infected individuals was reported officially, i.e., the reporting rate is 10% [22]. By using the sets of parameter values taken from the top 1,000 simulations scored by MSE (acceptance rate = 1%), the posterior distributions of parameters were inferred. Figure 3 displays the inferred distributions for parameters Tr, α, and β.

As to β, which is the recovery rate, the inference does not appear to have converged sufficiently since the distribution seems uniform. However, the mean value of distribution (i.e.,

TABLE I. HYPERPARAMETERS OF DISTRIBUTIONS

Parameter	Distribution	Hyperparameter
Activity a	$Ba^{-\gamma}$	$B = 1, \gamma = 2.2$
Susceptibility s	$N(\mu, \sigma^2)$	$\mu = 0.5, \sigma = 0.2$
Transmission rate Tr	$U(a, b)$	$a = 0.5, b = 1.0$
Probability α	$U(a, b)$	$a = 0.1, b = 0.4$
Probability β	$U(a, b)$	$a = 0.1, b = 0.4$

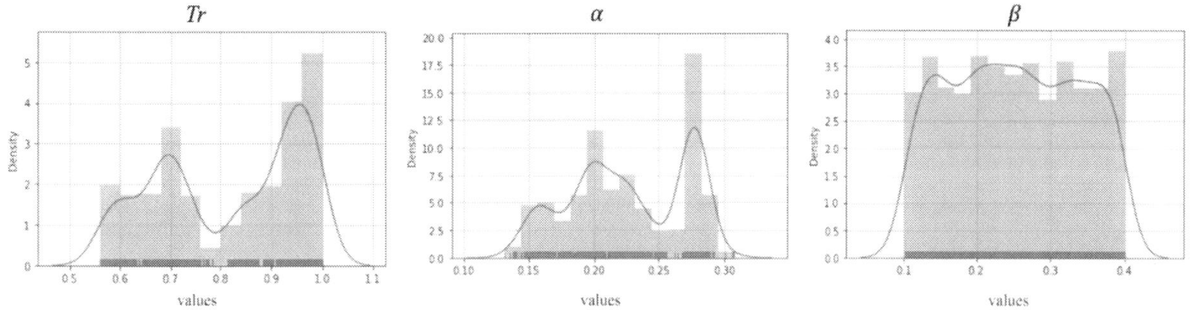

Figure 3. Inferred distributions of parameters *Tr* (left), *α* (center), and *β* (right).

0.25) coincides adequately with the length of infectious period that empirical research suggests [23]. The median time of infectious period suggested in research is 4.1 days, so it is the inverse of the mean value of distribution estimated for recovery rate. With respect to *α* which is the probability of becoming infectious, the distribution appears to gradually converge around the value 0.27, although the shape of the distribution is not evident enough. The mean of the distribution could have converged to approximately this value, had we carried out far more simulations. The inverse of the value 0.27 coincides with the median time of incubation period, i.e., 4-5 days, as suggested by empirical research [24]. As for *Tr*, i.e., transmission rate, the distribution seems to converge moderately between 0.9 and 1.0, while its shape is somewhat ambiguous. If the mean of the prior for *Tr* had been larger and many more simulations had been run, the shape of distribution could have been more obvious.

To validate our model, we compared the simulation results with real data, in terms of the 7-day average number and the cumulative number of newly infected agents, by calculating Pearson correlation coefficient. As for the 7-day average, the top 10 simulation results scored by MSE reached approximately 0.90 (p<1e-40) in Pearson correlation coefficient, as indicated in Figure 4. For the cumulative number, the top 10 results evaluated by MSE reached as high as 0.993 (p<1e-100) in Pearson correlation coefficient. Therefore, we appear to have sufficiently validated our model through parameter inference that fits the model to the observed data, and we have succeeded in identifying the corresponding parameter values. The values identified for parameters *Tr*, *α*, and *β* are 0.99, 0.26, and 0.31, respectively.

With these parameter values identified to represent the actual data, we performed additional simulations under imaginary conditions. The simulations suggest the results that could have been realized when people's activity had not been restricted. Without restriction on people's activity, the number of daily infected cases would have reached over 150,000 and more than half of the people could have been infected, leading to *herd immunity*. However, on the other hand, as Figure 5 shows, the cumulative number of social links in the networks fitted to real mobility data is 33% less than that in virtually generated activity-driven networks in which the activities of agents do not decline. The decrease of links in the networks can be considered as the economic and social cost to restrain the spread of infection with COVID-19.

Although it will be extremely difficult to evaluate the effectiveness as well as legitimacy for measures like 'state of emergency declaration', predictions using a well-validated simulation model may help do that more rationally.

V. Vaccine Strategies

While vaccines can arguably be a 'game-changer' in the pandemic, their supply is still inadequate globally. Examination of the effectiveness of various vaccine strategies using a model well-fitted to the observed data will be practically needed in this context.

A. Comparison between various strategies

Utilizing virtual activity-driven networks in which agents' activities are not restricted, we demonstrate a comparison of the effectiveness of three vaccination strategies through simulations of our model with parameter values identified in Section IV.

We examine the following three vaccine strategies:

1) Random: vaccinating randomly chosen agents at each timestep.
2) Priority for highly susceptible people: preferentially vaccinating the most susceptible 30% of agents, e.g., elderly, then randomly.
3) Priority for agents relatively active in networks: preferentially vaccinating the most active 30% of agents, then randomly.

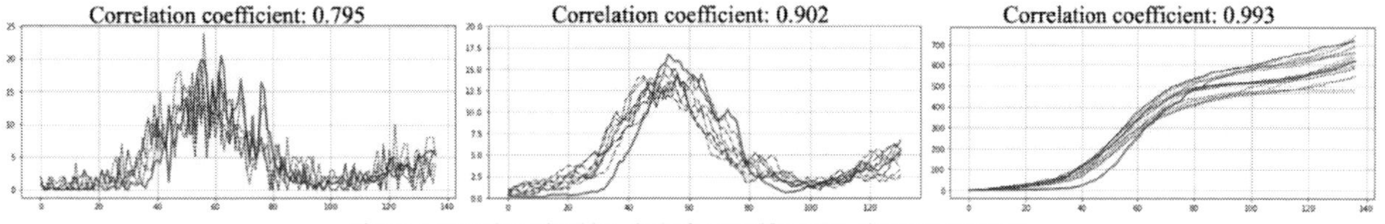

Figure 4. Top 10 results (blue, dashed) scored by MSE, observed data (red), daily(left), 7-day average(center), cumulative(right).

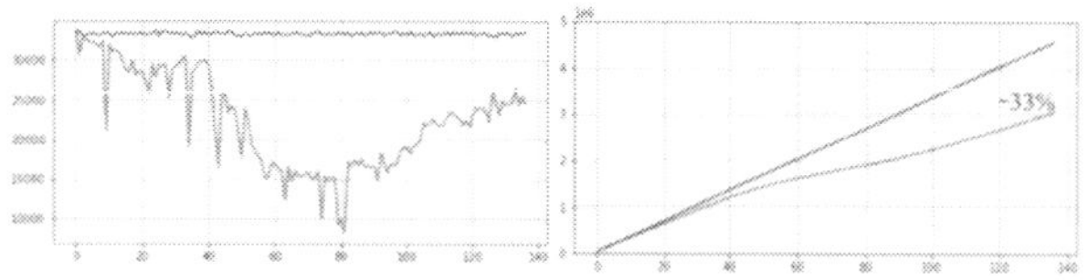

Figure 5. Daily links(left), cumulative links(right) real mobility data(red), no restriction(blue).

In addition, we run simulations under the following different conditions:

a) Vaccine availability: 1,000 shots (1% of the people) or 500 shots (0.5% of the people) at each timestep.
b) Vaccine efficacy: reducing the viral susceptibility of the agents by 80% or 30% (e.g., against variants).

The availability of vaccines and their efficacy may affect the evaluation of the performance of a vaccine strategy, so simulations are performed with these different conditions in mind. We run simulations over activity-driven networks with no governmental restrictions on the agents' activities. The vaccination starts from the 40th timestep in these simulations.

Figure 6 displays the courses of the number of newly infected agents when each of three strategies is performed under four different conditions. It is observed that preferential vaccination for agents who are more active in the networks is the most effective strategy under all conditions. It is also apparent that the difference in effectiveness between the three strategies is eminent when vaccines are abundant and effective. As the speed of vaccination slows down, or the effects of vaccines against viruses decline, the three strategies differ less evidently in their performance.

Figure 7 shows the cumulative number of infected agents among the highly susceptible group (e.g., elderly) when each of the three strategies is undertaken under four different conditions. Though it may be counterintuitive, the number of infected agents among the highly susceptible ones is lower when active agents are prioritized than when highly susceptible agents are vaccinated first.

Taking these observations together, it can be implicated that preferentially vaccinating for more active individuals in the network is a promising strategy, though it may be practically difficult to carry out.

B. *Vaccine passport*

Once people are vaccinated, they will probably be enthusiastic to resume their activities they have been forced to abandon during the pandemic. 'Vaccine passport', which allows vaccinated people to restart their business as well as leisure activities is practically needed. However, can vaccine passport really achieve both restraint of virus spreading and stimulation of social activity? It will make sense to give a clue to this question by running simulations with a model that represents well the observed data.

Therefore, we compared a vaccine passport scenario with other scenarios with respect to the mitigation of infection as well as the decrease of social links. We examined the following three scenarios.

1) Vaccine passport: agents are allowed to increase their activity by 20% after being vaccinated.
2) Sustained restriction on activity: agents are forced to reduce their activities even after vaccination.
3) No restriction on activity: no restriction on agents' activities is executed.

Simulations of our model are carried out over activity-driven networks where the activities of all agents are initially reduced by 5%. The vaccination starts from the 40th timestep.

In terms of the three scenarios, Figure 8 shows the courses of cumulative number of infected agents among the highly susceptible group (left) and the comparison of total number of social links generated in the networks (right).

When compared with no restriction scenario, vaccine passport scenario reduces the number of infected agents by 73% while it only loses social links by 4.8%. Sustained restriction scenario reduces the spread of infection more efficiently while decreasing social links more significantly.

susceptibility reduced by 80% — (1,000 shots per day) (500 shots per day)
susceptibility reduced by 30% — (1,000 shots per day) (500 shots per day)

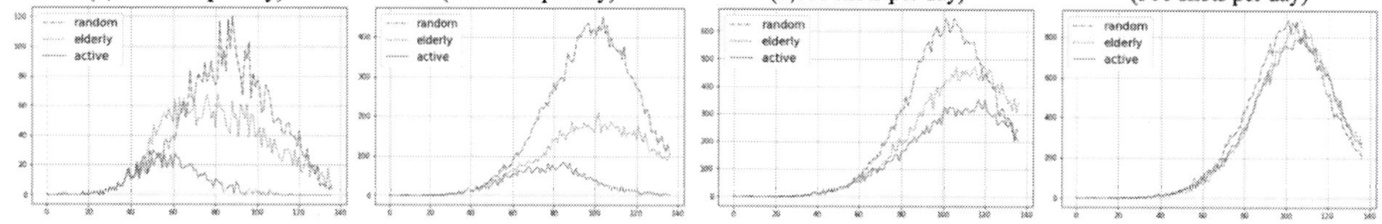

Figure 6. Comparison of 3 vaccine strategies under 4 different conditions.

susceptibility reduced by 80% — (1,000 shots per day) (500 shots per day)
susceptibility reduced by 30% — (1,000 shots per day) (500 shots per day)

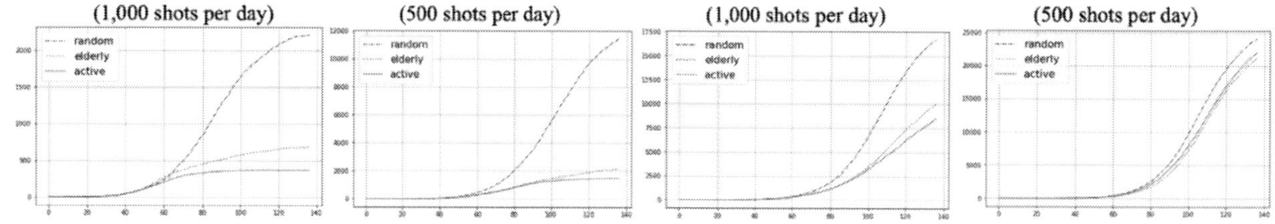

Figure 7. Cumulative number of highly susceptible agents who are infected.

Based on these observations, it may be suggested that vaccine passport definitely helps the activity of society resume while mitigating the spread of infection considerably. Thus, provided that the vaccine's efficacy is sufficient as expected among individuals and health care system is unlikely to be overloaded, vaccine passport could be a promising means to improve the situation of COVID-19.

VI. CONCLUSION AND FUTURE WORK

We have developed an agent-based model of COVID-19 infection with activity-driven networks that are fitted to actual mobility data. We inferred the parameters of our model via approximate Bayesian computation with 105,000 results of simulations. Through additional simulations under certain conditions, we also examined the effectiveness of several vaccination strategies and suggested promising one.

In future work, we will attempt to infer posterior of parameters more sufficiently by using deep learning [19] as summary statistics in approximate Bayesian computation.

ACKNOWLEDGMENT

We appreciate Google for providing useful data.

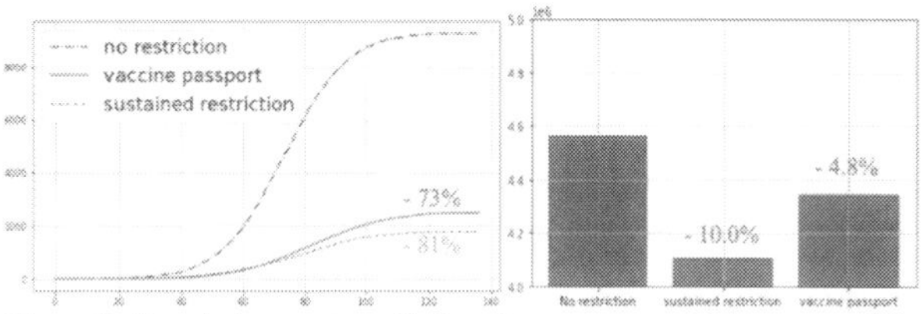

Figure 8. Cumulative number of infected agents among highly susceptible ones(left), cumulative number of links in the networks(right).

REFERENCES

[1] U. Wilensky and W. Rand, "An introduction to agent-based modeling: Modeling natural, social, and engineered complex systems with Netlogo," MIT Press ISBN978-0-262-73189-8 2015.

[2] H. Arduin, M. Domenech de Cellès, D. Guillemot, L. Watier, and L. Opatowski, "An agent-based model simulation of influenza interactions at the host level: insight into the influenza-related burden of pneumococcal infections," BMC Infectious Diseases 17:382 2017.

[3] N. Hoertel et al., "A stochastic agent-based model of the SARS-CoV-2 epidemic in France," nature medicine letters vol.26 pp. 1417-1421 Sep. 2020.

[4] G. Rossetti, L. Milli, S. Citraro, and V. Morini, "UTLDR: an agent-based framework for modeling infectious diseases and public interventions," working paper arXiv:2011.05606v1 [cs.SI] 11 Nov. 2020.

[5] P. C. L. Silva, P. V. C. Batista, H. S. Lima, M. A. Alves, F. G. Guimarães, and R. C. P. Silva, "COVID-ABS: An agent-based model of COVID-19 epidemic to simulate health and economic effects of social distancing interventions," Chaos, Solitons and Fractals 139 110088 2020.

[6] A. Aleta et al., "Modelling the impact of testing, contact tracing and household quarantine on second waves of COVID-19," nature human behavior vol 4 pp. 964-971 Sep. 2020.

[7] A. Nishi et al., "Network interventions for managing the COVID-19 pandemic and sustaining economy," PNAS vol.117 no.48 pp. 30285-30294 Dec. 1 2020.

[8] T. Kano, K. Yasui, T. Mikami, M. Asally, and A. Ishiguro, "An agent-based model of the interrelation between the COVID-19 outbreak and economic activities," Proc.R.Soc.A 477:20200604.

[9] J. Li and P. Giabbanelli, "Returning to a Normal Life via COVID-19 Vaccines in the United States: A Large-scale Agent-Based Simulation Study," JMIR Med Inform vol.9 iss.4 e27419 pp. 1-19 2021.

[10] S. M. Moghadas et al., "Evaluation of COVID-19 vaccination strategies with a delayed second dose," PLOS Biology 19(4):e3001211.

[11] P. Holme and J. Saramäki, "Temporal networks," Phys. Rep. vol.519 iss.3 pp. 97-125 Oct. 2012.

[12] N. Masuda and P. Holme, "Introduction to temporal network epidemiology," in N. Masuda and P. Holme(editors), "Temporal Network Epidemiology," Springer ISBN 978-981-10-5286-6 2017.

[13] M. Karsai, N. Perra, and A. Vespignani, "Time varying networks and the weakness of strong ties," Sci.Rep.4:4001 2014 doi: 10.1038/srep04001.

[14] M. Karsai and N. Perra, "Control strategies of contagion processes in time-varying networks," in N. Masuda and P. Holme(editors), "Temporal Network Epidemiology," Springer ISBN 978-981-10-5286-6 2017.

[15] Google COVID-19 Community Mobility Reports https://www.google.com/covid19/mobility/ [retrieved: June 2021].

[16] E. v. d. Vaart, M. A. Beaumont, A. S. A. Johnston, and R. M. Sibly, "Calibration and evaluation of individual-based models using Approximate Bayesian Computation," Ecological Modelling 312 pp. 182-190 2015.

[17] M. A. Beaumont, "Approximate Bayesian Computation," Ann.Rev.Stat. Appl 2019.6 pp. 2.1-2.25.

[18] B. Lambert, A. L. MacLean, A. G. Fletcher, A. N. Combes, M. H. Little, and H. M. Byrne, "Bayesian inference of agent-based models: a tool for studying kidney branching morphogenesis," J.Math.Biol. 76 pp. 1673-1697 2018.

[19] M. Kesson, P. Singh, F. Wrede, and A. Hellander, "Convolutional neural networks as summary statistics for approximate Bayesian computation," a preprint arXiv:2001.11760v4 [stat.ML] 14 Sep 2020.

[20] J. L. Schultze and A. C. Achenbrenner, "COVID-19 and the human innate immune system," Cell 184, April 1, 2021.

[21] N. Perra, B. Gonçalves, R. Pastor-Satorras, and A. Vespignani, "Activity driven modeling of time varying networks," Sci.Rep.2:469 2012 doi:10.1038/srep00469.

[22] G. Kobayashi, S. Sugasawa, H. Tamae, and T. Ozu, "Predicting intervention effect for COVID-19 in Japan: state space modeling approach," BioScience Trends Advance Publication doi: 10.5582/bst.2020.03133.

[23] H. Y. Cheng, S. W. Jian, D. P. Liu, T. C. Ng, W. T. Huang, and H. H. Lin, "Contact Tracing Assessment of COVID-19 Transmission Dynamics in Taiwan and Risk at Different Exposure Periods Before and After Symptom Onset," JAMA Intern Med. 2020:180(9) pp. 1156-1163.

[24] Centers for Disease Control and Prevention (CDC) in the United States, "Clinical Presentation: incubation period," https://www.cdc.gov/coronavirus/2019-ncov/hcp/clinical-guidance-management-patients.html [retrieved: June 2021].

[25] COVID-19 Information Website Tokyo Metroplitan Gov. https://stopcovid19.metro.tokyo.lg.jp/en/ [retrieved: June 2021].

The Shin-Life Career Game: Pursuing Your New Life Style through Gaming Simulation

Akinobu Sakata
Department of Computational Intelligence and System Science
Tokyo Institute of Technology
Yokohama, Japan
e-mail: sakata.a.aa@m.titech.ac.jp

Takamasa Kikuchi
Graduate School of Business Administration
Keio University
Yokohama, Japan
e-mail: takamasa_kikuchi@keio.jp

Ryuichi Okumura
Career Innovation Division
Mitsubishi Research Institute,Inc.
Tokyo, Japan
e-mail: okuty@mri.co.jp

Masaaki Kunigami
Department of Computer Science
Tokyo Institute of Technology
Yokohama, Japan
e-mail: mkunigami@gakushikai.jp

Atsushi Yoshikawa
Department of Computer Science
Tokyo Institute of Technology
Yokohama, Japan
e-mail: at_sushi_bar@dis.titech.ac.jp

Masayuki Yamamura
Department of Computer Science
Tokyo Institute of Technology
Yokohama, Japan
e-mail: my@c.titech.ac.jp

Takao Terano
Chiba University of Commerce
Ichikawa, Japan
e-mail: terano@cuc.ac.jp

***Abstract*— The purpose of this study is to propose a serious game: the Shin-Life Career Game, which allows players to construct various careers. The name of this game is come from the most famous classic game: the Life Career Game developed by Boocock. In the field of career education, various serious games have been developed as a means for students to learn about career planning and development in a practical way. However, in conventional serious games for career education, the diversity of careers constructed by the players is low compared to the reality of today's working society. We propose a new serious game: the Shin-Life Career Game which eliminates the restriction on the number of occupations a player is able to take at the same time. We plan to use this game to explore the possibilities of various lifestyles for people.**

Keywords—Serious game; career education; gaming simulation; resource allocation.

I. Introduction

The purpose of this research is to propose a gaming simulation: the Shin-Life Career Game, which provides players with the experience of constructing various careers. Gaming simulation is a simulation in which humans participate as players in the context of the simulation, and which is operated through the decisions of those players [1].

In the field of career education, serious games have been developed to help school students learn about career planning and development [2] [3]. It has been reported that students who learn through serious games are motivated to learn, acquire factual knowledge, and gain confidence in the real-world application of what they have learned [2].

A variety of serious games have been developed in the field of career education [2]-[4]. However, these games are not designed to take into account the diversification of careers faced by today's working society [5]. Specifically, in conventional career education games, players cannot work in more than one occupation at the same time. In addition, players is not able to choose the type of work when they enter a certain occupation. If there were a realistic career simulator that reflected the diversity of careers, it would be of use in revealing the lifestyles of various people. Therefore, we developed a new serious game: the Shin-Life Career Game in which players are able to work in multiple occupations at the same time and to choose the type of work (employed or independent). This game inherits the features of the original life game [6], as well as the Life Career Game, an early serious game for career education.

Therefore, we developed a new serious game: the Shin-Life Career Game in which players are able to work in multiple occupations at the same time and to choose the type of work (employed or independent). This game inherits the features of the original life game [6], as well as the Life Career Game, an early serious game for career education. Boocock's the Life Career Game has been played by students of all ages, from elementary school to university. Of course, our game can be used to educate students of all ages as well. On the other hand, we are considering having adults who have a lot of life experience play our games. This is because analyzing the games played by adults who have worked in the society and gained various experiences may help us to find their unique wisdom and perspectives on worldly affairs.

In this study, we conducted an experiment to verify the behavior of the Shin-Life Career Game. The goal of this experiment is to confirm that the game players experience a significant reduction in income when they experience an economic recession. To achieve this goal, we first prepared a scenario in which game players experience an economic recession. Next, we created four software agents with decision-making rules and made them participate in gaming. As a result of the experiment, we found that (1) the income of the players temporarily dropped when they experienced an economic recession in all the strategies, and (2) the strategy of devoting resources only to the core business (permanent work) may result in less money resources acquired through gaming than the strategy of distributing resources to the core business and other activities.

II. Related Work

To overcome the contradiction between the way secondary school youth see the career world and the way adults see it, Boocock developed a life career game that plays much like the original life game [2]. In the game, players experience a hypothetical life, playing various roles and spending their resources (money, time, etc.) on various activities with the goal of maximizing their present satisfaction and the possibility of a good life in the future. As a result, they acquire knowledge related to career development and develop understanding and confidence. These characteristics have been partially inherited by other serious games for career education that have been developed since then (e.g. [3], [4]).

In today's world, many workers have the opportunity to build a variety of careers [5]. There is a growing population of workers worldwide who choose non-traditional ways of earning a living, such as those who work more than one occupation at the same time, those who are independent of organizations and earn a living through contract work using highly specialized skills, and those who earn efficient rewards from simple labor online [5]. However, in traditional games, players are expected to make a living from only one job. In addition, players is not able to choose the type of work (Players should have a variety of options, such as working as an employee or as an independent contractor) when they take a certain occupation. Therefore, we have developed a new game that takes into account these modern workers' circumstances. The features of the game are shown in Table 1. A career simulator that reflects the realities faced by today's workers could be applicated to reveal the lifestyles of different people.

III. The Shin-Life Career Game

In this section, we describe the features of the Shin-Life Career Game in detail.

A. Overview

The Shin-Life Career Game is a kind of turn-based life game. Players experience a virtual worker's life in the game. The players are given several kinds of resources by the game system, and allocate them to various activities according to the game rules, restrictions, and their own will, resulting in the gaining or losing of new resources.

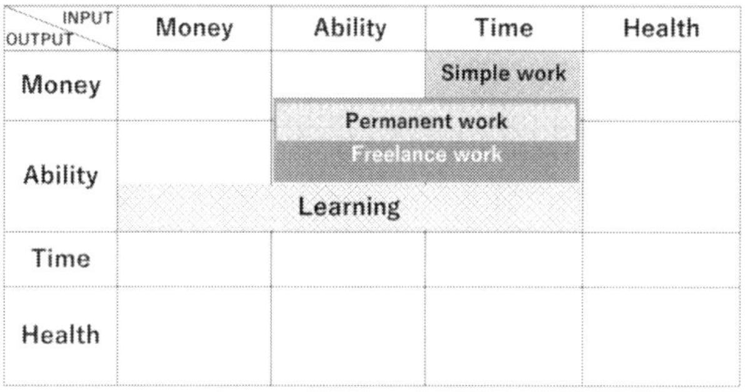

Fig. 1. MATH model for agents in the game.

B. Agent model

1) Resource variables: We used MATH model [7] to represent the activities of agents that gain and lose resources by allocating resources to various activities (See Figure 1). Our agent model contains three types of resource variables: money resources, ability resources, and time resources. The following sections describe the resource variables and activities that make up the model.

The variable of money resource corresponds to an asset in the real life. Human beings use monetary assets to support their lives. The variable of money resource has extensive property and does not have an upper limit.

The variable of ability resource corresponds to knowledge and skills for work in the real life. Human beings use their skills and knowledge to engage in labor and get paid for it. The variable of ability resource has intensive property and does not have an upper limit.

The variable of time resource corresponds to time for real life. Human beings live their lives by spending their time in a variety of activities. The variable of time resource has extensive property and an upper limit.

2) Activity: Next, we describe the agents' activities. In this game, agents allocate their resources to several activities, "Permanent work (PW)," "Freelance work (FW)," "Simple work (SW)," and "Learning (LN)," in each turn according to the constraints of the game and their own will. The features of each activity are summarized in Table II, and the details are described below.

PW is a work style in which workers are employed by an organization until they reach retirement age and receive remuneration for their labor. The characteristics of PW are described below. First, the remuneration for PW is stable. In reality, full-time workers are less likely to experience unemployment due to the effects of the economy than part-time workers [8]. Second, the remuneration for PW is higher than that for SW. In reality, the income of full-time workers is much higher than that of part-time workers [9]. Third, if a player's ability resources increase, the reward for PW will be higher. In the personnel evaluation system in companies, it is customary to reflect the medium- to long-term accumulation of capabilities by regular workers in the increase of their basic salary and the promotion of their qualification grade [10]. Fourth, engaging in PW increases the ability resources

TABLE I
COMPARISON OF FEATURES BETWEEN THE SHIN-LIFE CAREER GAME AND TRADITIONAL GAMES FOR CAREER EDUCATION

Feature	Conventional Games[a]	The Shin-Life Career Game
Number of occupations a player can have at the same time.	One	Multiple
Diversity of labor forms.[b]	Low	High

[a] The target games are "the Life Career Game [2]," "the Real Game [3]," and "MeTycoon [4]".
[b] In the real world of labor, workers earn their living not only through traditional full-time employment, but also through freelance work, part-timejobs, gig work, and many other forms of work. Conventional games do not make a clear distinction between these forms of work.

TABLE II
FEATURES OF EACH ACTIVITY

Feature	Activity			
	PW	FW	SW	LN
Type of activity[a]	W	W	W	L
Income level[b]	M	H	L	-
Positive impact of ability level on income level[c]	P	P	N	-
Stability of income[b]	H	L	L	-
Ability growth[c]	P	N	N	P

[a] W and LN stand for "Work" and "Learning," respectively.
[b] H, M, and L stand for "High level," "Middle level," and "Low level," respectively.
[c] P and N stand for "Positive" and "Negative," respectively.

of players. Firms provide regular workers with education and special jobs that encourage their growth [11]. Fifth, a player has to provide a certain amount of time resources for PW. In general, the law sets minimum and maximum working hours for regular employees. Sixth, a player is not able to decide the amount of time resources to be allocated to PW at will. In general, in regular employment, workers are obligated to engage in overtime and holiday work according to the orders of their supervisors.

FW is a way of working that is independent of a particular organization and is paid by providing expertise and skills to a contracted party. FW has the following characteristics. First, the income of workers who engage in FW is unstable. The income of real freelancers is also unstable [12]. Second, as a player's ability resources increase, the reward for FW increases. In online job brokerage services used by real freelancers, workers with high value-added skills have a chance to get high-paying jobs [13]. Third, a player's ability resources do not increase when the player engages in FW. Employers spend less time training the self-employed than do employees [14]. Fourth, a player is free to decide the amount of time resources to be allocated to FW. Since freelancers do not have an employment contract, they have no obligation or responsibility to have their working hours controlled by others [15].

SW is a form of work in which workers provide their time to their employers or contractors and are paid for it. In this game, SW is the kind of work that manual workers do in the real world, such as part-time jobs, day labor, and gig work, which do not require any special skills or qualifications. SW has the following characteristics. First, the money resource, which is the reward for labor, increases in proportion to the amount of time resource the player allocates to SW. In general, the wages of part-timers are determined by the length of time they work. The wages of day laborers and gig workers are determined by the unit cost and number of jobs that can be completed in a short period of time. Regardless of the type of labor engaged in, the longer the time spent in labor, the more the worker's income is expected to increase roughly proportionally. Second, the amount of a player's ability resource do not affect the amount of compensation for SW. In fact, many managers do not require part-time workers to have special job performance skills [16]. Third, the income of a player who engages in SW is unstable. If the economy is strong, the reward of simple workers' will be stable, but if the economy worsens, simple workers' jobs will be reduced or they will be laid off [17]. Fourth, a player's ability resource does not increase when the player engages in SW. Many companies keep the training costs they pay for part-timers to a minimum [16]. Finally, a player has the flexibility to adjust his/her working hours to engage in SW. Workers who earn money from one-time jobs, such as on-call work or gig work, and part-time workers can flexibly manage their working hours [18].

LN is the act of taking extra time to develop competencies in order to nurture one's work capacity. People who hold core positions in organizations or who do business with their expertise as freelancers engage in lifelong learning to develop professional competencies that will keep them eligible for work [19]. Self-employed individuals with unstable incomes spend more time on work-related learning than employees of firms [14].

Based on each of the above characteristics, we examined the structure of resource acquisition by each activity. The amount of remuneration for regular employment labor is thought to increase monotonically in proportion to the product of working hours and the worker's ability. The amount of remuneration for freelance labor increases monotonically in proportion to the product of working hours and ability, but there is uncertainty in terms of income. The amount of compensation for simple labor is expected to increase monotonically with the number of hours worked. The more time a worker spends in formal labor, the more work experience he or she will gain and the more education he or she will benefit from. Therefore, the ability acquired through formal employment is expected to increase monotonically as total hours worked increase. However, if a worker works for a particular company for a long time, the growth potential will gradually decrease. Finally, the ability of a worker is expected to increase monotonically in proportion to the product of

TABLE III
VARIABLES AND CONSTANTS IN EQUATIONS

Variable/Const	Name
$I_{PW}(t)$	Reward for PW in turn t (money resources))
$I_{FW}(t)$	Reward for FW in turn t (money resources)
$I_{SW}(t)$	Reward for SW in turn t (money resources)
$G_{LN}(t)$	Reward for LN in turn t (ability resource)
$A(t)$	Agent's ability resources as of turn t
$A_{PW}(t)$	Ability resources that an agent has developed in PW by turn t
$M_{LN}(t)$	Money resources allocated to LN in turn t
$T_{PW}(t)$	Time resources allocated to PW in turn t
$T_{FW}(t)$	Time resources allocated to FW in turn t
$T_{SW}(t)$	Time resources allocated to SW in turn t
$T_{LN}(t)$	Time resources allocated to LN in turn t
c_{PW}	Reward per unit time for PW (constant)
c_{FW}	Reward per unit time for FW (constant)
c_{SW}	Reward per unit time for SW (constant)
c_{LN}	Reward per unit time for LN (constant)
a_0	Intercept of equation (2) (constant)
$\epsilon_{FW}(t)$	A random number generated according to a continuous distribution whose probability density function is constant on a finite interval $[\alpha,\beta]$ and zero outside the interval.
$T_{PW\_TOTAL}(t)$	Total time resources allocated to PW by turn t

working hours, learning fees to the power of 0.5 , and working capacity. Based on the above, we have prepared equations (1) through (5). See Table 2 for the variables and constants that make up each equation.

$$I_{PW}(t) = C_{PW} \times A(t-1) \times T_{PW}(t) \quad (1)$$

$$A_{PW}(t) = a_0 + \frac{1}{1 + \exp(r \times (T_{PW\_TOTAL} - d))} \quad (2)$$

$$I_{FW}(t) = \epsilon_{FW} \times C_{FW} \times A(t-1) \times T_{FW}(t) \quad (3)$$

$$I_{SW}(t) = C_{SW} \times T_{SW}(t) \quad (4)$$

$$G_{LN}(t) = (C_{LN} \times T_{LN}(t) \times \sqrt{M_{LN}(t)}) \times A(t-1) \quad (5)$$

Equations (1) and (2) are used to determine the money resources and ability resources that are the rewards of PW, respectively. Because of the sixth characteristic of PW, players cannot determine the value of T_{PW} by themselves. The value of T_{PW} is determined by the system using a random number generator according to given conditions. The given condition is the range of values that T_{PW} can take. This condition reflects the fifth characteristic of PW. Next, equations (3) and (4) are the equations for calculating the money resource, the reward for FW, and the money resource, the reward for SW, respectively. Finally, equation (5) is an equation for calculating the ability resources gained from LN.

C. Happening

In the real world, events that cannot be avoided by individuals, such as natural disasters and economic recessions, can occur. Whenever people experience such events, they try to rebuild their lives by making various decisions. In this game, an "economic depression" is implemented, which temporarily reduces the amount of resources acquired by each activity. When an economic depression occurs in a given turn, the rewards for various types of labor are forcibly reduced. At this time, once a player has allocated resources to labor, he will eventually only receive the amount of reward he would have received if he had invested the least amount of resources in labor. In this game, a player who engages in PW are not laid off, so he/she is able to secure some income even if an economic recession occurs. However, workers who engage in FW and SW experience a significant temporary decrease in income.

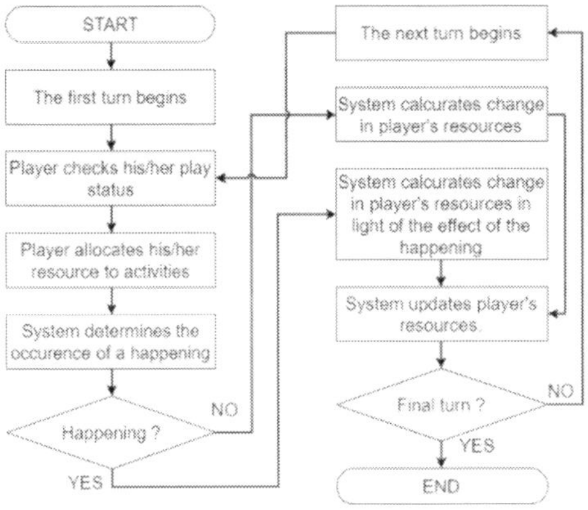

Fig. 2. Flowchart for gameplay

D. Instructions for Gameplay

In this section, we describe the procedure for playing the game. Figure 2 illustrates the procedure for playing the game. The player has to make a decision about resource allocation at each turn. First, when his turn comes, the player gets a chance to check the game information. Here, the player is allowed to check the amount of resources he currently has, the history of his past resource allocation activities, and information about the game environment. The player decides the policy of resource allocation based on the information obtained in this stage. Next, the player allocates resources to each activity. After the resource allocation is completed, the game system updates the player's resource variables. At this time, if the game system considers that a financial crisis event has occurred, the effect is reflected in the calculation results. Finally, the calculation results are fed back to the player, and the turn ends. When a turn ends, a new turn begins. The game is repeated for a predetermined number of turns.

IV. METHOD

In this section, we describe in detail the methodology of the experiment.

A. Agent

A software agent has a policy for resource allocation, and allocates resources to various activities according to the contents of that policy. Software agents allocate resources to various activities. Each software agent has one policy for resource allocation. This policy consists of three components

TABLE IV
CORRESPONDENCE BETWEEN POLICY AND RESOURCE ALLOCATION BEHAVIOR

Policy	Explanation of policy about resource allocation by agents	Policy[a]			Resource allocation behaviour[bc]			
		SI	HI	AG	PW	FW	SW	LN
A	Agents with Policy A hope to work in a way that allows them to earn a stable and high income and to grow in their abilities.	○	○	○	Rand.	-	Rest/2	Rest/2
B	Agents with Policy B hope to work in a way that allows them to earn a stable and high income.	○	○		Rand.	-	Rest	-
C	Agents with Policy C hope to work in a way that allows them to earn a stable income and to grow in ther abilities.	○		○	Rand.	-	-	Rest
D	Agents with Policy D are satisfied as long as they have a stable income.	○			Rand.	-	-	-

[a] SI, HI, and AG stand for "Stability of income," "Higher income," and "Ability growth," respectively.
[b] Rand represents the amount of resources determined by the random number generator.
[c] Rest is the amount of resources of time held at the beginning of each turn minus Rand.

TABLE V
VALUES OF THE PARAMETERS OF THE MATH MODEL IN THIS EXPERIMENT

Parameter	Value	Parameter	Value
C_{PW}	5.5	r	-2.5×10^{-3}
C_{FW}	5.5	d	1.5×10^{3}
C_{SW}	3.0	α	-1.0
C_{LN}	2.0×10^{-4}	β	3.0
a_0	1.0		

("stable income," "high income," and "growth"), each of which can be either "important" or "unimportant" (there are eight policies in total). Each policy is associated with a strategy and action rules for resource allocation. Each software agent allocates resources according to the action rule corresponding to its policy. In this study, we tested the behavior of the gaming system using only the software agent with the policy that emphasizes stable income. The test evaluation using the software agent with the remaining four policies is a future work. In this study, we tested the behavior of the gaming system using only the software agent with the policy that emphasizes stable income. The correspondence between each policy and the resource allocation behavior is summarized in Table IV. The following is a description of the behavior of the software agent with each policy. A software agent with Policy A allocates resources to PW, FW (or SW), and LN, because he considers stable income, high income, and ability growth to be all important. A software agent with Policy B allocates resources to PW and FW (or SW) because they consider stable income and high income to be important. A software agent with Policy D allocates resources to PW only, because it considers only stable income to be important. A software agent with Policy A or Policy C is subject to special rules that do not apply to a software agent with other policies. Because these policies emphasize ability growth, they allow software agents to allocate additional time resources to LN that were not allocated to labor due to the economic recession. In addition, the money resources spent on LN by a software agent with Policy A and a software agent with Policy C are fixed at 50.

B. System

The software for simulation is written in C#. The simulation was carried out using Intel(R) core(TM) 4600U CPU @ 2.10GHz PC with 16GB RAM, Windows10 Pro, 64bit OS.

C. Game scenario

In this experiment, we checked the behavior of the system and the changes in the resources of the software agents when an economic recession occurs. In our scenario, each software-agent experiences just one economic recession in a gaming. The recession occurs on turn 30 (the worker is in his/her 50s).

D. Procedures

We prepared four software agents, each with a different policy. Each software agent was ordered to play 40 turns per gaming session. We assumed that one turn of the game corresponds to one year in the real world. Therefore, 40 turns corresponds to the period from entry to retirement for a standard permanent worker. Each software agent played the game under the aforementioned scenario.

V. RESULTS AND DISCUSSION

In this section, we describe and discuss the results of our experiments.

A. Results

As a result of the experiment, it was observed that the money resources of each agent gradually increased as the game progressed (See Figure 3). It was also observed that the income level of each agent gradually increased as the game progressed (See Figure 4). Finally, the pace at which the ability resources of the software agent with Policy B and the software agent with Policy D increased, gradually accelerated in the first half of the game and gradually decelerated in the second half of the game (None of the agents allocated any resources to the LNs, so their lines overlap on the graph.). While the ability resources of software agents with the other policies increased software agents with the other policies did not decelerate in the second half of the game (See Figure 5).

B. Impact of economic recession on agents' income

When we check the income of each agent in turns 30 in Fig.4, we can see that the income of all software agents has fallen uniformly. The impact on software agents with Policy

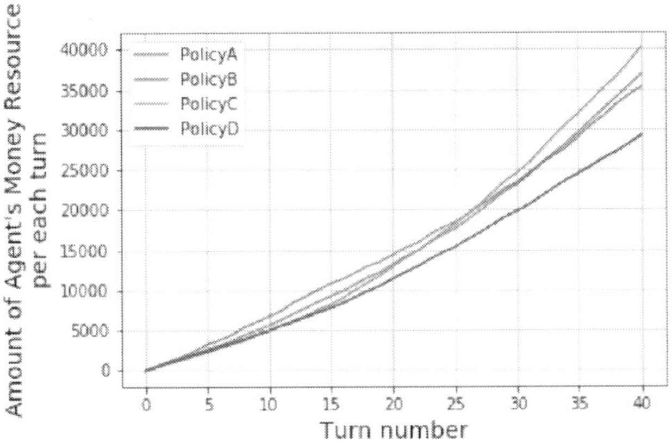

Fig. 3. Figure for time series change in money resource

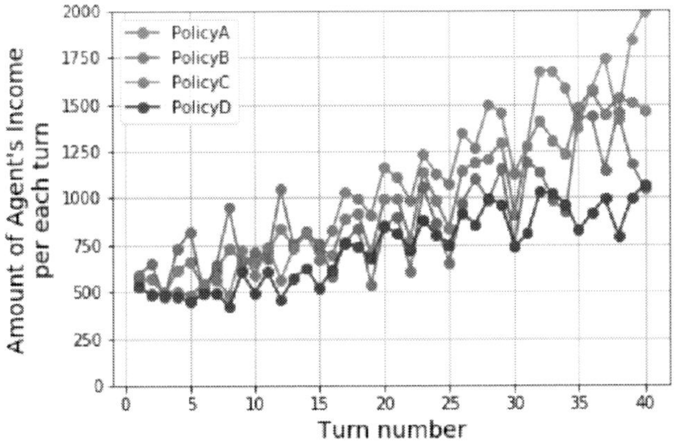

Fig. 4. Figure for time series change in income

A or Policy B, which allocate resources to FW and SW in addition to PW, seems to be relatively large. The reason for the large drop in the income of these software agents is that their income from labor other than PW was cut off due to the economic recession. The recent collapse of Lehman Brothers and the pandemic of the new coronavirus caused many non-regular workers and freelancers to reduce their income significantly or lose their jobs. This result may reflect this reality.

C. A relationship similar to that between ants and grasshoppers

Among the four software agents prepared in this experiment, it can be seen from Figure 3 that the money resources finally earned by the software agent with Policy D that considers only income stability to be important are less than those earned by the software agents who chose other policies. This software agent allocates resources only to PW, while other software agents invest resources in various activities in addition to PW, and succeed in increasing their income. In particular, software agents with Policy A or Policy B allocated resources to LN and engaged in skill development. Even as the speed of ability growth in PW slowed in the second half of their working lives, They continuously grew their

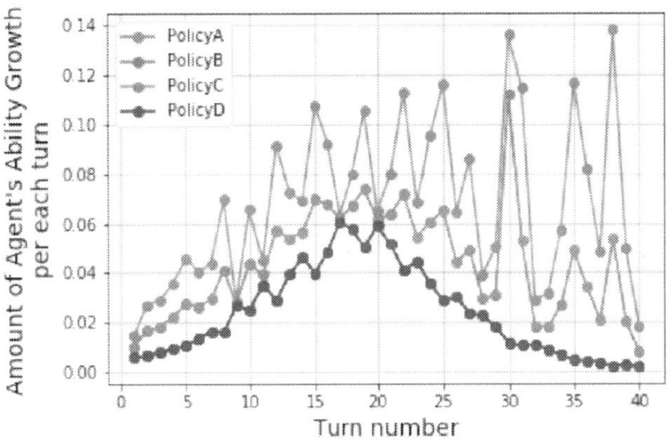

Fig. 5. Figure for time series change in ability growth

skills (see Figure 5) and increased their income (see Figure 4), The difference between the two groups is similar to the relationship between the ant and the grasshopper in Aesop's fable, "The Ant and the Grasshopper. The grasshopper (Agent with Policy D) seems to have widened the gap in income with the ant (Agent with Policy A, Policy B, or Policy C), which steadily accumulates resources, over the course of 40 turns.

VI. Conclusion

In this study, we proposed a gaming simulation: the Shin-Life Career Game, which allowed players to choose various careers. To test the behavior of the game, we conducted a gaming experiment using software agents that had different policies and behaviors regarding resource allocation. As a result of the experiment, we found that (1) the income of the players temporarily dropped when they experienced an economic recession in all the strategies, and (2) the strategy of devoting resources only to the core business (permanent work) might result in less money resources acquired through gaming than the strategy of distributing resources to the core business and other activities.

References

[1] C. S. Greenblat, "Designing games and simulations: An illustrated handbook," SAGE Publications, Incorporated, 1988.

[2] S. S. Boocock, "The life career game," The Personnel and Guidance Journal, Vol. 46 No. 4, pp. 328-334, 1967.

[3] A. J. Edwards and A. G. Watts, "The Real Game: Evaluation of the Initial Field Trials," Cambridge: National Institute for Careers Education and Counselling (mimeo), 1998.

[4] I. Dunwell et al., "MeTycoon: A game-based approach to career guidance", in 2013 5th International Conference on Games and Virtual Worlds for Serious Applications (VS-GAMES), Poole, 2013, pp. 1-6.

[5] C. Kelliher, J. Richardson, and G. Boiarintseva, "All of work? All of life? Reconceptualising work-life balance for the 21st century," Human Resource Management Journal, Vol. 29, No. 2, pp. 97-112, 2019.

[6] J. Ferrara, "Games for Persuasion: Argumentation, Procedurality, and the Lie of Gamification," Games and Culture, Vol. 8, No. 4, pp. 289-304, 2013.

[7] M. Kunigami, R. Okumura, T. Kikuchi, A. Sakata, and T. Terano, "Agents' Resources Allocation and Growth Modeling for Social and Organizational Agent Simulations," In: Editor, F., Editor, S. (eds.) JSAI Special Interest Group on Business Informatics 17th, 2021. (in Japanese)

[8] Statistics Bureau of Japan, "Monthly Results," Labour Force Survey, March 2021, [Online]. Available: https://www.stat.go.jp/english/data/roudou/index.html. [Retrieved: 05, 2021] (in Japanese)

[9] Statistics Bureau of Japan, "労働力調査（詳細集計）2020年 平均結果 (Labour Force Survey (Detailed Tabulation) 2020 Average Results)," 2020. [Online]. Available: https://www.stat.go.jp/data/roudou/sokuhou/nen/dt/. [Retrieved: 05, 2021] (in Japanese)

[10] H. Kakizawa and O. Umezawa, "評価・賃金・仕事が労働意欲に与える影響 ― 人事マイクロデータとアンケート調査による実証分析 (The impact of evaluation, wages, and work on work motivation - An empirical analysis using human resources micro data and questionnaire surveys)," JILPT Research Report No. 598, pp. 67-82, 2010. (in Japanese)

[11] Y. Zhu, "Responding to the challenges of globalization: human resource development in Japan," Journal of World Business, Vol. 39, No.4, pp. 337-348, 2004.

[12] C. Brown and M. Reich, "Developing skills and pay through career ladders Lessons from Japanese and US companies," California Management Review, Vol. 39, No. 2, pp. 124-144, 1997.

[13] S. Horowitz et al., "The Rise of the Freelance Class: A New Constituency of Workers Building a Social Safety Net," Brooklyn, NY: Working Today, 2005.

[14] A. G. Kazi, R. M. Yusoff, A. Khan, and S. Kazi, "The Freelancer: A Conceptual Review," Sains Humanika, Vol. 2 No.3, 2014.

[15] J. Kirchner and K. Wilhelm, "Employee or Freelance Worker," Key Aspects of German Employment and Labour Law. Springer, Berlin, Heidelberg, pp. 45-52, 2018.

[16] C. Inman and C. Enz, "Shattering the myths of the part-time worker," Cornell Hotel and Restaurant Administration Quarterly, Vol. 36, No. 5, pp. 70-73, 1995.

[17] Cabinet Office, "日本経済 2010 (Japan Economy 2010)," 2010. [Online]. Available: https://www5.cao.go.jp/keizai3/2010/1210nk/nk10.html. [Accessed: 6-May-2021] (in Japanese)

[18] J. Rubery, A. Keizer, and D. Grimshaw, "Flexibility bites back: the multiple and hidden costs of flexible employment policies," Human Resource Management Journal, Vol. 26, No. 3, pp. 235-251, 2016.

[19] R. Preston and C. Dyer, "Human capital, social capital and lifelong learning: an editorial introduction," Compare: A Journal of Comparative and International Education, Vol. 33, No. 4, pp. 429-436, 2003.

A Knowledge Extraction from Epidemic Control Simulation

Masaaki Kunigami
Department of Computer Science
Tokyo Institute of Technology
Yokohama, Japan
0000-0001-7377-622X
email: mkunigami@gakushikai.jp

Takamasa Kikuchi
Graduate School of Business Administration
Keio University
Yokohama, Japan
0000-0002-9183-6457
email: takamasa_kikuchi@keio.jp

Takao Terano
Chiba University of Commerce
Ichikawa, Japan
0000-0002-2364-6950
email: terano@cuc.ac.jp

Abstract—**In a social simulation of infection control policies using an epidemic model, it is necessary to consider the latent perspectives of stakeholders focusing on various costs or effects. Therefore, we classify the simulation results produced by various combinations of control policies from the perspective of latent evaluation. In this paper, we use the data envelopment analysis (DEA) method to classify the results of epidemic control simulations. DEA is an analytic method that measures and compares the efficiency of multiple input multiple output systems' performance data. From various latent evaluation perspectives, DEA classification allows us to endogenously extract knowledge about the superiority of each control policy over the others from various latent evaluation perspectives. This approach is a good example of classification and knowledge extraction for a set of social simulation logs.**

Keywords- epidemic model; Data Envelopment Analysis; DEA classification

I. INTRODUCTION

It is impractical to evaluate the results of a simulation using only a specific objective function when simulating the control of a society with various stakeholders. In this paper, we use an infectious disease model as an example to classify a set of simulation output logs without assuming a specific objective function. Furthermore, we extract the knowledge about which output logs are dominant over others under which the objective function, and which logs are not dominant under any objective function.

Since Kermack-McKendrick's proposal of the proposal of the Susceptible-Infectious-Recovered (SIR) model [1][2], there have been numerous studies on epidemic modeling and simulations describing the spread of infectious diseases in society. The study of infectious disease control using those epidemiology models has roughly directed two mutually related directions. One direction is theoretical research, which refines the social structure and diffusion process of infectious diseases and discovers ways to control them. The other direction is empirical research, which uses data on infectious diseases incidence to estimate key parameters for the spread and control of infectious diseases.

Many studies that use epidemic models focus on the number of infected people as the primal state variable and effective reproduction number as a key parameter. However, for practical research, we must consider more state variables as the model sophistication. We should also consider various control variables such as policy costs for infection control and economic side effects. For these multiple variables, various stakeholders may have their objective functions with different weights from different standpoints.perspectives. Our problem is to extract the knowledge related to the superiority or inferiority of simulation results for the various possible objective functions.

This study does not target for a specific infection, such as Corona-virus Disease (COVID). However, this methodology is open to study into the actual control of current and future infectious diseases.

Our approach is as follows. In Section II, we briefly outlook data envelopment analysis (DEA), which is a method for analyzing the efficiency of multiple inputs and outputs systems, to classify the results of epidemic simulation runs. In Section III, considering that the epidemic control simulation has multiple control and state variables, we consider each run of the simulation as a multiple inputs and outputs system. In Section IV, DEA allows us to extract knowledge about which simulation runs are dominant over others under what objective function, as well as which set of runs is dominated by which dominant run.

II. DATA ENVELOPMENT ANALYSIS

DEA [3][4], proposed by Charnes, Cooper, and Rhodes in 1978, is a method for efficiency comparison among decision making units (DMUs) that have multiple inputs and multiple outputs. In DEA, each DMU is characterized by a reference set consisting of DMUs with greater optimal efficiency. The envelopment generated by connecting the reference sets allows us to compare the relative positions of DMUs.

A. Concept of Data Envelopment Analysis

Charnes Cooper and Rhodes (CCR) method [3] is the most basic DEA method, its concept is as follows: a) weighted efficiency of DMUs with multiple inputs and outputs, b) efficiency comparison among DMUs through optimization of the evaluative weights of the various DMUs, and c) characterization by a reference set, which is a collection of DMUs with greater optimal efficiency than the DMUs under consideration.

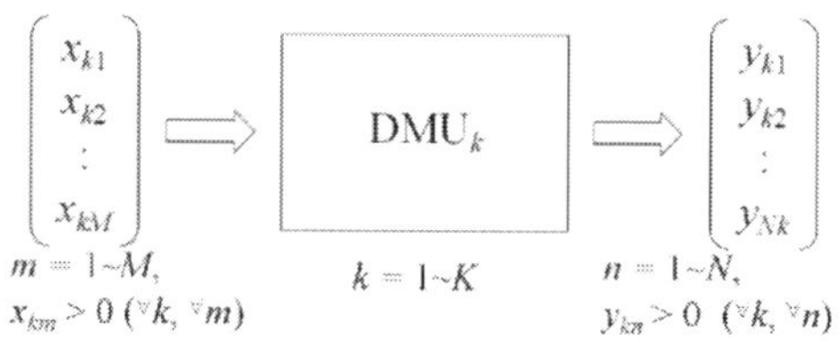

$$\Theta_k(\boldsymbol{\eta}, \boldsymbol{\xi}) = \frac{\boldsymbol{\eta}_k \cdot \mathbf{y}_k}{\boldsymbol{\xi}_k \cdot \mathbf{x}_k} = \sum_{n=1}^{N} \eta_{kn} y_{kn} \Big/ \sum_{m=1}^{M} \xi_{km} x_{km}$$

Figure 1. DMUs and efficiency Θ

The first step is to use a reference set to characterize the DMUs. First, we assume that each DMU$_k$ ($k = 1\sim K$) of the K DMUs generates an N-component output $\mathbf{y}_k$ $\{y_{kn} > 0 \mid n = 1\sim N\}$ from an M-component input $\mathbf{x}_k = \{x_{km} > 0 \mid m = 1\sim M\}$. At this point, the efficiency Θ_k of each DMU$_k$ can be defined as $\Theta_k(\boldsymbol{\eta}_k, \boldsymbol{\xi}_k) \equiv (\boldsymbol{\eta}_k \cdot \mathbf{y}_k) / (\boldsymbol{\xi}_k \cdot \mathbf{x}_k) = \sum_{n,m}\{(\eta_{kn}\, y_{kn}) / (\xi_{km}\, x_{km})\}$ with the evaluative weights $\boldsymbol{\xi}_k = \{\xi_{km} > 0\ (m = 1\sim M)\}$ and $\boldsymbol{\eta}_k$ ($\eta_{kn} > 0$ ($n = 1\sim N$)) attached to the input $\mathbf{x}_k$ and output $\mathbf{y}_k$ (see Figure 1).

In this case, the evaluative weights $\boldsymbol{\xi}_k$ and $\boldsymbol{\eta}_k$ can be moved as much as desired, changing the efficiency Θ_k. The evaluative weights $\boldsymbol{\xi}_k$ and $\boldsymbol{\eta}_k$ are optimized so that the efficiency Θ_k of each DMU$_k$ is the most advantageous while maximizing the efficiency across all DMUs ($\Theta_k \leq 1$). However, the key point is optimizing the evaluative weights $\boldsymbol{\xi}_k$ and $\boldsymbol{\eta}_k$ so that no efficiency of other DMU$_h$ surpasses a value of 1 ($\Theta_h \leq 1$). Therefore, DEA is formulated as the fractional programming problem shown below (see Figure 2).

$$\max_{\eta,\xi} \ \Theta_k(\boldsymbol{\eta}_k, \boldsymbol{\xi}_k) = \frac{\sum_{n=1}^{N} \eta_{nk} y_{kn}}{\sum_{m=1}^{M} \xi_{mk} x_{km}} \quad (k = 1\sim K)$$

Efficiency Θ_k of DMU$_k$

$$\text{s.t.} \begin{cases} \dfrac{\sum_{n=1}^{N} \eta_{nk} y_{hn}}{\sum_{m=1}^{M} \xi_{mk} x_{hm}} \leq 1 \quad (h = 1\sim K), \\ \eta_{nk} \geq 0 \quad (n = 1\sim N), \\ \xi_{mk} \geq 0 \quad (m = 1\sim M) \end{cases}$$

Under $\boldsymbol{\eta}_k$, $\boldsymbol{\xi}_k$ any other h^{th} efficiency keeps $\Theta_h \leq 1$.

All weights $\boldsymbol{\eta}_k$, $\boldsymbol{\xi}_k$ are not negative.

Figure 2. Optimization problem to find the efficiency Θ_k of the kth DMU

If no optimization of the evaluative weights can bring the efficiency Θ_k to 1 and it is less than the $\Theta_{k'}$ values of other DMU$_k$s, then DMUk is inefficient. In this case, the DMU$_{k'}$ whose optimal efficiency is 1, is referred to as reference set E_k of DMU$_k$, and it can be used as a reference for improving the efficiency of DMU$_k$ (see Figure 3).

$$E_k = \left\{ k' \,\middle|\, \Theta_{k'}(\boldsymbol{\eta}_k^*, \boldsymbol{\xi}_k^*) = \frac{\sum_{n=1}^{N} \eta_{nk}^* y_{nk'}}{\sum_{m=1}^{M} \xi_{mk}^* x_{mk'}} = 1 \ (k' = 1\sim K) \right\}$$

When the optimal efficiency $\Theta_k(\boldsymbol{\eta}_k^*, \boldsymbol{\xi}_k^*) < 1$, there exist other DMU$_{k'}$ such that $\Theta_k(\boldsymbol{\eta}_k^*, \boldsymbol{\xi}_k^*) < \Theta_{k'}(\boldsymbol{\eta}_k^*, \boldsymbol{\xi}_k^*) = 1$.

Figure 3. Reference set E_k of DMU$_k$.

In Figure 2, the DEA optimization is formulated as a fractional programming problem. In practice, it can be solved by converting it into the equivalent linear programming problem shown in Figure 4.

$$\max_{\eta,\xi} \ \Theta_k(\boldsymbol{\eta}_k, \boldsymbol{\xi}_k) = \sum_{n=1}^{N} \eta_n y_{kn} \quad (k = 1\sim K)$$

$$\text{s.t.} \begin{cases} \sum_{m=1}^{M} \xi_{mk} x_{km} = 1 \\ \sum_{n=1}^{N} \eta_{nk} y_{hn} \leq \sum_{m=1}^{M} \xi_{mk} x_{hm} \quad (h = 1\sim K) \\ \eta_{nk} \geq 0 \quad (n = 1\sim M) \\ \xi_{mk} \geq 0 \quad (m = 1\sim M) \end{cases}$$

Fixed denominator

Linear inequalities

⇓

Equivalent reference set

$$E_k = \left\{ k' \,\middle|\, \sum_{n=1}^{N} \eta_{nk}^* y_{k'n} = \sum_{m=1}^{M} \xi_{mk}^* x_{k'm} \quad (k' = 1\sim K) \right\}$$

Figure 4. The equivalent forms of the optimization (Figure 2) and the reference set (Figure 3) as linear programming problem

One of the advantages of using DEA is that its optimization process (described above) automatically solves the problem of determining weights when measuring the efficiency of a multiple inputs multiple-outputs system.

In addition to empirical research on organizational efficiency, DEA is applied to simulation research for optimization of production systems, etc. [5]-[8].

B. *Classification by Data Envelopment Analysis*

DEA is also used for data classification.[9] As a data classification methodology, DEA has a different approach than other distance-based methodologies such as cluster analysis.

In DEA, the reference set E_k of a given DMU$_k$ is an object of reference for improving DMU$_k$, the reference set of an efficient DMU is itself. If we draw a scatter plot of DMUs in the space of input-output variables, the envelopes of the DMUs are shaped by all efficient DMUs. The minimal convex region containing the efficient DMU and the origin also contains inefficient DMUs whose reference set is the efficient DMU. Therefore, this set of DMUs can be classified as sharing the same reference set (see Figure 5).

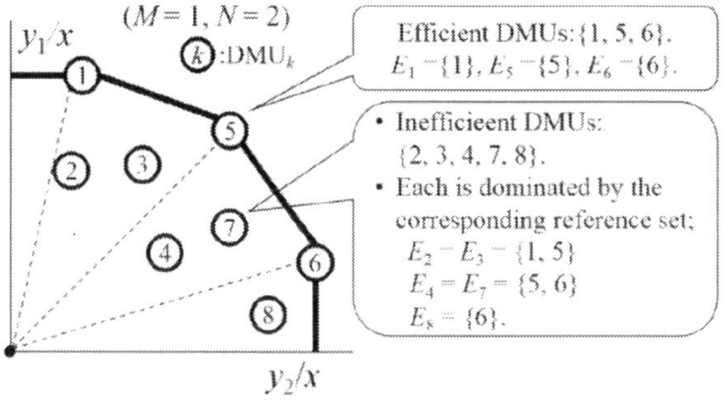

Figure 5. Dividing the envelope by efficient DMUs (reference set) allows classification of inefficient DMUs by common reference sets.

DMUs with the same reference set have similar weighting to improve efficiency. Those weightings are generated by DEA. Thus, the advantage of using DEA is that it allows for endogenous knowledge extraction on the relationship between the DMUs dominating the others in the group (the reference set and the optimal weights) and other subordinated DMUs.

Another advantage of using DEA as a classifier is that it is simple to consider group similarity. The number of overlapping elements of two reference sets indicates the similarity between those groups. The more common reference sets are shared between two groups, the closer they are.

DEA is applicable to data classification in fields other than the social sciences. For example, Hoshino [10] attempts to apply DEA to the classification of gene expression data.

III. Epidemic Control Simulation

Here, we present a simple epidemic control simulation to demonstrate knowledge extraction using DEA. As an epidemic model, we use the SIR model for mortal infection by Kermack-McKendrick [2]. Furthermore, we add input variables for infection control and medical care, to implement multiple-input multiple-output decision-making.

A. Epidemic Control Model

As an example, the epidemic control model used is a system of difference equations (1)–(2). Figure 6 shows the state transitions. Equation (3) shows the effects of social infection suppression and medical care on patient survival.

Equation (1) shows the time variation of the state variable, whereas (2) shows the initial values of the dependent and state variables. Equation (3) shows the time variation of the coefficients due to the control variable.

The state variables are $S(t)$ for the uninfected susceptible population, $I(t)$ for the infected population, $R(t)$ for the recovered non-susceptible population, and $D(t)$ for the deceased population, where the dependent variable $P(t)$ is the surviving population. The infection rate c, healing rate h, and mortality rate m are variables that can be changed by the control variables $u(t)$, $v(t)$, and $w(t)$. When there is no control input, the positive constants c_0, h_0, and m_0 denote the values of $c(t)$, $h(t)$, and $m(t)$, respectively.

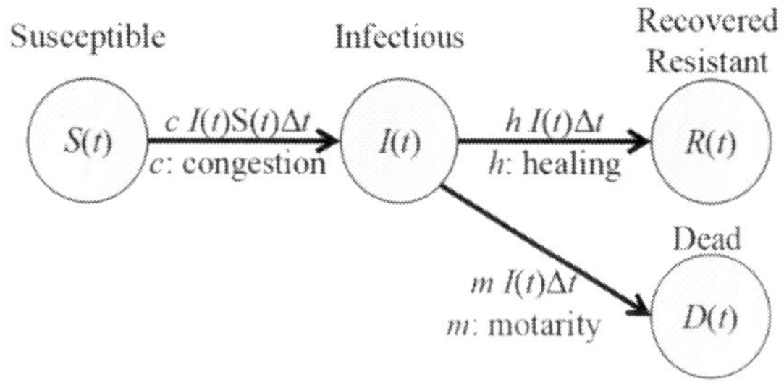

Figure 6. State transitions of the epidemic model

$$\begin{cases} S(t+1) = S(t) - c(t)S(t)I(t), \\ I(t+1) = I(t) + c(t)S(t)I(t) - h(t)I(t) - m(t)I(t), \\ R(t+1) = R(t) + h(t)I(t), \\ D(t+1) = D(t) + m(t)I(t). \end{cases} \quad (1)$$

$$\begin{cases} P(t) = S(t) + I(t) + R(t), \quad \text{population alive}, \\ P(0) = P_0, \quad \text{initial population}, \\ S(0) = P_0 - \varepsilon, \ \ I(0) = \varepsilon,, \ \ R(0) = 0, \ D(0) = 0. \end{cases} \quad (2)$$

$$\begin{cases} c(t) = \dfrac{c_0}{1 + \alpha_u \cdot u(t)}, \quad \text{: contagion}, \\ h(t) = h_0 (1 + \alpha_v \cdot v(t)),\text{: healing}, \\ m(t) = \dfrac{m_0}{1 + \alpha_w \cdot w(t)}, \quad \text{: mortality}. \end{cases} \begin{cases} u(t), v(t), w(t) \geq 0 \\ u(t) + v(t) + w(t) \leq 1 \end{cases} \quad (3)$$

Among the control variable $u(t)$, $v(t)$, and $w(t)$, $u(t)$ represents control measures to suppress the infection rate $c(t)$. With increasing $u(t)$, $c(t)$ asymptotically decreases. The positive constants α_u represents the sensitivities of $u(t)$ to $c(t)$. The larger α_u, $c(t)$ steeper decreases with respect to $u(t)$.

The variable $v(t)$ represents control measures to improve the healing rate $h(t)$, which is an increasing function of $v(t)$. The positive constants α_v is the sensitivities of $v(t)$ to $h(t)$. The larger α_v means steeper increasing $h(t)$ with respect to $v(t)$.

Furthermore, $w(t)$ represents control measures to suppress the mortality rate $m(t)$. With increasing $w(t)$, $m(t)$ asymptotically decreases. The positive sensitivity constants α_w means that the larger α_w changes $m(t)$ steeper with respect to $w(t)$.

Although the costs and effects of these measures differ, the differences are expressed only in terms of the sensitivities α_u, α_v, and α_w without losing generality by standardizing on costs, according to the cost constraint $u(t) + v(t) + w(t) \leq 1$.

B. Epidemic Control Simulation

The model is then run to obtain simulation data for epidemic control. Table 1 shows the common initial conditions and coefficients for the simulation run. Table 2 shows the simulation execution (RUN) settings following the 10 different control input assignments.

TABLE I. COMMON SIMULATION SETTING

Common Simulation Setting				
Initial Conditions	$S(0)$: Susceptibles	$I(0) = \varepsilon$: Infectives	$R(0)$: Recovered	$D(0)$: Dead
	9990	10	0	0
	$P(0)$: Population Alive =10000			
Coefficients	c_0 Contagion	h_0 Healing	m_0 Mortality	
	0.00002	0.01	0.01	
Control Sensitivities	α_u	α_v	α_w	
	10	15	20	

TABLE II. SIMULATION RUN SETTING(CONTROL VARIABLES)

Simulation Run Setting		stage-0			stage-1			stage-2			stage-3		
Time stage		t = 0~29			t = 30~89			t = 90~179			t = 180~500		
Control variables		$u(t)$	$v(t)$	$w(t)$	$u(t)$	$v(t)$	$w(t)$	$u(t)$	$v(t)$	$w(t)$	$u(t)$	$v(t)$	$w(t)$
RUN # (DMU #)	0	0.0	0.0	0.0	0.0	0.0	0.0	0.0	0.0	0.0	0.4	0.3	0.3
	1				1.0	0.0	0.0	1.0	0.0	0.0			
	2				1.0	0.0	0.0	0.0	1.0	0.0			
	3				1.0	0.0	0.0	0.0	0.0	1.0			
	4				0.0	1.0	0.0	1.0	0.0	0.0			
	5				0.0	1.0	0.0	0.0	1.0	0.0			
	6				0.0	1.0	0.0	0.0	0.0	1.0			
	7				0.0	0.0	1.0	1.0	0.0	0.0			
	8				0.0	0.0	1.0	0.0	1.0	0.0			
	9				0.0	0.0	1.0	0.0	0.0	1.0			

The simulation summary values of the execution results obtained from the above settings are shown in Table 3. The summary values were used because the number of runs in this example was small. Note that DEA requires that the output variables be positive, and the larger output variables, the better the characteristics.

Two control inputs and three outputs are used as summary variables. The two control inputs are Cs and Cm, and the three outputs are BtmActP, AvgActP, and AlvPE. Here, Cs denotes the time average of the contact infection control measure and its sensitivity ($u{\cdot}\alpha_u$) for population $P(t)$, which means the social cost of measures (such as lockdown or vaccination) to reduce the contact infection rate $c(t)$. Cm denotes the time average of cures and their sensitivity plus life-saving measures and their sensitivity ($v{\cdot}\alpha_v + w{\cdot}\alpha_w$) for the infected population $I(t)$. It represents the medical cost of promoting recovery and reducing deaths.

Furthermore, BtmActP is the minimum value of the sum of the uninfected population $S(t)$ and the recovered population $R(t)$. It represents the depth of the trough of social and economic activities. Furthermore, AvgActP is the time average of the active population ($P(t) - I(t)$). It represents the average of social and economic activities over the period. Finally, AlvPE is the minimum value of the population $P(t)$. It represents the population that survived in the end.

TABLE III. SIMULATION RESULTS (SUMMARY VALUE DATA)

		Simulation Result (Summary Values)				
		Input:		*OutPut:*		
		Cs	Cm	BtmActP	AvgActP	AlvPE
		Social Cost	Medical Cost	Bottom Active Population	Average Active Population	Alive Poplation at the end
		Avg[P(t)·αu·u(t)]	Avg[I(t)(αv·v(t)+αw·w(t))]	Min[P(t)-I(t)]	Avg[P(t)-I(t)]	Min[P(t)]
Run # (DMU #)	0	13,574	231	1,915	5,112	5,296
	1	49,693	340	8,176	8,590	8,638
	2	34,737	617	8,371	9,011	9,072
	3	34,481	19,220	2,514	7,974	8,967
	4	41,879	912	8,650	9,560	9,603
	5	24,652	919	8,650	9,575	9,619
	6	24,328	6,776	6,505	9,147	9,488
	7	33,203	15,244	1,906	6,589	7,235
	8	24,088	15,932	1,906	8,663	9,399
	9	24,418	29,615	1,906	8,082	9,524

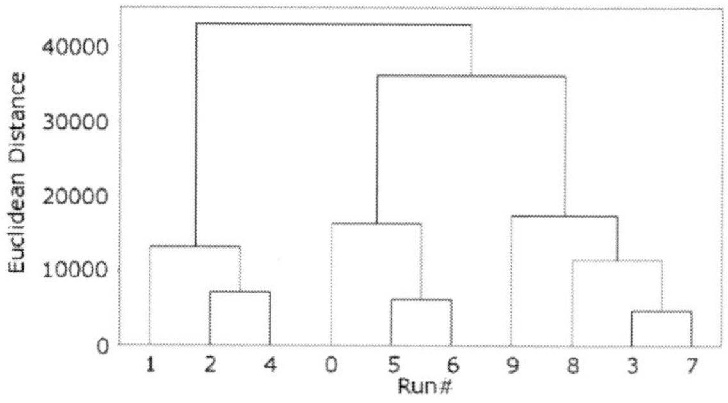

Figure 7. Clustering of input–output summary values

C. *Classification by Clustering*

Before applying DEA, the simulation run was classified by clustering. The results of hierarchical clustering of the simulation run shown in Table 3 using the Ward method with Euclidean metric are shown in Figure 7. Intuitively, as shown, the runs with similar summary value data are clustered together.

Nowadays, cluster analysis is a commonly used and convenient method, and it is also used to classify results of simulation runs [11][12]. However, when defining the distances between data with multiple variables in cluster analysis, we require exogenous weights on the variables. Furthermore, the relationship between data in the same cluster is explained only by the distance between them.

In empirical research, DEA and cluster analysis are compared in studies of the efficiency of educational systems [13].

IV. KNOWLEDGE EXTRACTION BY DATA ENVELOPMENT ANALYSIS

There are thousands of studies that use DEA. Some of those DEA studies include optimization with simulation models and clustering of data. However, in research on epidemics and infectious diseases, the application of DEA is limited to several empirical studies [14]-[20].

TABLE IV. DEA RESULTS FOR THE SUMMARY VALUES IN TABLE III

DEA_CCR		DEA Score Θ	Reference Set	Input Weights ξ		Output Weights η		
				ξ Cs	ξ Cm	η BtmActP	η AvgActP	η AlvPE
Run # (DMU #)	0	1.0	{0, 1, 2}	0.4	22.4	1.8	0	1.2
	1	1.0	{1}	0	29.4	1.2	0	0
	2	1.0	{1, 2}	0.1	8.4	1.2	0	0
	3	0.6665	{8, 5}	0.3	0	0	0	0.7
	4	0.7903	{0, 2, 5}	0.1	5.3	0.5	0.4	0
	5	1.0	{5}	0.4	0	1.2	0	0
	6	0.9995	{8, 5}	0.4	0	0	0	1.1
	7	0.5584	{8, 5}	0.3	0	0	0	0.8
	8	1.0	{8}	0.4	0	0	0	1.1
	9	0.9997	{8}	0.4	0	0	0	1.0

Using DEA, we attempt to extract knowledge from the results of the previous section's epidemic control simulation runs. The knowledge to be extracted here is, first, the classification, reflecting the characteristics of the simulation run results, and second, the information on which run results are better than others under what evaluative weights.

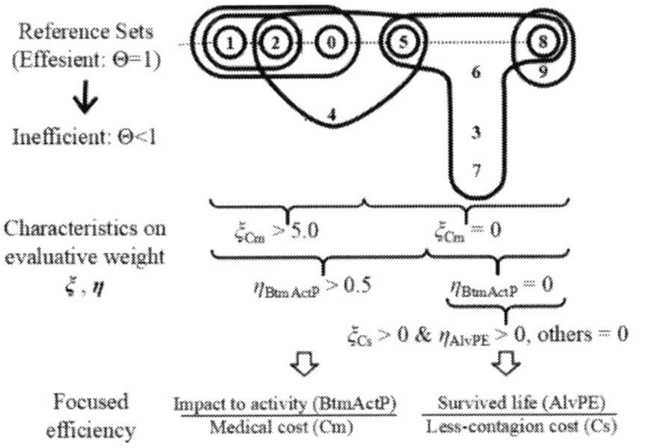

Figure 8. Classification and weight characterization by DEA

Table 4 shows the optimal efficiency Θ (DEA Score), reference set (reference set), and optimized weights for the input and output summary values (Input Weight, Output Weight) obtained by DEA (CCR method) from the simulation input-output summary value data (Table 3). For calculation of the CCR method, we used the Python code by Namiki [21].

The DEA results (Table 4) show that runs {0, 1, 2, 5, 8} are efficient (Θ = 1) while runs {3, 6, 7} are inefficient (Θ < 1). Because those inefficient runs share runs {5} and {8} as common reference sets, the weights ξ, η tend to be close in value.

As for the efficient runs {0, 1, 2, 5, 8}, runs 8 and 5 serve as reference sets for other classification groups. Runs 0, 1, and 2 serve as reference sets for one another, indicating that there is little difference between them. However, a large difference is evident between runs {8} and runs {0} and {1}, as no common reference set shares between them.

Evaluative weight ξ, η characterize that these reference sets are efficient under what posture. The runs {0, 1, 2} are efficient under the posture that focuses on the lowest number of the uninfected population divided by the medical cost. However, run {8} is efficient under the posture that focuses on the number of finally survived population divided by the infection prevention cost.

These results are summarized in Figure 8. The execution results are grouped according to their shared reference set. This also reveals which data can be used as a reference to improve group efficiency within the group.

This efficiency also characterizes the groups in terms of what posture is focused on. Thus, by endogenously determining these evaluative weights without prior knowledge, DEA enables us to extract knowledge of latent evaluative weights and the superiority or inferiority of simulation results under the weights.

V. CONCLUSION

In this paper, we used DEA to extract knowledge from the results of epidemic control simulation. The DEA classified epidemic simulation results using a method other than cluster analysis. Furthermore, DEA endogenously discovered evaluative weights that define the efficiency of simulation results and shows the potential evaluative weights and superiority of epidemic simulation results based on them. This method was a good example of classification and knowledge extraction for a set of social simulation results.

As a future research, we are going to apply DEA classification to simulation log analysis for agent-based social simulation and business gaming.

ACKNOWLEDGMENT

The ideas in this paper are inspired by Prof. Takeuchi's commentary [22]. We would like to express our deep appreciation to him. This work is partly supported by the Grant of the foundation for the Fusion Of Science and Technology. The authors would like to thank Enago (www.enago.jp) for the English language proofreading.

REFERENCES

[1] W. O. Kermack and A. G. McKendrick, "A Contribution to the Mathematical Theory of Epidemics", Proceedings of the Royal Society, vol.115A, pp.700–721, 1927, doi:10.1098/rspa.1927.0118, (reprinted Bulletin of Mathematical Biology, Vol.53, pp.33-55, 1991)

[2] W. O. Kermack and A. G. McKendrick, "Contributions to the Mathematical Theory of Epidemics-II. the Problem of Endemicity", Proceedings of the Royal Society, Vol.138A, pp.55–83, 1932, doi:10.1098/rspa.1932.0171, (reprinted in Bulletin of Mathematical Biology, Vol.53, pp. 57-87, 1991)

[3] A. Charnes, W.W. Cooper and E. Rhodes, "Measuring Efficiency of Decision Making Units", European Journal of Operational Research, Vol.2 , pp.429-444, 1978, doi:10.1016/0377-2217(78)90138-8.

[4] W.W. Cooper, L.M. Seiford and K. Tone, "Data Emvelopment Analysis, A Comprehensive Text with Models, Applications, References and DEA-Solver Software" (2nd. Ed.) , Springer, 2007, doi:10.1007/978-0-387-45283-8

[5] A. Azadeh, T. Nazari and H. Charkhand, "Optimisation of Facility Layout Design Problem with Safety and Environmental Factors by Stochastic DEA and Simulation Approach", International Journal of Production Research, Vol.53, pp.3370-3389, 2015.

[6] D. Berre, J. Vayssières, J.P. Boussemart, H. Leleu, E. Tillard and P. Lecomte, "A Methodology to Explore the Determinants

of Eco-efficiency by Combining an Agronomic Whole-farm Simulation Model and Efficient Frontier", Environmental Modelling and Software, Vol.71, pp.46-59, 2015.

[7] S. Hossein and A. Meysam, "A Simulation-Based Data Envelopment Analysis (DEA) Model to Evaluate Wind Plants Locations", Decision Science Letters, Vol.4, pp.165-180, 2015.

[8] E. Shadkam and M. Bijari, "Multi-Objective Simulation Optimization for Selection and Determination of Order Quantity in Supplier Selection Problem Under Uncertainty and Quality Criteria", The International Journal of Advanced Manufacturing Technology, Vol.93, pp.161–173, 2017.

[9] R-W. Po, Y-Y. Guh and M-S. Yang, "A New Clustering Approach Using Data Envelopment Analysis", European Journal of Operational Research, Vol.199, pp.276–284, 2009. doi:10.1016/j.ejor.2008.10.022

[10] M. Hoshino, H. Oono and H. Inazumi, "A Step Towards New Clustering Algorithm using DEA -for Gene Expression Data-", The 19th Annual Conference of the Japanese Society for Artificial Intelligence, 3A1-01, 2005. (In Japanase)

[11] Y. Tanaka , M. Kunigami, T. Terano, "What can be Learned from the Systematic Analysis of the Log Cluster of Agent Simulation", Studies in Simulation and Gaming Vol.27, pp.31-41, 2017,.doi:10.32165/jasag.27.1_31. (In Japanese)

[12] T. Kikuchi,M. Kunigam, H. Takahashi, M. Toriyama and T. Terano, "Explaining Log Data of Agent-Simulation Results with Managerial Decision-Making Description Model", Studies in Simulation and Gaming Vol.29, pp.36-48, 2019, doi:10.32165/jasag.29.1_36. (In Japanese)

[13] Y. Yuan, Q. Ying and M. Shan, "Using DEA and CA Approachs for Educational Production Efficiency: Evidence from ShangHai PISA Measurement", International Journal of Simulation: Systems, Science and Technology, Vol.17, pp.10.1-10.5, 2016.

[14] S.H. Zanakis, C. Alvarez and V. Li, "Socio-economic determinants of HIV/AIDS Pandemic and Nations Efficiencies", European Journal of Operational Research, Vol.176, pp.1811-1838, 2007.

[15] A.L. Pakyz and Y.A. Ozcan, "Use of Data Envelopment Analysis to Quantify Opportunities for Antibacterial Targets for Reduction of Health Care–Associated Clostridium Difficile Infection", American Journal of Medical Quality, Vol.29, pp.437-444, 2014.

[16] M. Tsakas, "Management Evaluation of Public Hospital Units Expenditures on Infections with the Use of Quantitative Analysis Methods",, Health Science Journal, Vol.5, pp.128-136, 2011.

[17] S. Mazo, C. Emparan, M. Vallejo and P. Soriano, "Hospital-In-The-Home Treatment of Surgical Infectious Diseases", An Economic Analysis. Surgical Infections, Vol.8, pp.567-574, 2007.

[18] C. Li, M. Sun, J.J. Shen, C.R. Cochran, X. Li and M. Hao, "Evaluation on the Efficiencies of County-Level Centers for Disease Control and Prevention in China: Results from a National Survey", Tropical Medicine and International Health, Vol.21, pp.1106-1114, 2016.

[19] J.F. Liao, J. Wang, L. Liang, Y.D. Wu, M.J. Huang, T.Q. Liu, L. Zhou and X.W. Wang, "An Evaluation Study of Research Efficiency of the Guangzhou Institute of Respiratory Diseases Based on Malmquist Index", Journal of Thoracic Disease, Vol.8, pp.2709-2716, 2016.

[20] E. Thanassoulis, M. Silva Portela and M. Graveney, "Identifying the Scope for Savings at Inpatient Episode Level: An Illustration Applying DEA to Chronic Obstructive Pulmonary Disease", European Journal of Operational Research, Vol.255, pp.570-582, 2016.

[21] M. Namiki, "Introduction to Mathematical Optimization with Python" , Asakura, 2018. (in Japanese)

[22] T. Takeuchi, "Introduction to DEA", http://blog.livedoor.jp/lionfan/archives/52682140.html, last accessed 2021/7. (In Japanese)

Survey and Application: Constructing Life Planning Support System for Retirement Planning Using Social Simulation

Takamasa Kikuchi
Graduate School of Business Administration
Keio University
Yokohama-city, Japan
takamasa_kikuchi@keio.jp

Hiroshi Takahashi
Graduate School of Business Administration
Keio University
Yokohama-city, Japan
htaka@keio.jp

Abstract—**This extended abstract focus on a life planning support system built based on data and social simulation. We present an overview of the simulation model and its applications.**

Keywords- life planning; finance; computational simulation

I. Introduction

Asset formation for the retirement generation is a common issue around the world and has been widely discussed in various countries. In the U.S., the empirical benchmark is a fixed withdrawal rate of 4% of initial assets [1]. On the contrary, there are critics who argue that a fixed withdrawal rate is inefficient [2] and that "rules" should be set to vary the withdrawal rate and amount [3] [4].

On the other hand, there have been reports of research using social simulation to solve problems in social science. For example, Yamada et al. [5] have proposed a method that utilizes both real data and agent simulation to solve problems faced by real businesses and industries. Such a level of elaborate analysis that is able to withstand decision-making in the field is expected to make a significant contribution to efficient decision-making in social and economic activities. In addition, there have been many reports of analysis through modeling based on real corporate behavior and finance theory [6][7].

In this study, we focus on a life planning support system built based on data and social simulation. In Sections II and III, we present an overview of the model and its application.

II. Methodology

In this Section, we present an overview of the simulation model used in this paper.

A. Outline

This system is designed to run simulations based on data of customer attributes, and to evaluate and validate measures for customers' retirement assets based on the data and simulation results (Fig. 1). The social simulation is constructed based on finance theory. And machine learning is used for the evaluation and verification of the policy measures [8].

Through these models, it will be possible to effectively discuss measures to avoid the depletion of retirement assets [9][10]. The proposed methodology is intended to be used by financial planners and others who develop life plans for their clients.

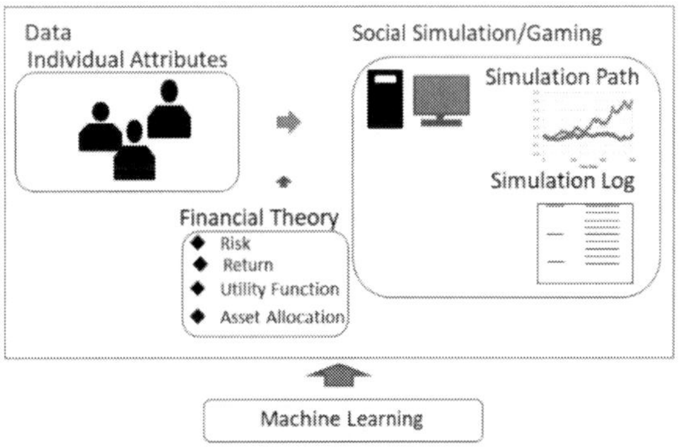

Figure 1. Basic Architecture of Life Planning Support System

B. Simulation model

We construct a computer simulation model that expresses asset formation and withdrawal before and after retirement (Fig. 1). This model is based on a model previously proposed by the authors [9][10].

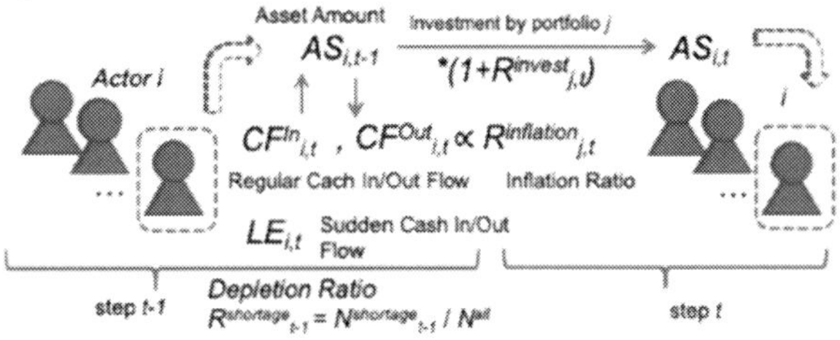

Figure 2. Conceptual Diagram of Simulation Model

The actors in the model have a specific asset balance at a certain age. Actors also have regular income and expenditure (cash inflow and outflow) and sudden income and expenditure (depending on life events) according to actor's own status (before and after retirement). The attributes of the actors can be grounded to statistical data. In addition, by manipulating the attributes of the actors, what-if analysis can be performed when a policy is implemented.

Next, the assets held by actors include cash, deposits, and risk assets. Risk assets are fully invested in a portfolio of traditional assets and provide returns according to the risk of the portfolio. In addition, the regular income and expenditure fluctuates according to the inflation rate. Here, the risk-return of the portfolio, inflation rate, and their variances are given as the external environment.

C. *Usefulness and limitation of the proposed system*

Conventional analysis has often focused on people with specific attributes to simulate asset depletion situations [11] [12]. In those studies, ad hoc analysis was required for each person in order to examine possible measures to be taken.

On the other hand, the proposed system is capable of comprehensively and semi-automatically specifying possible life planning measures for each person.

One of the limitations of this analysis is that there is arbitrariness on the part of the modeler as to which attributes of the targeted individuals are reflected in the simulation model.

III. APPLICATION

In this Section, we show an application of our methodology.

A. *Dataset: Individual attributes*

We use the individual questionnaire data from the "Awareness Survey on Life in Old Age for Before and After Retirement Generations" conducted by the MUFG Financial Education Institute [13]. The survey target was men and women aged 50 and over. The survey area was Japan, and the number of valid responses was 6,192 samples. This questionnaire comprehensively investigated the asset status of each individual (current asset balance and expected income/expenditure in old age), the planned asset succession amount, stance on investment, and outlook for old age, etc.

B. *Sample of Simulation Results*

Based on the above individual questionnaire data, we established several patterns of "possible person attributes" through segmentation by feature analysis. Based on these attributes, the simulation model described in the Section II was used to simulate measures for asset formation and withdrawal. Then, we estimated the asset depletion status of representative people who were typified by the individual questionnaire data (TABLE I) [9].

TABLE I. SIMULATION RESULT (SAMPLE): DEPLETION RATES

# of cluster	Depletion rates by inflation scenario					
	(1) No inflation		(2) Moderate inflation		(3) 2% inflation	
	Age: 90 (%)	Age: 100 (%)	Age: 90 (%)	Age: 100 (%)	Age: 90 (%)	Age: 100 (%)
#4	34	75	60	86	93	98
#1	0	0	0	0	0	0
#3	100	100	100	100	100	100
#2	0	34	0	94	0	100
#5	0	0	0	1	0	5

In addition, we conducted a hypothetical simulation in which the actors made various decisions to control asset depletion. By calculating feature importance using machine learning methods, we examined the effectiveness of these decisions (TABLE II) [9].

TABLE II. ASSUMED COUNTERMEASURES FOR EACH CLUSTER

# of cluster	Countermeasures (example)
#4	Appropriate risk taking for inflation hedging, increase retirement age
#1	Appropriate and steady asset succession
#3	Curbing expenditure, expanding social security
#2	Curbing expenditure
#5	Avoid excessive risk to prevent price fluctuations

REFERENCES

[1] Bengan, W. P., "Determining Withdrawal Rates Using Historical Data," Journal of Financial Planning, pp.767-777, 1994.

[2] Scott J.S., W.F. Sharpe and J.G. Watson, "The 4% Rule – At What Price ?," Journal of Investment Management, Third Quarter, 2008.

[3] Guyton, W.T. and Klinger, W., "Decision rules and maximum initial withdrawal rates,", Journal of Financial Planning, vol.19, article 6, 2006

[4] Spitzer, J.J., "Retirement withdrawals: an analysis of the benefits of periodic "midcourse" adjustments," Financial Services Review, vol.17, pp.17-29, 2008.

[5] Yamada, H., Ohori, K., Iwao, T., Kira, A., Kamiyama, N., Yoshida, H. and Anai, H., "Modeling and managing airport passenger flow under uncertainty: A case of Fukuoka Airport in Japan," 9th International Conference on Social Informatics (SocInfo), LNCS 10540, pp.419-430, 2017.

[6] Kikuchi, T., Kunigami, M., Yamada, T., Takahashi, H. and Terano, T., "Agent-based Simulation of Financial Institution's Investment Strategy under Easing Monetary Policy on Operative Collapses," Journal of Advanced Computational Intelligence and Intelligent Informatics, vol.22, no.7, pp.1026-1036, 2018.

[7] Takahashi, H., Takahashi, S. and Terano, T., "Analyzing the validity of passive investment strategies employing fundamental indices through agent-based simulation," In KES International Symposium on Agent and Multi-Agent Systems: Technologies and Applications, Springer, Berlin, Heidelberg, pp.180-189, 2011.

[8] Bishop, C.M., Pattern Recognition and Machine Learning, Springer New York, 2006.

[9] Kikuchi, T. and Takahashi, H., "Policy Simulation for Retirement Planning Based on Clusters Generated from Questionnaire Data," In: Jezic G., Chen-Burger J., Kusek M., Sperka R., Howlett R.J., Jain L.C. (eds) Agents and Multi-Agent Systems: Technologies and Applications 2021. Smart Innovation, Systems and Technologies, Springer, Singapore, vol.241, pp.285-298, 2021.

[10] Kikuchi, T. and Takahashi, H., "Policy Simulation on Retirement Planning Considering Individual Attributes," Journal of the Japan Society for Management Information, Research Note, to be published, 2021.(in Japanese)

[11] Yokoyama, et al., "Futureforecast policy simulation analysis on private asset formation," MURC report, 2018.(in Japanese)

[12] Kato, Y., "Post-retirement asset management framework," Secur. Anal. J. vol.56, no.8, pp.19–28, 2018.(in Japanese)

[13] Awareness Survey on Life in Old Age for Before and After Retirement Generation, MUFG Financial Education Institute, 2019.(in Japanese) last accessed 2021/2/9.

Supporting Augmented Reality Industry 4.0 Processes with Context-aware Processing and Situational Knowledge

Gregor Grambow, Daniel Hieber, Roy Oberhauser and Camil Pogolski

Dept. of Computer Science
Aalen University
Aalen, Germany
e-mail: {gregor.grambow, daniel.hieber, roy.oberhauser, camil.pogolski}@hs-aalen.de

***Abstract*—Production processes in Industry 4.0 settings are usually highly automated. However, many complicated tasks, such as machine maintenance, must be executed by human workers. In current smart factories, such tasks can be supported by Augmented Reality (AR) devices. These AR tasks rely on high numbers of contextual factors like live data from machines or work safety conditions and are mostly not well integrated into the global production process. This can lead to various problems like suboptimal task assignment, over-exposure of workers to hazards like noise or heat, or delays in the production process. Current Business Process Management (BPM) Systems (BPMS) are not capable of readily taking such factors into account. Therefore, this contribution proposes a novel approach for context-integrated modeling and execution of processes with AR tasks. Our practical evaluations show that our AR Process Framework can be easily integrated with prevalent BPMS. Furthermore, we have created a comprehensive simulation scenario and our findings suggest that the application of this system can lead to various benefits, like better quality of AR task execution and cost savings regarding the overall Industry 4.0 processes.**

Keywords*—*Business Process Management Systems; Augmented Reality; Fuzzy Logic; Business Process Modeling Notation; Resource Assignment Automation.

I. INTRODUCTION

Today's manufacturing industry heavily relies on smart factories which enable a better customer orientation as well as more efficient and individual production. In this context, the term "Industry 4.0" is used for the fourth industrial revolution driven by digitalization. Machines with built-in sensors and information technology form Cyber-Physical Systems (CPS) [1], enabling comprehensive optimization of production with regard to criteria, such as costs, resource consumption, quality or availability. Despite the focus on a high automation level and autonomous systems, human involvement in complex processes still plays a crucial part. Human workers often have to make important decisions or perform complex tasks, like machine maintenance.

In modern smart factories, such human tasks are often supported with AR devices. With AR, the worker can receive additional information for a task, contributing to its quality, performance, and repeatability. However, the integration of such activities in the global production process remains a challenge. A primary reason for this is that human AR tasks depend on a myriad of factors that are not represented in the global process. This includes the following factors:

- The AR tasks rely on different contextual data sets, e.g., external information sources supporting task execution, such as maintenance manuals, alternative procedures, checklist variability, live data from external systems or sensors of machines, the task executor and their decisions, and context-sensitive AR data like the relative position of the worker or the machine.
- For maximal effectivity and efficiency, the task must be assigned to the best suitable worker. Simple Staff Assignment Rules (SARs) of contemporary BPMS governing the production processes are only capable of determining if an agent is able to perform a task, but not their level of suitability. For AR tasks in complex Industry 4.0 settings, however, many parameters should be taken into account, like the position of the worker and the task, the qualification of the worker, or the workload of each worker. Otherwise, task execution might be suboptimal or too expensive, e.g., because of overqualification of the worker or long distances between him and the task. Furthermore, work safety is usually enforced by legal regulations and workers' exposure to hazards like heat and noise must be strictly limited.
- Usually, workers processing AR tasks are able to communicate via the AR device. However, as the AR tasks are not integrated with the global process, decisions or information provided by the worker cannot be used in that process, leading to delays or incorrect activity choices.

Contemporary BPMS lack facilities for representing and exploiting such data sets and contextual factors. Usually, these systems utilize standard BPM languages like the Business Process Modeling Notation (BPMN) [2], which were not designed to integrate such information into the process templates. Subsequently, live data and situational knowledge cannot be utilized in the process instances based on these templates.

In prior work [3][4][5], we developed an approach for contextual process management. However, our prior approach was tailored towards software engineering processes and did not involve the complex specifics of Industry 4.0 nor AR processes. To overcome the aforementioned limitations, this contribution proposes an integrated framework extending current BPMS with the following features:

1) Facilities to model processes that incorporate contextual

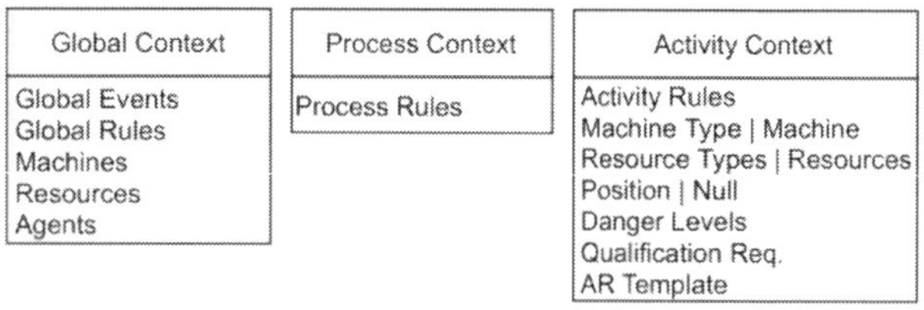

Figure 1. Context data model.

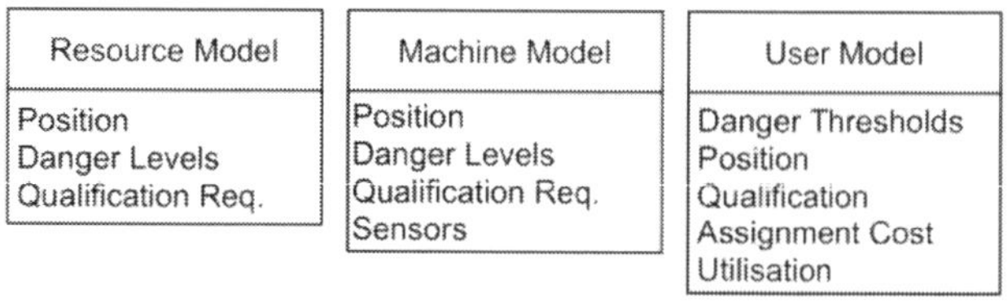

Figure 2. Actor models.

factors crucial for human AR tasks.

2) Incorporating real-time context data in BPM-Processes, enabling context dependent decision making and execution support.
3) An AR activity interface that can be used in such processes, enabling bi-directional communication between the process and the AR-supported worker.
4) An intelligent task assignment component capable of utilizing contextual data for fine-grained suitability levels to be able to match the optimal worker for any task.
5) Easy integration into existing BPMS.

The remainder of this paper is structured as follows: Section II describes the concept and solution approach, while Section III provides realization details. Thereafter, Section IV evaluates the feasibility and efficiency of the implemented system. Section V elaborates the background of the research as well as related work. Finally, Section VI provides a conclusion and outlook on future work.

II. Solution Approach

This section describes our concept for a context-aware system with AR support, called AR-Process (ARP) Framework (ARPF). It is conceived as a generic extension that any BPMS can readily integrate, providing facilities for representing contextual and AR information in executable processes in conjunction with an enactment component.

A. *Contextual Processes*

To enable the application of the ARPF in both new and existing processes and enable easy integration in any BPMS, the contextual information will be integrated into the processes via a generic BPMN 2.0 extension. Extending the BPMN standard not only allows an easy integration (requirement 2), but also allows the reuse of the existing BPMN service and script activities [6], heavily reducing implementation efforts. Such activities provide an intuitive interface between the BPMS and the ARPF. With this approach it is possible to decouple the ARPF from the process itself and provide it as a service to any BPMS supporting BPMN 2.0.

In the following, we will elaborate on the context data and rules or conditions crucial for contextual ARP execution. The context is separated into three major parts: global, process, and activity. A model can be seen in Figure 1.

The *global context* represents a cross-process entity containing all required global information. This includes information about different entities external to the BPMS. In particular, all machines, resources, and available agents. Further, the global context should provide facilities for defining conditions regarding the context that must be verified and fulfilled before an activity can be executed (requirement 2), e.g., check if an agent has the required danger clearance for an activity. This is realized by a *global rule set*. Another important factor is external context information that must be provided to the ARPF, e.g., priority changes for customer orders. Such data is incorporated via a global event system. in this manner, real-time context integration into BPM processes on a global level (requirement 2) can be achieved.

In addition to such global information, each process type may also have specific contextual conditions, e.g., if a specific process should only access a subset of the available machinery. To achieve this, a *process context* is employed that can overlay applicable portions of the global context if required. It further contains an additional *process rule set*. The latter is similar to the global rule set, but is limited to the processes of this type.

The third important entities requiring contextual information are concrete activities. To support these, an *activity context* is defined. It contains specific information for a single activity of a specific activity type and can be further specified during the ARP execution. As for the process and global context, an *activity rule set* is present to enable fine grained conditions on the activity level. On this level, however, a set of additional contextual information is required to enable an efficient assignment of the best suitable worker for each task. This incorporates data like the danger levels the task may involve, the qualification to successfully complete it (both defined as a dynamic set of key value pairs, containing values between 0 to 1), and the position of the activity represented by a three-dimensional vector X, Y, Z. Machine types can also be defined, as well as additional resources required for the activity, allowing the inclusion of machine context data directly into the process. Finally, the information, which AR-Component should be displayed to the worker while executing the activity (requirement 3) must be present. This is achieved by the AR Template.

B. *Data Models*

In addition to the contextual information added to the processes that governs how activities should be executed efficiently, the ARPF also requires information about the physical entities involved in process execution. In particular, three entities are crucial: the workers, the machines where activities (e.g., a maintenance task) are executed and their position, and resources required for such activities, like materials or tools.

To provide such information to the ARPF, three models are created, which can be found in Figure 2.

As simple BPM engines do not provide entries for resources and machines, new models must be created. Both contain a position, connected danger levels (e.g., noise with machines or chemical hazards with resources), and the required qualification to safely and efficiently work with the machine/resource. Machines usually also contain sensors providing real-time information about important production parameters. These are also included in the model.

Finally, the BPMS user/agent concept has to be extended, as current BPMS lack sufficient information to support AR activities intelligently. In order to assign agents to activities, the BPMS must possess compatible models. This can be achieved by extending the agent model of a BPM engine with values for position, qualification, and danger thresholds. Further, in most cases, cost-effective activity execution is also a requirement. Therefore, we incorporate information about the additional cost of an assignment of this agent (e.g., salary of an external worker, or weekend surcharge if it is not part of the contract) and the current utilization of the worker to avoid unbalanced workloads.

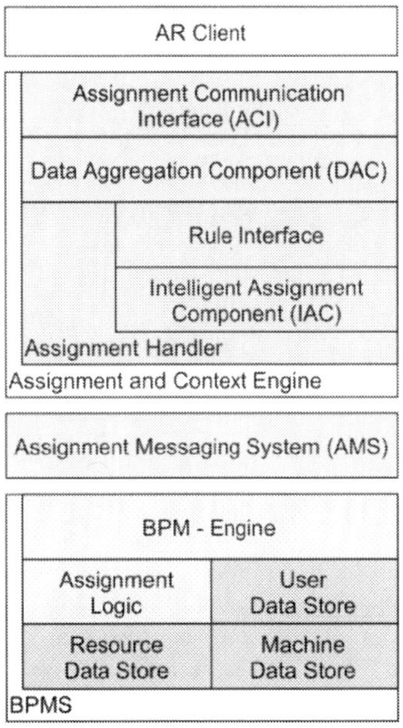

Figure 3. ARPF concept architecture.

C. *Process Modeling*

In current BPMS, there are rather limited and generic facilities to add context data to processes. This concerns the process modeling tools as well as the processes themselves. To overcome these limitations, our approach for adding contextual data for ARP execution is to realize such datasets as an extension for the most prevalent process language currently, BPMN 2.0. That way, the integration in a BPMS can be readily achieved, as any BPMN 2.0 compatible modeling tool can be easily extended (cf. requirement 1). To show the feasibility of this approach, we provide a prototype implementation of our extensions into a prevalent BPM modeling tool.

With an extended modeling tool at hand, a process engineer can add all contextual information and dependencies crucial for ARP execution support to new as well as existing process models without programming knowledge. Users, machines, and additional resources can be specified, including relevant parameters like their position. With appropriate data structures in place, relevant live data (e.g., from machine sensors) can be incorporated in the processes as they are executed. This data, in turn, is utilized by the components of the ARPF to provide more efficient task assignments and more effective support of the AR activities in the process.

D. *AR - Process Enactment*

The core architecture of the ARPF for contextual ARP enactment is depicted in Figure 3.

The core component of ARP process enactment is the Assignment and Context Engine (ACE). To provide a generalized and independent solution, this component is decoupled from the utilized BPMS. This permits a finer engineering of the ACE independent of the utilized suite. To achieve this, the ARPF incorporates two language- and platform-neutral generic communication components. The Assignment Communication Interface (ACI) enables communication between the ACE and both the BPMS, as well as the client software on AR devices, while the Assignment Messaging System (AMS) manages live data from the ARPF environment. That way, the ACE can be realized independent of any preexisting programming language or BPMS limitations. This allows the usage of the ARPF with a wide range of existing BPMS (requirement 5).

Many BPMS are provided as a standalone BPM engine (e.g., Camunda [7], jBPM) and therefore require external software to build a fully functional BPMS capable of managing all crucial data sets for contextual process enactment. To overcome these limitations and provide an easy way to extend BPM engines, we provide three generic Data Stores (DS): a User-DS, a Resource-DS, and a Machine-DS. These contain additional context information as specified by the aforementioned data models, like a more refined user model, machines used in the factory, and resources required to complete tasks. This extended context data is required in the assignment process and during the activity execution in the AR-Client.

The Assignment Logic Component (ALC) of the BPM engine is used as a bridge between engine and ACE. It aggregates all required context data for assignments; however, it is also possible to integrate the assignment request completely in the process itself via service or script tasks defined in the BPMN 2.0 standard [6] (requirement 5).

If an assignment request is sent to the ACE via the communication interface, the request is forwarded to the Data Aggregation Component (DAC) and validated for completeness. If some required context data is missing, the DAC will request it from the corresponding DS. Afterwards, the assignment request is forwarded to the Assignment Handler. The handler can then calculate a specific assignment score for the requested

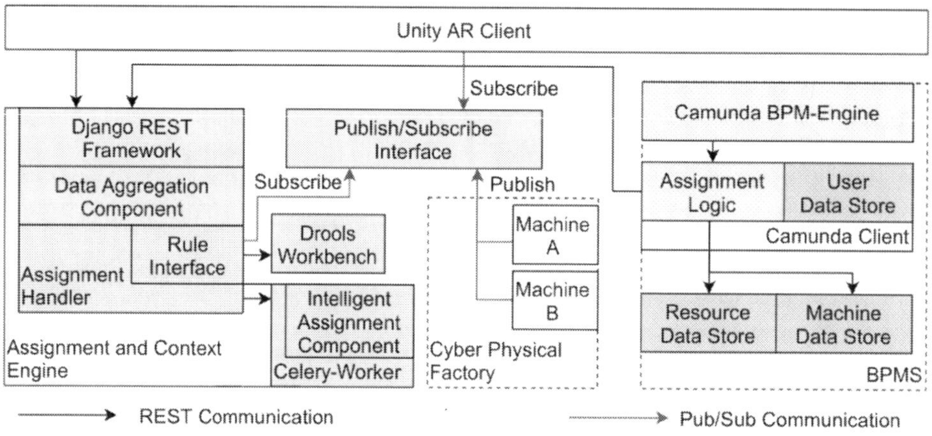

Figure 4. ARPF camunda implementation.

activity and agents in the Intelligent Assignment Component (requirement 4). If required, a presorting can be applied in a rule engine via the Rule Interface. Further preconditions of assignments (e.g., only assign the task if a sensor value is below a certain threshold) can be handled by the rule interface. To guarantee an optimal fine granular assignment score calculation fuzzy sets are utilized [8]. In this case, these are to be preferred to other solutions like Machine Learning (ML) and chaining. In contrast to ML approaches, with fuzzy sets no preexisting data sets are required nor is a training phase required, as weights can be defined directly and transparently according to the user's own knowledge and experience. Further, a fine granular calculated score between 0 and 1 is possible instead of the simple true or false of a chaining approach.

The final component of the ARPF is the AR-Client. The latter should be implemented as generic as possible to be available to a wide range of AR devices, e.g., tablets, goggles and even smartphones. The client is able to request all relevant process data via the ACI, and activities can be started, executed and completed in the AR-Client without the need to change to another software client e.g., a PC-interface, or web-client (requirement 3). Thanks to the provided AMS, it is further possible to consume real-time context changes on multiple levels (e.g., a global change of activity priorities or sensor data send from a machine connected to the activity being executed) (requirement 2).

III. Realization

This section describes the technical realization of the ARPF. It further details the communication between the components. While this section describes its integration with Camunda as a BPM engine and the AristaFlow BPM Suite [9] to demonstrate its capabilities with two mature and prevalent BPMS, the framework can be used with all BPM-Engines supporting REST-calls or external code execution.

Our prototype was implemented using Python. This approach was chosen for its rapid prototyping capabilities while still providing a large spectrum of libraries. As a base image for the ACE, a Django server was used which can be readily scaled for production deployment. To implement the ACI, the Django REST framework was integrated, providing a REST interface on top of the Django service. For the AMS, handling the real-time machine sensor communication, the Publish/Subscribe (Pub/Sub) system MQTT [10] was chosen, utilizing the Eclipse Mosquitto broker as the main component. As both technologies use well-defined industrial standards, an easy integration in BPMS is supported.

Figure 4 shows the architecture for the implementation of the ARPF with Camunda. Compared to the concept from Figure 3, some minor changes were made and the communication specified. The implementation of the AristaFlow BPM-Suite follows the same base architecture, however the full suite is provided by AristaFlow, removing the need for our own Data-Stores or an ALC. The communication is symbolized by colored arrows in Figure 4.

While the AristaFlow Suite does not require extensions, the Camunda solution requires implementation of a minimal BPM-Suite around the engine itself. This could either be realized as a single Java application relying on the Camunda Java API or using REST. In order to stay consistent with the general architecture, we use REST for our minimal BPM-Suite and split it into three sections. The Camunda BPM engine in its base version, a Camunda Client Django server containing the Assignment Logic, and the User-DS as well as a final Django Server containing the Resource and Machine Data Store. In order to connect the ARPF to a BPMN process template, it is required to create a service or script task sending a REST call to the Camunda Client. This call must contain the process instance id that can be acquired during process runtime in the same activity. During the process execution, the Camunda engine then calls the Assignment Logic via the created activity and triggers the assignment process. The Assignment Logic confirms the request to the engine and then spawns a new process handling the request. It then aggregates all data required for this assignment and sends an assignment request to ACE.

The Django REST Framework based ACI receives the assignment request and then executes the data aggregation component, validating that all required data for an assignment is available. In the Camunda implementation all required data is already present, in the AristaFlow implementation, the required data can be received from predefined endpoints. Afterwards the Assignment Handler is called. If preconditions are implemented (e.g., confirming the temperature of a machine sensor), the Rule Interface takes action. It first subscribes to all required machine sensor data endpoints via the Mosquitto Broker and then calls the connected rule engine via REST. In the implementation Drools is used for the Camunda Implementation while AristaFlow provides its own XPath-based solution. The preconditions can either be run in a loop (e.g., waiting for a sensor to cool down) until the condition is fulfilled, or in single-shot mode, aborting the assignment if the check is negative.

If the assignment is aborted, a response is sent to the Camunda Client/AristaFlow suite which are then required to provide a fallback plan, e.g., a retry after some time, a fallback process, or human intervention.

If the preconditions have been fulfilled, the assignment request is forwarded to the Intelligent Assignment Component (IAC), which itself is detached from the ACE to a celery worker. Utilizing the Celery Python framework, all assignment calculations are outsourced from the ACE and do not bind resources, therefore the I/O operations of the backend are not affected, even if many concurrent assignments are calculated. Each fuzzy assignment calculation is assigned its own processor for optimal execution speed. After the calculation is finished the IAC sends the assignment to the Celery Client/AristaFlow Suite handling the assignment update in the BPM engine.

The AR-Client is implemented using the Unity AR Foundation framework, this allows the creation of a generic AR frontend usable with a majority of present AR devices like AR goggles, tables, or phones. Instead of communication with the BPM-Suite itself, the AR-Client communicates via REST with the ACE and all requests to other sources are handled by the ACE. This enables the creation of a truly generic frontend independent of the BPMS, as all requests are parsed to the required model in the ACE. With this approach combined with a powerful AR interface, the user is able to complete and perform all activities in the AR-Client without the need to utilize another software solution or device. As the BPM workflow is still handled solely by the BPMS, it is however possible to switch at any moment to another solution (e.g., the Camunda Tasklist or the AristaFlow Client) if the worker deems it more beneficial, e.g., filling a long form.

While all process management communication is handled via REST between the AR-Client and ACE, the client can also access the Pub/Sub data via the Pub/Sub interface. It is therefore possible to see all relevant sensor values of a machine while working on it, or receive global updates (e.g., a change of priority or information a new assignment).

The final component of the ARPF is the Pub/Sub Interface, handling all MQTT messages. This contains all machines sensor data for the Rule Interface or the AR-Client, as well as global worker specific updates like a new assignment or priority updates. While the Camunda Client makes no use of global events via MQTT, the event feature is implemented in the AristaFlow suite.

In our prototype a Cyber Physical Factory is simulated using the OPC-UA protocol to connect machines' sensor data to the ARPF. As OPC-UA supports MQTT, this can be achieved in an easy and generic way, further easing the implementation into existing production environments.

To enable the creation of context-aware processes, a new BPMN modeler is created as an extension of the open source Camunda Modeler. While it is possible to create processes using the ARPF with any BPMN 2.0 modeler, a specific implementation comes with certain advantages. The modeler is linked to the different data stores and can therefore display all available machines, resources, and workers as specific entities or groups (e.g., CNC mill, maintenance workers, etc.) during the modeling of processes. This allows the process engineer to easily include the context during process creation. Further, it is possible to see available rules of the connected rule engine, enabling their integration as preconditions to activities. Moreover, the ARPF specific assignment request is moved to the background of activities, removing them from the eye of the user reducing the potential for user interface overload.

IV. Evaluation

The framework was evaluated using AnyLogic simulation software instead of a physical factory. This allowed for a more controlled and reproducible evaluation in a safe environment. Camunda was integrated as a BPM engine and Drools used as a rule engine.

The complete framework was deployed on a virtual server with 90GB main memory. However, the memory consumption never exceeded 24GB during our evaluation and can easily be halved by removing the Drools rule engine. The AnyLogic simulation was run on a Lenovo T495 with 14GB main memory utilizing Arch Linux as an operating system. To simulate values for the machine sensor, an OPC-UA server was hosted, utilizing a common industrial standard for this use case.

The evaluation was used to compare a BPMS using the ARPF against a plain BPM engine. To simulate workers and a realistic workflow, an AnyLogic simulation model was created and two simulation setups were configured.

As an environment, a factory with $21504m^2$ and a total of 29 machines requiring maintenance every 16 hours were created. The first maintenance was scheduled between 0 to 16 hours after start of the simulation. Further, the machines had an average breakdown interval of 36 hours. If a machine required maintenance or repair, a new Camunda process instance with the required worker qualification and the machine's position was started. The activity takes between 1 to 3 hours and requires an engineering qualification of 4 for maintenance and 6 for repairs. Other qualifications (electric, computer, bio_chemical) were not required and set to 0. As most modern manufacturing environments contain hazards requiring special training and regulations dangers were implemented in the simulation represented by values for noise: 0.01, heat: 0.03, electricity: 0.05, and chemicals: 0.02. While these values are quite abstract, they can easily be further refined and specified. A total of 5 workers (the agents in this use case) were available to complete these activities. Four internal workers, waiting in a maintenance building in the factory hall and one external worker, waiting 165 meters away. The external worker is used to display the need for highly trained personal which often has to be contracted by external service providers. The internal workers had engineering qualifications of 4, 5, 6 and 7 while the external worker had an engineering qualification of 8. The other qualification values were set to 0 to avoid bias. Their danger thresholds were set to 0.7 for all values. The usage of the external worker further was connected to an additional cost of 25000 (250€/activity), while the usage of internal workers incurred no additional costs. In their idle state, an worker checked every 5 minutes if a new activity was available. If they were working, they immediately checked after completion of their current activity for another enqueued activity. If no activity was enqueued, they switched back to the idle state and moved to their starting position. The simulation was separated into 5 work-shifts (each 8 hours long) with a break of 4 hours between shifts. During this break, workers were allowed to complete their current activity, but could not start new ones nor was it possible for machines to create a new task during the break. At the beginning of each work-shift, all tasks are reassigned and the danger thresholds of workers are reset to their default.

In the Camunda Setup (called CMD-Setup in the following), the workers fetched their activities directly from Camunda. All activities of the simulation were available to all of the workers and no further verification performed. If an activity is available to the group, the workers try to claim it and, if successful, work on it. In the ARPF Setup (further called ARP-Setup), the workers checked their personal worklist at the Assignment Engine REST API. If their personal worklist contains an activity, they start to work on it, otherwise they remained idle.

The five workdays were simulated for both configurations, using the same seed for the simulations random number generator. This process was repeated 10 times with different seeds to get statistically relevant test data. For the ARPF the model introduced in Section III was used. The qualification value was weighted half, to increase utilization of the more qualified workers and reduce the downtime of the machines. Further adjustment of the weighting could lead to heavily deviating results. An optimal weighting has to be configured according to the needs of the activities.

Table I shows a general comparison between the CMD and ARP simulation, while Table II shows a detailed comparison of internal and external worker stats in both simulations. In the following, values from Table I will be discussed and argued with the values from Table II.

TABLE I. ANYLOGIC ARP EVALUATION.

	ARP	Camunda
work_time	2103.31	2310.60
idle_time	524.49	396.38
avg_overqual	0.12	0.08
avg_tasks_day	3.52	3.62
violations	0.00	5.12
traveled_distance	9304.40	9502.27
cost	2000.00€	4600.00€
max_avg_underqual	0.00	-0.02
downtime_maintain	439.83	293.14
downtime_repair	218.90	249.32

The average work time and total activities per worker are lower in the ARP run, while the utilization of the internal workers (ARP-int) is slightly increased and the external utilization (ARP-ext) is heavily reduced. The average idle time is increased, which results from the low external utilization. The heavily reduced average cost of a simulation run, if using the ARPF instead of a plain BPM engine is due to the preferred use of internal workers. The increase in overqualification while using ARP instead of plain Camunda can be explained with the low weighting of qualification in the algorithms and no under-qualification, in opposition to the CMD-Setup, where under-qualification was generally present (to make it more realistic, under-qualified workers required 60 minutes longer than qualified workers). Taking a look at Table II, the main source of overqualification in the ARP simulation comes from the usage of the external worker, who was mainly used for activities below their qualification. This happened because the workload was too high and could be resolved by employing another internal worker with lower qualification to help out with these activities. This would lead to reduced costs and downtime. Optimization in the simulation or company values is needed rather than an adaptation of the algorithm.

The traveled distance for the internal workers is slightly increased in the ARP simulation compared to the CMD run. This correlates with the increased workload, and a stronger weight regarding the distance could reduce this effect. While the time for maintenance in the ARP run is around 40% higher than in the CMD-Setup, the actual down time for repairs could be reduced. This would increase the overall efficiency, as machines scheduled for maintenance still function properly while fast intervention is required on broken down machines. Further, the cost could be reduced to 43% of the CMD-Setup.

While the ARPF also utilized rules via Drools to validate if the work on the machine was safe by checking the values of the machine's temperature sensor against a max threshold, the base BPM engine did not provide such features. Violations against this precondition can be found under violations in Table II. In a real environment this would either lead to a safety regulation violation or would require a change of tasks for the worker, leading to even lower performance.

Finally, the ARPF could support workers more efficiently with their tasks, as it displays AR-instructions according to the qualification of the user. This could lead to a further speedup which has to be evaluated in a real-world setup.

Concluding, the ARPF worked as expected and the IAC

TABLE II. ANYLOGIC WORKER EVALUATION.

	ARP-int	ARP-ext	CMD-int	CMD-ext
work_time	2358.93	1080.83	2336.76	2205.95
idle_time	324.34	1325.07	381.82	454.65
avg_overqual	0.04	0.42	0.05	0.19
cost	0.00	200.00	0.00	460.00
avg_tasks_day	4.00	1.60	3.60	3.68
violations	0.00	0.00	4.88	6.10
traveled_distance	9952.32	6712.70	9386.80	9964.14
max_avg_ underqual	0.00	0.00	-0.02	0.00

produced comprehensible results. The utilization of ARPF in the simulations reduced the downtime of machines through failure and prevented any safety regulation violations.

V. RELATED WORK

Generalized context models are difficult to achieve and are not prevalent, as a survey on context models conclude [11]. An example is presented in [12]. The model is heavily tailored towards general pervasive computing scenarios and lacks several components crucial for industry 4.0 AR processes. In contrast, the ARPF context model presented is rather specific and yet readily extensible, due to its three layer context based on global, process, and activity context. Furthermore, the integration of context into process languages is challenging because they are not flexible enough, as stated in [13]. The contribution also proposes a BPMN extension for context integration, which is, in turn, tailored heavily towards mobile processes and not suitable for industry 4.0 production.

Focused on context processing the Java Context Aware Framework [14] is a technical object- and service-oriented framework targeting modeling context changes via rules. However, the processing of such rules is forwarded to the application layer. In JCOOLS [15], this limitation is overcome by by integrating JCAF with the Drools rule engine. The approach taken is rather complicated and generic, lacking support for both programmers and end users.

Examples of context modeling approaches include Coutaz and Crowley [16] and Ghiani, Manca, and Paternò [17]. However, these approaches primarily target the creation of context rules by the application developer that can later be completed with concrete values by end users, without providing the execution infrastructure.

There are also contextual approaches for Industry 4.0 production. Giustozzi et al. [18] provides a context model for industry 4.0 processes. Some of the mentioned entities are similar to the ones in the ARPF. However, the model is ontology-based and the paper primarily deals with logical relations of the concepts, which makes concrete implementation in an industry-ready system problematic. Furthermore, only a model is presented, lacking other components for integration process enactment. Another model for industry 4.0 production based on ML is presented in [19]. This model, however, is also not applicable for enactment of AR processes, as it primarily deals with predicting the degradation of the state of machines.

Another approach is taken by Tasdemir and Toklu [20]: it focusses on fuzzy task assignment and integrates BPM concepts. The described system is not suitable for the Industry 4.0 scenario, as it focuses on teams and the social relationships of the worker in the team. In addition, it lacks other components like a real-time data context model.

In summary, ARPF provides a unique approach for contextual processing for Industry 4.0 processes with human AR tasks, supporting integration with existing BPMS and utilizing a BPMN extension to include AR and context in new and existing process models. Other approaches lack the inclusion of information needed for representing processes and their connection to AR devices and workers, machines, and resources with their specific contextual properties and rules. In addition, most of these approaches do not present an integrated framework for comprehensively supporting process enactment in such complicated domains utilizing real-time data.

VI. CONCLUSION

This contribution described our ARPF approach for incorporating contextual factors crucial for AR tasks into industry 4.0 production processes. The presented framework incorporates components for integrating such factors when modeling the processes and utilizes live data from different sources while executing them. That way, contextually supported process enactment becomes possible, providing improved task assignment capabilities and better support for the AR activities. Furthermore, by providing bi-directional communication interfaces between the process and the AR task, the latter can be seamlessly integrated into the process.

We further implemented a prototype integrating our approach with two prevalent BPMS. The prototype shows that the integration with real BPMS is feasible and achievable with little effort. Further, we conducted an evaluation executing a comprehensive simulation scenario with our prototype. Our findings suggest that our approach can lead to various improvements for Industry 4.0 processes with AR tasks. Task assignments can be improved by incorporating contextual factors. Further, AR task execution can be better supported with matching contextual information. Thus, the overall process execution can be improved, resulting in better resource usage and cost savings. Moreover, other factors, like worker safety can also be taken into account and be seamlessly integrated into the processes.

Future work includes: the optimization of our context-integrated process editor to improve its appearance and usability; integration of ARPF with further BPMS; application of ARPF to other domains; further improvements to the BPMN 2.0 extension; and a comprehensive empirical evaluation in a real production environment.

ACKNOWLEDGMENTS

The authors wish to acknowledge Felix Gräber's contribution regarding the technical foundation of the IAC. This work was partially funded via the PARADIGMA project by "Zentrales Innovationsprogramm Mittelstand" (i.e., the "Central Innovation Programme for small and Medium-Sized

Enterprises (SMEs)"), of the Federal Ministry for Economic Affairs and Energy of the Federal Republic of Germany.

References

[1] R. Baheti and H. Gill, "Cyber-physical systems," *The impact of control technology*, vol. 12, no. 1, pp. 161–166, 2011.

[2] T. Allweyer, *BPMN 2.0: introduction to the standard for business process modeling*. BoD–Books on Demand, 2016.

[3] G. Grambow, R. Oberhauser, and M. Reichert, "Contextual injection of quality measures into software engineering processes," *Int'l Journal on Advances in Software*, vol. 4, no. 1&2, pp. 76–99, 2011.

[4] G. Grambow and R. Oberhauser, "Towards automated context-aware software quality management," in *2010 Fifth International Conference on Software Engineering Advances*. IEEE, 2010, pp. 347–352.

[5] G. Grambow, R. Oberhauser, and M. Reichert, "Towards automatic process-aware coordination in collaborative software engineering," in *6th Int'l Conference on Software and Data Technologies*. ScitePress, 2011, pp. 5–14.

[6] *Business Process Model and Notation(BPMN) - Version 2.0.2*. Object Management Group, 12 2013, retrieved: 2021.06.10. [Online]. Available: https://www.omg.org/spec/BPMN/2.0.2/PDF

[7] Camunda. Last Visited: 2021.06.10. [Online]. Available: https://camunda.com

[8] L. A. Zadeh, "Fuzzy logic," *Computer*, vol. 21, no. 4, pp. 83–93, 1988.

[9] M. Reichert, "Enabling flexible and robust business process automation for the agile enterprise," in *The Essence of Software Engineering*. Springer, Cham, 2018, pp. 203–220.

[10] G. C. Hillar, *MQTT Essentials-A lightweight IoT protocol*. Packt Publishing Ltd, 2017.

[11] C. Bolchini, C. A. Curino, E. Quintarelli, F. A. Schreiber, and L. Tanca, "A data-oriented survey of context models," *SIGMOD Rec.*, vol. 36, no. 4, p. 19–26, Dec. 2007.

[12] K. Henricksen, J. Indulska, and A. Rakotonirainy, "Modeling context information in pervasive computing systems," in *Pervasive Computing*. Berlin, Heidelberg: Springer Berlin Heidelberg, 2002, pp. 167–180.

[13] J. Dörndorfer and C. Seel, "A meta model based extension of bpmn 2.0 for mobile context sensitive business processes and applications," *Proc WI 2017*, pp. 301–315, 2017.

[14] J. Bardram, "The java context awareness framework (jcaf) – a service infrastructure and programming framework for context-aware applications," vol. 3468, 05 2005, pp. 98–115.

[15] J. Park, H.-C. Lee, and M.-J. Lee, "Jcools: A toolkit for generating context-aware applications with jcaf and drools," *Journal of Systems Architecture*, vol. 59, no. 9, pp. 759–766, 2013.

[16] J. Coutaz and J. L. Crowley, "A first-person experience with end-user development for smart homes," *IEEE Pervasive Computing*, vol. 15, no. 2, pp. 26–39, 2016.

[17] G. Ghiani, M. Manca, and F. Paternò, "Authoring context-dependent cross-device user interfaces based on trigger/action rules," *Proceedings of the 14th International Conference on Mobile and Ubiquitous Multimedia*, pp. 313–322, 2015.

[18] F. Giustozzi, J. Saunier, and C. Zanni-Merk, "Context modeling for industry 4.0: an ontology-based proposal," *Procedia Computer Science*, vol. 126, pp. 675–684, 2018.

[19] J.-R. Ruiz-Sarmiento *et al.*, "A predictive model for the maintenance of industrial machinery in the context of industry 4.0," *Engineering Applications of Artificial Intelligence*, vol. 87, p. 103289, 2020.

[20] C. Tasdemir and C. Toklu, "Qos driven dynamic task assignment for bpm systems using fuzzy logic," in *Emerging trends and challenges in information technology management*. Hershey, Pennsylvania (701 E. Chocolate Avenue, Hershey, Pa., 17033, USA: IGI Global, 2006.

Generating Market Comments on Stock Price Fluctuations Using Neural Networks

Ibuki Sekino
Major in Computer and Information Sciences
Graduate School of Science and Engineering,
Ibaraki University
email: 21nm734a@vc.ibaraki.ac.jp
4-12-1, Nakanarusawa, Hitachi, Ibaraki, 316-8511, Japan

Minoru Sasaki
Dept. of Computer and Information Sciences
Faculty of Engineering, Ibaraki University
email: minoru.sasaki.01@vc.ibaraki.ac.jp

Abstract- In recent years, there has been a lot of interest in techniques for generating market comments from stock prices automatically. However, even today, it is still manually generated by analyst. In this paper, we propose a method for generating "comments on stock price fluctuations" included in market comments in order to reduce the workload of analysts. The proposed method learns stock price fluctuations and the corresponding expressions, generates comments, and completes market conditions comments by assigning them to prepared canned sentences. As a result of our experiments, we found that the features used to generate them are effective and the proposed method can accurately generate market comments.

Keywords; Generate market comments; Stock price fluctuation;Nikkei Stock Average

I. INTRODUCTION

In recent years, there has been an increase in the use of data in various fields, such as weather, sports, medicine and finance. However, when the data is large or complex, it is difficult for a person without expert knowledge to understand it, and even if he or she is an expert, it takes time to understand the data and extract the important elements. One way to make effective use of such data is the data-to-text technology. This is a technology that expresses the outline of data in text to make it easier for humans to interpret, and it has been gaining attention due to its increased demand in recent years.

The task of generating market comments from stock price data, which is the subject of this research, is also a type of data-to-text technology. Currently, market commentary is generated by analysts, who are experts in researching and analyzing social conditions, etc. They analyze stock prices after they are released and generate market comment. However, it takes a lot of time and effort for analysts to generate full-text market comments from stock prices. Therefore, in this paper, we propose a method for generating a part of the market comment in order to reduce the effort required for analysts to generate market comment. Specifically, we extract expressions related to the price movements of stock prices and their fluctuation ranges, and then generate comments by learning the price movements of stock prices and expressions through machine learning. By applying the generated comments to the pre-prepared format, the system automatically generates the quantitative analysis results in the market comment, and as a result, analysts can concentrate on their core business, such as factor analysis.

In this paper, we extract various features from the time series data and convert them into text based on the task of generating market comments on the Nikkei Stock Average. First, we form long-term and short-term time series data to capture the changes in the time series stock price data. Next, we extract 12 important phrases from NQN(Nikkei Quick News) so that we can generate a expression in NQN. These phrases are frequent occurrences in the first sentence of the market comment, and the four main expressions are "続落 (continued to decline)", "続伸(continued to rise)", "反発 (rebound)", and "反落(reactionary fall)", with "大幅 (large)" and "小幅(small)" added for a total of 12. By mapping these expressions to the price movements of stock prices, we create a single data set for learning.

In order to compare our results with those of a previous study by Murakami et al [1], we unified the similar expressions among the generated ones. In addition, we omit sentences that do not need to be generated automatically using the neural network. We will verify if there is any change in the experimental results.

II. RELATED WORK/METHODS

In this section, we present a related work and related methods that this paper referred to.

A. *Related works*

Various studies have been conducted on data-to-text technology, which automatically generates a summary of time-series data in text that is easy for humans to interpret. For example, research has been conducted to automatically generate text about weather forecasts from time-series weather information [2], to generate text from clinical data to assist doctors and nurses in decision making [3], and to generate feedback text for students from time-series data that records their learning status within a certain period [4]. In the past, the mainstream of data-to-text research has been the generation of text using manually created rules. However, in recent years, with the development of information and communication technology, large-scale and complex data has become readily available, and interest in machine-learning type methods that generate text based on large-scale correspondence between data and text has been increasing. For example, research has been conducted on the use of machine learning in various data-to-text techniques, such as image caption generation [5], which generates descriptions from image data, and weather forecast text generation from molded weather data [6].

B. Related methods

There are various approaches to the technology of generating market comment from various perspectives. For example, there are techniques to generate factors of change, such as events that are said to have affected the price movement of the Nikkei Stock Average and information on other stocks [7], to control the generated text by inputting topics that represent the content of the generated market comment in addition to the Nikkei Stock Average data [8], and to generate characteristics, such as the history of the price of the stock and time-dependent expressions [1].

In this research, we are working on a technique to generate text by appropriately selecting words that represent the direction of price movement and the range of fluctuation of stock prices.

III. PROPOSED METHOD

In this section, we present a method for extracting words and phrases that represent the price movement and fluctuation range of stock prices from the Nikkei Stock Average and NQN, and the data used in this paper.

A. Overview

Figure 1 below shows the execution procedure of the proposed method.

First, we molded the data in order to create a correspondence between stock price data and article data. Since the article data contains many noisy expressions, we set the conditions to remove the noise and extracted the original phrases of the expressions generated from the article data. The details will be described later.

Next is the stock price data, which also contains a lot of noise and is inefficient for machine learning, so we molded it into a form that is easy to learn.

We then created a correspondence between three days of stock price data and a single expression and used it to start learning. For machine learning, we used a Multilayer Perceptron (MLP), which is commonly used as an encoder.

Finally, using the trained data, we input test data including stock price data to predict the expression. The predicted expressions are then substituted into the prepared format, and the market condition comments are completed. F value between the predicted expression and the correct data is calculated and used as an evaluation criterion.

B. Dataset

In this paper, we use the Nikkei Stock Average as stock price data and NQN as article data. The data used are for the four years from 2014 to 2017. TABLE I and TABLE II show examples of the Nikkei Stock Average and NQN used in this study. The Nikkei Stock Average is the five-minute version, and the NQN is used for the part that can extract the expressions to be generated.

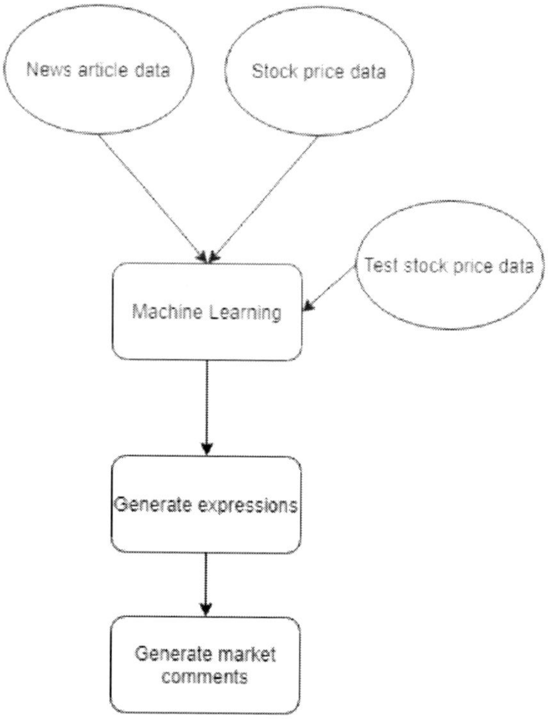

Figure 1. Flow of the proposed method

TABLE I. PART OF THE NIKKEI STOCK AVERAGE 5-MINUTE TTIMEFRAME 〔2017/01/04〕

Time	Opening Price	High price	Low price	Closing price
9:00:00	19298.68	19351.47	19277.93	19351.47.1
9:05:00	19354.42	19362.40	19335.90	19352.44
9:10:00	19358.04	19390.47	19358.04	19387.76

TABLE II. PART OF NQN

No	Headline
166	<NQN>◇日経平均先物、夜間取引で下落　60 円安の 1 万 9040 円で終了 (Nikkei 225 futures fell in overnight trading, closing 60 yen lower at 19,040 yen.)
392	<NQN>◆日経平均、反発で始まる　184 円高の 1 万 9298 円 (Nikkei 225 begins to rebound, up 184 yen to 19,298 yen)
411	<NQN>◇日経平均、反発して始まる米株高で市場心理が好転 (Nikkei 225 starts to rebound, market sentiment improves on high US stock prices)

C. *Pre-processing*

In various fields, such as image processing and natural language processing, it is common to perform prepr- -ocessing in order to generalize machine learning models and to remove noise from data. Also in this paper, preprocessing is applied to the Nikkei Stock Average data, which is numerical data. We used the standardization and the difference from the previous day as the preprocessing methods for the numerical data. The equations of the processing methods used are shown below.

$$x_{std} = (x_i - \mu)/\theta \quad (1)$$

$$x_{move} = x_i - r_i \quad (2)$$

x_i represents the stock price.

In (1), standardization is performed using the data x, mean value μ, and standard deviation θ used for learning.

In (2) calculates the difference between the price x_i at each time step from the previous day's closing price r_i in order to capture the change in price from the previous day's closing price.

As in the previous study [1], Prepared "XShort", a one-day stock price data consisting of 62-time steps and "XLong", a long-term stock price data using the past closing price as an input, as a short-term time series data to capture short-term and long-term stock price fluctuations. However, it was difficult to extract the expression of the short-term data from the articles, so this paper mainly deals with the long-term stock price data.

As for the molding of the article data, since there is more than one expression extracted from NQN in a day, the first expression of the day is treated as the expression of the date.

IV. EXPERIMENT

TABLE III compares the data set used in the previous study with the data set used in this study. The comparison with the previous paper is made only where the expressions are covered. The reason for the difference in the data used in the training data is that the data of the Nikkei Stock Average for 2013 was in a different format from the data of other years, making it difficult to extract the data. Although there are some differences between the Nikkei 225 data of 2013 and 2017, the differences have been compensated by increasing the number of train data. In addition, the test data are all the same, so the results are expected to be fine.

TABLE III. DATASET FOR PREVIOUS PAPER AND THIS PAPER

	Previous paper	This paper
Training data	Nikkei Stock Average/ Nikkei QUICK News in 2013,2014,2015	Nikkei Stock Average/ Nikkei QUICK News in 2014,2015,2017
test data	Nikkei Stock Average / Nikkei QUICK News in 2016	Nikkei Stock Average / Nikkei QUICK News in 2016
Expressions that describe changes in stock prices	10/ Four expressions were used as references for comparison with this study	12
Others/Differences from this study	the previous study incorporated expressions that depend on the time of day and where the actual stock price values are calculated in the encoder-decoder.	-

V. RESULT

In this experiment, we use a combination of time series data Xlong and Xshort and preprocessing methods std and move, with one time series data as a reference and one or both preprocessing methods applied to it. The number of expressions used in the previous study was four, and they are shown in TABLE IV. TABLE IV includes the experimental results.

TABLE IV. RESULTS

Expression	Xlong_move	Xlong_std	Xlong_move_std	Xshort_move	Previous study
Rebound	0.9	0.85	0.91	0.98	0.803
Reactionary fall	0.94	0.90	0.90	0.98	0.748
Large reactionary fall	0.62	0.38	0.60	-	-
Large rebound	0.55	0.60	0.44	-	-
Large, continued to decline	0.00	0.77	0.00	-	-
Large, continued to rise	0.60	0.69	0.63	-	-
Small, rebound	0.00	0.00	0.00	-	-
Small, reactionary fall	0.00	0.00	0.00	-	-
Small, continued to rise	0.00	0.00	0,46	-	-
Small, continued to decline	0.00	0.00	0.50	-	-
Continued to rise	0.90	0.89	0.88	1.00	0.814

Continued to decline	0.89	0.87	0.90	1.00	0.753

Several methods have been used in previous studies as well as in this paper, and the results here refer to the method that produced the highest F value. The red letters represent the best results within Xlong. The blue letters are the ones with good results, but without the expression for the stock price fluctuation range. This is because when generating comments, NQN does not produce expressions at five-minute version, so I used a rule base to generate expressions without stock price fluctuation ranges. Although it is not directly related to the experimental results, it is described following the execution results of previous studies.

In this table, we can see that the two types of preprocessing give the best results in terms of Xlong alone.

VI. DISCUSSIONS

In this section, we will discuss the results.

A. *Expressions about stock price fluctuations and Xshort.*

NQN does not produce expressions for every 5 minutes, but only for important time periods (9:00, 12:00, 15:00). Therefore, in the case of short-term data that deals with five-minute data, it is necessary to extract expressions mechanically or by using other data as training data and extracting expressions by predicting them. In this paper, the former method was used. In producing the expressions for short-term data, we used the difference from the previous day in two steps. Specifically, two steps of the previous day's difference are used, with a positive value indicating "続伸(continue to rise)" and a negative value indicating "続落(continue to decline)". However, the thresholds for large or small at this time are not defined, resulting in the results shown in Table3. The NQN shows several instances of large and small falls, but the conditions for their appearance could not be determined because of only two steps of difference from the previous day, so it was not possible to set a threshold. The reason for this is that the analysts who write the market commentary assign "large" and "small" according to their sensitivity.

Therefore, the results show a high F value because there were only four expressions for three years of data. One of the future tasks will be to determine the threshold for mechanically generating expressions related to the range of fluctuation.

B. *Extraction methods considered based on differences with previous studies.*

TABLE V shows the comparable areas in this paper and previous studies. The present study produced high F values for all comparable expressions. This is thought to be due to the fact that similar expressions in the previous studies, such as "反発(rebound)" and "上げに転じる(start to move up)", were treated as the same in this study. In order to improve the accuracy of expression generation, we unified the expressions in this study. It was found that unifying the expressions increased the accuracy by about 10-20%.

TABLE V. COMPARISON OF PREVIOUS STUDIES AND THIS STUDY

Expression	This Paper	Previous paper
Continued to decline	0.91	0.803
Continued to rise	0.90	0.748
Rebound	0.88	0.814
Reactionary fall	0.90	0.753

C. *Number of expressions and number of data References*

The results show, there are some expressions whose occurrence rate is 0, and the problem is that the number of data is too large for the number of expressions prepared.

The following is a table of the number of expressions that exist in the data (TABLE VI.) and the occurrence rate of the expression that represents the fluctuation range of stock prices in the data used (TABLE VII). The red letters in TABLE VI and TABLE VII are the three selected from the lowest values.

Looking at TABLE VII, we can see that there are several expressions that are never generated. As in the case of Short, if the training data is biased, the result will be like this, so it is desirable to have training data where all expressions are generated to some extent. Or it is necessary to review the expressions to be extracted.

TABLE VI. THE NUMBER OF EXPRESSIONS THAT EXIST IN THE DATA

Expression	Xlong_move_std F-value
Continue to rise	184
Rebound	150
Reactionary fall	147
Continue to decline	111
Lage rebound	24
Large, continue to decline	24
Small continue to decline	20
Large Reactionary fall	17
Small continue to rise	17
Small reactionary fall	14
Large continue to rise	13
Small rebound	8

TABLE VII. OCCURRENCE RATE OF THE EXPRESSION THAT REPRESENTS THE FLUCTUATION RANGE

Expression	Xlong_move_std F-value
Large rebound	0.6
Large reactionary fall	0.44

Large continue to rise	0
Large continue to decline	0.63
Small rebound	0
Small reactionary fall	0
Small continue to rise	0.46
Small continue to decline	0.5

VII. CONCLUSION

In this paper, we extracted expressions related to the price movements of stock prices and their fluctuation ranges using the Nikkei Stock Average and NQN, learned the expressions and price movements by machine learning, and generated expressions for given stock prices. We compared the generated expressions with those extracted from the original article and verified which training data was superior in terms of correct answer rate and F value.

In conclusion the results of the training data with two types of preprocessing implemented exceeded those of the previous study. This is thought to be due to the unification of similar expressions in the previous study.

In addition, when generating expressions related to the range of variation of values, such as "大幅(Large)" and "小幅(Small)," it turned out to be difficult to generate them unless the training data contained this expressions with a certain degree of probability.

Future tasks include setting the threshold for generating expressions related to the range of variation mechanically, creating better training data, and reviewing the expressions.

REFERENCE

[1] S. Murakami, A. Watanabe, A. Miyazawa, K. Goshima, T. Yanase, H. Takamura, and Y. Miyao, "Learning to Generate Market Comments from Stock Prices" Proceeding of the 55th Annual Meeting of the Association for Computational Linguistics, pp. 1374-1384, 2017.

[2] B. Anja, "Probabilistic Generation of Weather Forecast Texts" Association for Computational Linguistics, pp. 164-171, 2007.

[3] F. Portet, E. Reiter, J. Hunter, and S. Sripada "Automatic Generation of Textual Summaries from Neonatal Intensive Care Data" Artificial Intelligence, Volume173, pp. 789-816 , 2009.

[4] D. Gkatzia, H. Hastie, and O. Lemon "Comparing Multi-label Classification with Reinforcement Learning for Summarization of Time-series Data." Association for Computational Linguistics, pp. 1231-1240, 2014.

[5] O. Vinyals, A. Toshev, S. Bengio, and D. Erhan "Show and Tell: A Neural Image Caption Generator" IEEE, Accession Number: 15524253, 2015.

[6] H. Mei, M. Bansal, and M. R. Walter "What to talk about and how? Selective Generation using LSTMs with Coarse-to-Fine Alignment" Association for Computational Linguistics, pp. 720-730, 2016.

[7] T. Aoki, A. Miyazawa, T. Ishigaki, K. Goshima, K. Aoki, I. Kobayashi, H. Takamura, and Y. Miyao "Generating Market Comments Referring to External Resources" Association for Computational Linguistics, pp. 135-139, 2018. (RELATED WORK/METHODS)

[8] K. Aoki, A. Miyazawa, T. Ishigaki, T. Aoki, H. Noji, K. Goshima, I. Kobayashi, H. Takamura, and Y. Miyao "Controlling Contents in Data-to-Document Generation with Human-Designed Topic Labels", Association for Computational Linguistics, pp. 323-332, 2019.

Predicting the Approval or Disapproval of each Faction in a Local Assembly Using a Rule-based Approach

Ryo Kato
Major in Computer and Information Sciences
Graduate School of Science and Engineering,
Ibaraki University
Hitachi, Ibaraki, Japan
21nm718s@vc.ibaraki.ac.jp

Minoru Sasaki
Dept. of Computer and Information Sciences
Faculty of Engineering,
Ibaraki University
Hitachi, Ibaraki, Japan
minoru.sasaki.01@vc.ibaraki.ac.jp

Abstract—**This paper uses the meeting minutes of the Tokyo Metropolitan Assembly and the Ibaraki Prefectural Assembly to create a rule base for predicting the approval or disapproval of each faction, and to examine the effectiveness of methods for extracting opinions from the meeting minutes and methods for estimating when opinions cannot be obtained. In recent years, the voter turnout in Japan has been on a downward trend. In order to solve this problem, we conducted this research because we believe that it is necessary to present materials to judge the credibility of politicians' statements by clearly indicating in an easy-to-understand manner what kind of opinion each faction has on each proposition and the direction of its argument. In the Tokyo Metropolitan Assembly, we used the meeting minutes of the plenary sessions, and from the statements made during the meetings, we assumed that the opinion of the faction to which the speaker belonged was the opinion of "for" or "against" the proposal. As a method of estimating opinions, we created and verified several methods of estimating opinions when they could not be read. In addition to the method used in the Tokyo Metropolitan Assembly, the Ibaraki Prefectural Assembly implemented an estimation method that applied the opinions of the Assembly Steering Committee and an estimation method that used machine learning. As a result, in the Tokyo Metropolitan Assembly, the method that applied the opinions of the minority group obtained the highest value. For the Ibaraki Prefectural Assembly, the method that applied the members of the Assembly Steering Committee obtained the highest value. For the estimation of the Tokyo Metropolitan Assembly's opinion, there are similar studies that have recorded higher values, and further improvement in accuracy can be expected by using machine learning.**

Keywords- stance classification, Approval or disapproval forecast.

I. INTRODUCTION

In this paper, we develop a system that allows each party to decide whether to support or oppose each proposal in a local assembly.

In recent years, the voter turnout in Japan has been on a downward trend, with 51.28% in the last Tokyo Metropolitan Assembly election and only about 40% in the lowest years. The low voter turnout rate among people in their twenties is particularly noticeable, and in the Tokyo Metropolitan Assembly election of 2009, the turnout rate was 26.44%, the lowest of any generation. One possible reason for this is that it is difficult for young people to judge what kind of agenda, what kind of opinions, and what kind of discussions are going on in politics itself. It is not easy to watch all the meetings of the Diet or to read through the minutes, and we think this is the reason why people are not interested in politics. For this reason, we think that clearly indicating in an easy-to-understand manner what kind of opinion each faction has on each agenda item and showing the direction of their arguments would be a material for judging the credibility of politicians' statements. Looking at the minutes of a given meeting, it is not difficult to estimate the approval or disapproval of the major political parties, but it is difficult to estimate the opinions of the factions with a small number of seats, since they rarely make statements themselves. The goal of this research is to estimate the opinions of the political parties to which the politicians belong from their statements, and to calculate the approval or disapproval of each proposal.

In section Ⅱ, we describe the implementation method of each experiment we conduct. Section Ⅲ describes the experiments conducted in this paper, and the conclusion of this study is given in section Ⅳ.

II. RULE BASED FOR STANCE CLASSIFICATION

We talk about the rule based we used in the stance classification in this section

A. *Whole picture*

We scan the minutes of each meeting and detect whether the speaker agrees or disagrees with the proposal. If we are able to detect the approval or disapproval of a proposition, we take it as the opinion of the party to which the speaker belongs. If we are unable to obtain the approval or disapproval of the proposal being discussed, we assign an opinion to each group according to the rule base described below. We will take the approval or disapproval thus obtained as our response.

B. *How to process text and classify agree and disagree*

We input the plenary session minutes data and extract the remarks containing the bill number and their speakers. We use the minutes of the last day of each plenary session. We classify the minutes by speaker and content. We use

MeCab(Ver.0.996.2) to morphologically analyze these statements and get a list of strings. We scan this list and investigate whether there is a word "agree" or "disagree". If we find one or the other, we divide the list into two parts based on the location of the word. If we find "○○bill" and the bill number in the first sentence, we judge the proposition to be the opinion of the found phrase. We then repeat the same action in the following sentence.

C. How to judge whether to agree or disagree of a proposal in the Tokyo Metropolitan Assembly

1) Batch processing of bills

There are some cases where a bill is described as " outside ○○ bill ".In this case, we convert the Chinese numerals in "○○" into alphanumeric characters. After that, we determine that the number plus one of the bills from the beginning of the bills whose Speaker is null in the minutes is an objection. For those proposals for which no opinion in favor or against was obtained by this method, we give the opinion of opposition to the Communist Party, which is often the opposition party, and the opinion of approval to the other parties provisionally.

2) Judgment of approval or disapproval by ruling party or opposition faction

In *1)*, we assigned affirmative opinions to the proposals on which no opinion was obtained. We now assign the labels of the ruling and opposition parties to the minority caucus and assign opinions accordingly. The minority group has very little to say during the assembly and it is difficult to extract approval or disapproval from the text of the meeting. For this reason, we collect the tendency of each minority group to agree or disagree with the opinion of the ruling party or the opposition party in advance, and assign opinions for or against each minority group accordingly. We estimated this tendency from Wikipedia's Tokyo Metropolitan Assembly page [9] and training data, and then we used the following data , a dictionary was created. We grant approval or disapproval if no approval or disapproval is obtained. For minority parties, we refer to the dictionary we created. A faction that is presumed to have "oppositional tendencies" is assigned the same opinion as the Communist Party, which is often the largest opposition party, as the opinion of that faction. This assigns an opinion to the minority party.

3) Decisions for and against by the ruling and opposition factions

We consider, as in *2)*, the manner in which opinion is presumed for the minority group. At the first meeting of each year of the meeting minutes, there is a discussion of the proposed budget. This budget proposal includes the "General Fund" and "Water Utility Account" and often the same budget proposal is discussed each year. We also estimate that all political parties often have a same opinion on this budget proposal every year. We gather from the Training data which budget proposals the various factions disagree with each year and create a dictionary. Using this dictionary, we determine whether the parties in question have ever held opposing views on the budget proposal, and if so, we assign opposing views to it as well.

D. How to judge whether to agree or disagree of a proposal in Ibaraki Prefectural Assembly

1) Judgment of approval or disapproval by ruling party or opposition faction

We use the same method as in *2)* to estimate agree or disagree. We use the training data to estimate whether the various factions tend toward the ruling party or the opposition party. We assign the same approval or disapproval to parties that are estimated to be "opposition leaning" as to the Communist Party, which is often the largest opposition party. We thus assign an opinion to the minority party.

2) Judgment using the minutes of the Parliamentary Steering Committee

At the Steering Committee meeting, each faction expresses its opinion in favor of or against the proposal. The attitude of each faction is described in order to ask the faction in favor to raise their hands when the vote is taken in the plenary session. We infer approval or disapproval from the confirmation of attitudes after the phrase "the vote will be taken by division" in the meeting minutes. We first extract each part of the agenda that is being voted on. There are cases where many bills are voted on at once, and cases where only a few are voted on. When we see the notation "Bills No.○○or ○○.", we handle the whole series of propositions from the first to the last one. We assign an opinion to each of these proposals. If there is the word "abstaining from voting" we label the group in that sentence as having no opinion. If it contains the phrase " A summary of the decision " we will label all factions in favor. If the wording is "rejection " the Communist Party will be labeled as in favor, and all other parties will be labeled as against. If there is a " showdown vote " we give the label of "remove" to the party described before the "except" language, if any, and the label of "for" to the other parties. If there is no "Remove" language, we give the label "agree" to the faction described before the " raising one's hand " and the label "disagree" to all others.

3) Rule base for Predicting Pros and Cons Using BERT

In this section, we use Bidirectional Encoder Representations from Transformers (BERT) to find the cos similarity of the opposing proposals and predict the approval or disapproval based on it. BERT(Bidirectional Encoder Representations from Transformers))\ is a model announced by Google in 2018, in which a learning model pre-trains a large amount of text data and can be applied to various tasks such as text understanding and sentiment analysis. There are two types of pre-training: one is to use the representation vector obtained from the pre-training as one of the features, and the other is to use the parameters obtained from the pre-training as initial values for the weights. In this experiment, we use the BERT(Bidirectional Encoder Representations from Transformers) pre-trained model [cl-tohoku/bert-base-japanese-whole-word-masking]. We first collect the bills that are opposed by each faction. We then compare them with the names of the bills in the currently estimated assembly. Using a pre-trained model, we extract the features of each proposition name. We calculate the cos similarity of the extracted features. If the similarity is 0.98 and 0.99, we also label the proposition as opposed. We collect the opposing bills from the first meeting in 2019 to the second meeting in 2020 after the election in 2008. We compare the names of the bills by deleting the parts of the bills that are not related to the contents of the bills, such as "HEISEI ○○ Fiscal year". We will compare the opposing bills with the bills submitted by the legislative bodies that we are judging.

4) Rule base for Predicting pros and cons using machine learning for BERT with training data.

In this section, we will build a machine learning/deep learning model to train the tendency of dissenting opinions of the Communist Party, and estimate it using the training results. We first create training data, in order to grasp the tendency of opposition to a particular proposition when the opposition to that proposition is also opposition to a particular proposition. For each opposing proposition, we collect related opposing propositions and label them as correct, and for unrelated propositions, we label them as incorrect. This training data is then used for learning. We use BERT(Bidirectional Encoder Representations from Transformers) to do the training. We apply this learning result to output the probability value of the target proposition. We set a threshold value of 0.5, and label the proposals whose probability value exceeds this value as the opposite.

III. EXPERIMENTS

In this section, we describe the experiments we performed and their results.

E. Date

1) Tokyo Metropolitan Assembly

The data to be used are the Tokyo Metropolitan Assembly meeting minutes (from the fourth regular session in 1999 to the first regular session in 2019), the Test data question file (4551 questions), and the Training data question file (23321 questions), as given in the Stance classification task in NTCIR15. The question file of Training data (23321 questions) is used. In this question file, the information of the meeting and the name of the agenda are described.

2) Ibaraki Prefectural Assembly

The data to be input will be the minutes of the last day of each session of the Ibaraki Prefectural Assembly (the 4th session of 2011 to the 2nd session of 2020) and the Assembly Steering Committee (the 1st session of 2016 to the 2nd session of 2020). The training data will be created from the period from the 4th session in 2011 to the 2nd session in 2020. In addition, a dictionary of opposing bills of each group (the 1st session of 2019 to the 2nd session of 2020) will be used.

F. Result

1) Tokyo Metropolitan Assembly

Four experiments will be conducted. ① When no one votes for or against a proposal submitted by the governor, the Communist Party is given an opposition opinion and the other factions are given an affirmative opinion. ②In the case where the opinion of approval or disapproval is not obtained for a proposal submitted by the governor, the opinion of approval is given to all the factions. ③ In addition to ② above, if the process of " outside ○○ bill " is given. ④ In addition to ③ above, when the minority party is given information on the tendency of the ruling and opposition parties. ⑤ In addition to ③ above, when the minority party is given information on the proposed budget.

The experimental results are summarized in Table 1.

TABLE I. TOKYO METROPOLITAN ASSEMBLY EXPERIMENT

	accuary	total	match	miss
①	0.9457	4307	4073	234
②	0.8870	4541	4028	513
③	0.9604	4541	4361	180
④	0.9639	4541	4377	164
⑤	0.9604	4541	4361	180

The method in ① predicted that the Communist Party would often take the position of the opposition party and oppose proposals submitted by the governor. Comparing the results of ① with those of ②, there was an improvement in accuracy of 6.15%. This is a result of the fact that the Communist Party also often gives its opinion in favor of the proposals submitted by the governor. In method ③, there was an improvement of 1.19% in accuracy. In method ④, we predicted the tendency of minority groups that could not speak and assigned an opinion. As a result, the highest performance was obtained, with an improvement of 0.35% over ③. The accuracy of ⑤ was the same as the accuracy of ③. The combined accuracy of the functions of ④ and ⑤ was 96.39%. This result confirms that the performance of ④ and⑤ overlap or the usefulness of the method in ⑤ is low.

2) Ibaraki Prefectural Assembly

Seven experiments will be conducted.(1) When the label of agree is given when agree or disagree is not obtained. (2) When the opinion of the minority group is given. (3) When the minutes of the Assembly Steering Committee are used. (4) (5) Using BERT (Bidirectional Encoder Representations from Transformers), with a threshold of 0.98 and 0.99 to predict approval or disapproval. (6) (7) In the case of predicting approval or disapproval with the results of machine learning with 20 and 100 EPOCs of BERT (Bidirectional Encoder Representations from Transformers) using training data.The experimental results are summarized in Table 2.

TABLE II. RESULTS OF THE IBARAKI PREFECTURAL ASSEMBLY BERTEXPERIMENT

	accuary	total	match	miss
①	0.8968	10312	9248	1064
②	0.8982	10312	9262	1050
③	0.9935	7190	7143	47
④	0.9122	10312	9407	905
⑤	0.9143	10312	9428	884
⑥	0.8958	10312	9237	1075
⑦	0.8964	10312	9244	1068

The highest accuracy and precision was obtained in experiment 2. It was found that the Parliamentary Steering Committee of the Ibaraki Prefectural Assembly could obtain the approval or disapproval of a proposal with a high probability. Among the methods used to estimate the approval or disapproval, the highest accuracy was obtained with the method set to 0.99 in (5). Compared to the formulation of 0.98, which used the same cos similarity, the number of wrong answers decreased by about 21. Since the number of correct objections has decreased, but the number of wrong objections has also decreased, we believe that 99% is an effective setting for the decision threshold.

IV. CONCLUSION

In this paper, we proposed a method for estimating the approval or disapproval of a faction for an agenda item from its statements, based on the minutes of the Tokyo Metropolitan Assembly and the Ibaraki Prefectural Assembly. In the Tokyo Metropolitan Assembly, we tested three techniques as estimation methods and compared their performance. One was to examine the way opinions were given when they were not obtained. The second was the estimation of opinions using a dictionary of the ruling and opposition parties to the minority party. Finally, we created a dictionary of budget proposals for the minority party and estimated opinions based on it. We examined the accuracy-of each method and investigated which method would result in the highest accuracy. As a result, the model with the highest accuracy was the one that used the ruling and opposition party dictionaries for the minority faction, which provided the highest performance with a correct answer rate of 96.39%.

For the Ibaraki Prefectural Assembly, we tested the method using our own rules and the method using BERT (Bidirectional Encoder Representations from Transformers). The method that collects opposing proposals in advance and directly asks for similarity to the proposals was effective.

REFERENCES

[1] Y. Kimura, K. Takamaru, T. Tanaka, A. Kobayashi, H. Sakaji, Y. Uchida, H. Ototake and S. Masuyama, Creating Japanese Political Corpus from Local Assembly Minutes of 47 Prefectures, *"Proceedings of the 12th Workshop on Asian Language Resources (ALR12)"*, pp.78-85.

[2] S. Andler, Predicate path expressions. In *"Proceedings of the 6th. ACM SIGACT-SIGPLAN Symposium on Principles of Programming Languages (POPL '79)"*.ACM Press, New York, NY,pp.226-236, Available from: https://doi.org/10.1145/567752.567774, 1979.

[3] I. Editor (Ed.), "*The title of book one* (1st. ed.)", The name of the series one, Vol. 9. University of Chicago Press, Chicago, Available from: https://doi.org/10.1007/3-540-09237-4, 2007.

[4] D. Kosiur. "*Understanding Policy-Based Networking* (2nd. ed.)". Wiley, New York, NY, 2001.

[5] Y. Kimura, H. Shibuki, H. Ototake, Y. Uchida, K. Takamaru, M. Ishioroshi, T. Mitamura, M. Yoshioka, T. Akiba, Y. Ogawa, M. Sasaki, K. Yokote, T. Mori, K. Araki, S. Sekine, and N. Kando. Overview of the NTCIR-15 QA Lab-PoliInfo Task, Proceedings of The 15th NTCIR Conference.

[6] T. Kudo, K. Yamamoto, and Y. Matsumoto, Applying Conditional Random Fields to Japanese Morphological Analysis, In *"Proceedings of the 2004 Conference on Empirical Methods in Natural Language Processing"*. pp.230–237, 2004

[7] MeCab: Yet Another Part-of-Speech and Morphological - Analyzer, Available from: https://taku910.github.io/mecab/

[8] NTCIR-15 QA Lab poliInfo, Available from: https://poliinfo2.net/stance-classification-task

[9] Assembly page (https://ja.wikipedia.org/wiki/東京都議会)

Japanese Word Sense Disambiguation Using Gloss Information of a Japanese Dictionary

Hiroki Okemoto
Major in Computer and Information Sciences
Graduate School of Science and Engineering,
Ibaraki University
e-mail: 21nm716g@vc.ibaraki.ac.jp
4-12-1, Nakanarusawa, Hitachi, Ibaraki, Japan

Minoru Sasaki
Dept. of Computer and Information Sciences
Faculty of Engineering, Ibaraki University
e-mail: minoru.sasaki.01@vc.ibaraki.ac.jp
4-12-1, Nakanarusawa, Hitachi, Ibaraki, Japan

Abstract— **Word Sense Disambiguation (WSD) aims to find an appropriate meaning of ambiguous words in a particular context. Traditional supervised WSD methods rarely take into account lexical resources, such as WordNet, but recent studies have shown the effectiveness of incorporating glosses into neural networks for WSD. However, since most of this research is based on WSD, such as English, it has not been shown whether Japanese gloss information, such as a Japanese dictionary is effective for WSD. In this study, we aim to evaluate the effectiveness of using glossary information of the Japanese dictionary for WSD. As results of experiments, we found it effective to use glosses of the Japanese dictionary in WSD.**

Keywords-WSD; Japanese Dictionary; Machine Learning.

I. INTRODUCTION

In this section, we present the purpose and background of our research.

A. Research background

A word may have multiple meanings depending on its context. For example, the word "合う" has multiple meanings, such as "同じ動作をする" (Do the same action), such as "あなたと話し合う"(Talk to you) and "一致する"(Match), such as "意見が合う"(To agree in opinion). Thus, there is WSD, a basic task of Natural Language Processing (NLP) aimed at finding the exact meaning of ambiguous words in a particular context.

WSD has been studied in various ways[1][2] to date, and there are several approaches. Knowledge-based techniques [3] use lexical knowledge, such as glosses, to infer the correct meaning of the meaning of ambiguous words in context. However, the biggest drawback of knowledge-based methods is that they perform worse than supervised methods. Also, supervised methods usually train separate classifiers for words. Therefore, we cannot easily extend to the WSD task of words which ambiguate all polysemes in the text. In addition, in the neural-based method, only the local context of the target word is considered, and it becomes impossible to distinguish the minority meaning which is not in the training data.

In recent years, Huang et al. [4] conducted experiments using several English word WSD benchmark datasets with glosses using a technique called "GlossBERT" to construct context-gloss pairs and showed that this approach significantly outperformed state-of-the-art systems.

B. Purpose of research

In this study, in order to solve the problem of the above background, the purpose is to analyze whether the use of the gloss of the Japanese dictionary is effective or not by creating data in which the gloss of the Japanese dictionary is combined with the example sentence whose semantic meaning is known in the WSD system. By using glosses in the Japanese dictionary, it is possible to capture information about meaning that does not exist in the training data, and it is possible to capture detailed meaning differences between meanings.

In Section 2, we describe the proposed method. In Section 3, we describe the experiments conducted in this research. In Section 4, we discuss the experimental results in Section 3. In Section 5, we describe the conclusion and future work of this research.

II. METHODS

This section describes the proposed WSD using glosses of Japanese dictionaries in WSD systems.

A. System overview

The WSD method proposed in this paper uses glosses of Japanese dictionaries in WSD systems. We show the general execution order of the proposed method in Figure 1.

First, training data combining Japanese dictionary glosses and example sentences are created.

Next, the prepared training data and the test data to be compared are converted into a context vector by using BERT (NWJC-BERT). Therefore, the data was morphemically analyzed and converted to a lexeme of Unidic, and then converted to a context vector by BERT.

Then, the cosine similarity between the CLS vector of the converted training data and the object word vector of the test data, and the cosine similarity between the object word vector of the training data and the object word vector of the test data are respectively obtained, and their average values are obtained, and the values become evaluation values. The number of evaluation values obtained in this process is the number of training data and the number of combinations of test data per target word.

Finally, we compare the obtained evaluation values, and the meaning of the target word of the training data corresponding to the maximum value becomes the meaning of the target word of the test data.

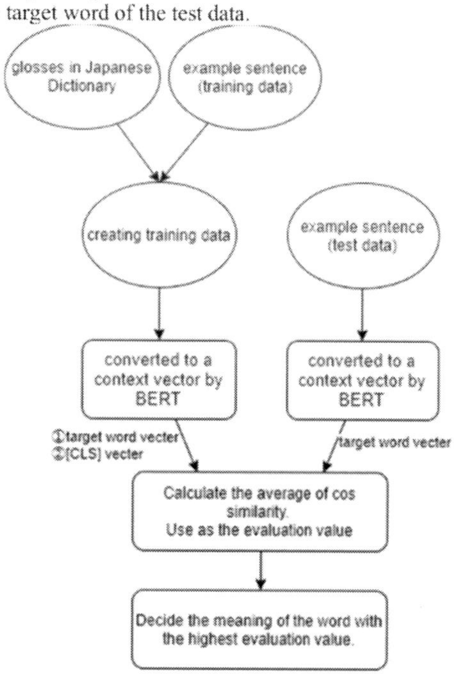

Figure 1. The general execution order of the proposed method

B. Description of the usage data

The target words in this study are 50 target words that are SemEval 2010 Japanese WSD task data (Okumura, Shirai, Komiya, Yokono, 2010). As the use data, 50 pieces of example sentence data using the word as training data and test data are respectively prepared from the modern Japanese written language balanced corpus (BCCWJ), and the Iwanami Japanese dictionary is used as the Japanese dictionary. This dictionary is the data distributed in SemEval -2010: Japanese WSD task.

C. Preparation of training data

First, when creating training data using the meaning glosses of the Japanese dictionary this time, the meaning and example sentence are extracted from the meaning definition sentence of the Iwanami Japanese dictionary. The format of the Iwanami Japanese Dictionary used this time is shown in Figure 2. The part enclosed by "「」" in the gloss is an example sentence, and the "-" part is used as one example sentence by complementing with a headword. In addition, the parts enclosed by "(())", "<>" and the parts following "▽" were judged to be irrelevant and removed. A sentence separated by the rest of the punctuation marks is used as one meaning. For example, if it is 166 − 0 -2 -3 − 0 in Figure 2, the meaning of the word is "物事に出会う。"(Encounter things), and the example sentence is "雨に遭う"(Get rain) or "ひどい目に合う"(Go through a bitter experience). Next, the definitions extracted from the Japanese dictionary and example sentences of example sentences and training data extracted from the Japanese dictionary are combined one by one to form one data. The format of the data is "gloss「example sentence」" as shown in Figure 3.

Headword あう【合う・会う・遭う・逢う・遇う】
166-0-0-0-0 ((五自))
166-0-1-0-0 <一>物・事が一つになり、離れていない、また矛盾がない。合
166-0-1-1-0 <1>寄り集まって一つになる。「三筋の流れが一つになって本流となる」▽普通、他の動詞の連用形につけて使う。「友人と駅で落ち—」
166-0-1-2-0 <2>《他の動詞の連用形を受けて》互いに同じ動作をする。「話し—」「なぐり—」
166-0-1-3-0 <3>互いに、また、一方が他方に、つり合う。「お前の手に—相手ではない」
166-0-1-3-1 <ア>ぴったりする。調和する。「帽子の色と服の色とがよく—」「服が体に—」
166-0-1-3-2 <イ>一致する。「意見が—」。理にかなう。「答えが—」
166-0-1-3-3 <ウ>費やしたものに対し、損をしない結果が出る。引き合う。「千円に見切っても—」「わない仕事だ」
166-0-2-0-0 <二>顔が合う(一)(1)。
166-0-2-1-0 <1>対面する。会見する。「応接間で客と—」
166-0-2-2-0 <2>偶然（人や物に）出会う。「道で旧友に—」
166-0-2-3-0 <3>物事に出会う。「雨に—」「ひどい目に—」▽(1)には「会」、(2)(3)には「遭」「遇」「逢」を使うのが普通。関連対面・初対面・面会・面接・お目にかかる・まみえる・お目見え・目通り・拝顔・拝謁・拝眉・引見・接見・謁見・会見・インタビュー・奇遇・遭遇・出会う・めぐりあい・邂逅（かいこう）・再会・見合い・顔合わせ・落ち合う・待ち合わせる・密会・ランデブー・デート

Figure 2. Format of Iwanami Japanese Dictionary

"物事に出会う。「ひどい目に遭う」"
"物事に出会う。「雨に遭う」"
"物事に出会う。「ら が 交通 事故 に 遭っ た 後 、 両手 +」"

Figure 3. Format of the created training data

D. Cosine similarity

In this study, we use cosine similarity [5] as a method to calculate similarity between vectors. We can calculate the cosine similarity with the following equation. The closer the maximum value is to 1, the more similar the vectors are.

$$\cos(\vec{p}, \vec{q}) = \frac{\vec{p} \cdot \vec{q}}{|\vec{p}| \cdot |\vec{q}|}$$

In the present method, a plurality of vectors, such as a CLS vector of training data and a target word vector of test data, and a target word vector of training data and a target word vector of test data are compared by one combination of the training data and the test data. Therefore, we determined the cosine similarity and used the average value as the evaluation value.

III. EXPERIMENT

In this section, we present the objectives, methods, and results of this experiment.

A. Purpose of the experiment

In this study, glosses of 50 test data sentences of 50 target words (Okumura, Shirai, Komiya, Yokono, 2010), which are

SemEval 2010 Japanese WSD task data, are determined up to the middle classification of Iwanami Japanese Dictionary using glosses of Japanese dictionaries in WSD systems. By doing so, we aim to verify the effective-ness of using glosses in Japanese dictionaries compared to when they are not used.

B. Experimental Methods

An experimental method based on the proposed method is presented.

1) Creating data using glosses

In this experiment, we experimented by changing the method of separating the example sentences of the training data, which was added after the meaning. This is because the length of the example sentence in the training data is not constant, and it is expected that when the sentence becomes long, there will be parts which are not related to the judgment of meaning. Table 1 below shows how to separate the example sentences used this time.

TABLE I. LIST OF HOW TO SEPARATE EXAMPLE SENTENCES

case	how to separate example sentences
A	not separate
B	separate by punctuation. And the part that contains the target word.
C	A total of 7 words, including 3 words before and after the target word
D	A total of 11words, including 5 words before and after the target word
E	A total of 15words, including 7 words before and after the target word
F	A total of 19 words, including 9 words before and after the target word

2) Target for comparison with test data

In this experiment, the average value of the cosine similarity between the target word vector of the test data and the target of comparison of the training data is used as the evaluation value. However, we are experimenting with different targets for comparison. In this study, we conducted experiments using two patterns: one with CLS vector and the other without CLS vector. This is because, since the target word is basically in the example sentence, the target word vector is considered to be more influenced by words around the example sentence, and the CLS vector is considered to reflect more the semantic context when it is added to the vector comparison object of the whole sentence.

3) Evaluation Method

In this experiment, the test data consists of 50 words as de-scribed in Section 2.2, and there are 50 data items per word. We compared them with the training data, determined the evaluation value, determined the meaning of the training data which became the maximum value as the meaning of the test data, and obtained the correct answer rate. We then determined the average of the correct answers of 50 words.

C. Results

First, Table 2 below shows the average of the correct answer rates of 50 words using training data that does not use Japanese dictionary glosses, which is the object of comparison with this method.

TABLE II. AVERAGE OF CORRECT ANSWER RATE OF WSD WITHOUT GLOSSES OF JAPANESE DICTIONARY

case	[CLS] vec + target word vec	target word vec
A	78.68%	79.00%

In order to show the effectiveness of glosses, we compare it with the method of supervised learning which does not use glosses of Japanese dictionary. We use a Multi-Layer Perceptron (MLP) as a classification model to learn training data and estimate the glosses of test data. In this method, the number of nodes in the middle layer is set to 50, the stochastic gradient descent method is used as an optimization method, the number of epochs as the number of learning iterations is set to 50, and the batch size is set to 200. Since the training data was small and the values were unstable with each execution, we conducted six tests to find the average value. The experimental results are shown in Table 3 below.

TABLE III. SUPERVISED LEARNING WITHOUT GLOSSES（MLP）

	correct answer rate
1	68%
2	63%
3	58%
4	64%
5	68%
6	61%
Ave	64%

Next, the experimental results based on this experimental method are shown in Table 4 below.

TABLE IV. AVERAGE OF THE CORRECT ANSWER RATES OF WSD USING GLOSSES OF JAPANESE DICTIONARIES

case	[CLS] vec + target word vec	target word vec
A	78.88%	78.32%
B	79.28%	79.16%
C	78.36%	79.24%
D	78.52%	79.16%
E	79.20%	79.68%
F	78.28%	79.44%

As a result, the highest percentage of correct answers was 79.28% for "case B" in the case of "CLS vector and target word vector" and 79.68% for "target word vector" in the case of "case E".

Comparing Table 2, Table 3, and Table 4, it can be seen that the method using glosses is more accurate.

IV. DISCUSSION

From the experimental results, the WSD using the gloss of the Japanese dictionary was slightly more correct than the WSD without the gloss. From this, we believe that it is effective to use glosses in WSD.

When the division method was changed, the word with the highest correct answer rate was "case B" with 79.28% in the case of "CLS vector and target word vector," and the word with the highest correct answer rate was "case E" with 79.68% in the case of "target word vector.". We think that this is because not only the gloss but also the example sentence had to be established as a sentence to some extent in order to consider the CLS vector and the target CLS word vector. In addition, in the case of the "target word vector", since a higher rate of correct answers is generally obtained when the words are separated by the number of words before and after the punctuation mark than when they are separated by the punctuation mark, we think that it is effective for example sentences to always have the context of words.

Based on these results, we think that by punctuating with the number of preceding and following phrases, we can maintain the context of the word to some extent while making it possible to maintain the context of the word, and thus we can further increase the rate of correct answers.

This time, the meaning of the word was judged by obtaining the cosine similarity of the object word vector. However, we expect improvements by using of MLP for semantic analysis. In addition, there was a bias in the number of examples depending on the meaning of the word. In addition, we expect improvements by increasing the amount of data and using related words because there are few or short definitions for a single meaning.

V. CONCLUSION AND FUTURE WORK

In this study, we conducted experiments to analyze whether it is effective to use glosses of Japanese dictionaries in WSD systems. In the experiment, we divided the comparison object with the object word vector of the test data into two types, the case in which the object word vector of the training data and CLS vector of the training data are included and the case in which it is not included. In addition, when combining meaning and example sentences, we changed the way of separating example sentences into six types.

As a result of the experiment, it was possible to obtain a higher correct answer rate of the data using the gloss, when the object to be compared with the object word vector of the test data includes the object word vector of the training data and the CLS vector of the training data, and when it does not include them. Therefore, we confirmed the effectiveness of using glosses of Japanese dictionaries in WSD systems.

Future work will include using other semantic methods, such as MLP, scrutinizing the data used, and increasing the amount of data.

REFERENCES

[1] Fuli Luo, Tianyu Liu, Qiaolin Xia, Baobao Chang, Zhifang Sui, "Incorporating Glosses into Neural Word Sense Disambiguation", Association for Computational Linguistics

[2] Fuli Luo , Tianyu Liu , Zexue He , Qiaolin Xia , Zhifang Sui , Baobao Chang, "Leveraging Gloss Knowledge in Neural Word Sense Disambiguation by Hierarchical Co-Attention", Association for Computational Linguistics

[3] Andrea Moro, Alessandro Raganato, Roberto Navigli ,"Entity Linking meets Word Sense Disambiguation: a Unified Approach", Transactions of the Association for Computational Linguistics

[4] Luyao Huang, Chi Sun, Xipeng Qiu, Xuanjing Huang,"GlossBERT: BERT for Word Sense Disambiguation with Gloss Knowledge", Association for Computational Linguistics

[5] Amit Singhal,"Modern Information Retrieval: A Brief Overview", Bulletin of the IEEE Computer Society Technical Committee on Data Engineering

Extraction of Causal Relationships across Multiple Sentences from Securities Reports

Takerou Aniya
Major in Computer and Information Sciences
Graduate School of Science and Engineering,
Ibaraki University
Email:21nm704f@vc.ibaraki.ac.jp
Nakanarusawa, Hitachi, Ibaraki, Japan

Minoru Sasaki
Dept. of Computer and Information Sciences
Faculty of Engineering, Ibaraki University
Email:minoru.sasaki.01@vc.ibaraki.ac.jp
Nakanarusawa, Hitachi, Ibaraki, Japan

Abstract— **One of the most important sources of investment decisions in the stock market is the textual data contained in securities reports by companies. Investors consider investment strategies based on the information. However, since these text data are updated and published every day, it takes a great deal of time and money to read through and obtain information from all of them. In this study, we devised a method for extracting causal expressions from multiple sentences in securities reports. We extracted candidate causal expressions using clue expressions, and trained SVM (Support Vector Machine) by combining the similarity with the previous sentence and common phrases with the features obtained from a single sentence and verified how effective the method is. The effectiveness of the newly added features of inter-sentence similarity and common usage was confirmed.**

Keywords-causal relationship extraction; securities report; pattern recognition

I. INTRODUCTION

One of the most important sources of investment decisions in the stock market is the text data contained in news reports, newspaper articles, financial summaries, and securities reports released after the end of a company's fiscal year. These text data contain important information. The information has a significant impact on a company's performance, such as past and current business results and initiatives, future prospect, development of new products, anticipated impact from overseas and political events, and measures to deal with scandals that have been discovered. This information can be used by investors to formulate investment strategies.

Since these text data are updated and published daily, it takes a great deal of time and money for investors to read through and obtain all the information. In the past, it was difficult to structure such text data, so investors could only obtain the content by reading it directly.

In recent years, there has been a great deal of research in the fields of machine learning, artificial intelligence, and natural language processing to efficiently extract the desired information from text. These include research on automatically obtaining expressions that influence business performance by focusing on single sentences that indicate business performance factors in securities reports and using keywords that provide clues to sentence structure and causal relationships in Japanese[1], and research on extracting causal relationship sentences from newspaper articles by focusing on sentence structures that contain causal relationships.[2]

These studies mainly focus on extracting causal expressions consisting of single sentences, and when causal relationships are described in more than two sentences in securities reports, they are often excluded from the analysis, and there are few studies that extract causal expressions spanning two sentences. Therefore, this study devised a method for extracting causal expressions spanning two or more sentences from securities reports and verified the effectiveness of the inter-sentence similarity and common usage used in the features for SVM.

In Section 2, we introduce the research and related methods relevant to this study. In Section 3, we explain the flow of the method devised in this study and the features used for machine learning. In Section 4, we show the experimental method using the research method, and in Section 5, we present the results. Section 6 discusses the results, and Section 7 concludes the study.

II. RELATED WORKS AND METHODS

This section presents the related works and methods related to our research.

A. Related works

In the study by Sato et al. [1], a discriminant model of causal sentences for single sentences was constructed using text data contained in the securities reports of the companies that make up the TOPIX 1000 from 2008 to 2016. Here, for example, in the sentence "猛暑日が連続したため、飲料水の売上が伸びた。" (Sales of drinking water increased due to a series of extremely hot days.), "ため" (due to) is used as a clue expression as it is an important clue to indicate causality and is used to obtain candidate causal sentences from the target text data. Also, referring to the study by Sakaji et al. [2], we extracted features from candidate causal sentences using four features: particle pairs, clue expressions in sentences, morphological unigrams, and morphological bigrams, and constructed a discriminant model using SVM.

In the study by Sakaji et al. [2], based on the clue expressions obtained from the Nikkei Shimbun newspaper from 1990 to 2005, the expression patterns of causal relationships and clue expressions were classified into five patterns, and a discriminant model was constructed using SVM while filtering the clue expressions (to remove the cases where the clue expressions have non-causal relationships).

In the study by Sato et al. [1], the objective was to extract from securities reports, but only single-sentence causal relationship was targeted, and causal relationships spanning multiple sentences were excluded from the target data. In addition, the study by Sakaji et al.[2] included up to two sentences in the sentence structure pattern, but the target data was the Nikkei Shimbun, not Securities reports and the feature extraction was based on the features that can be extracted from a single sentence. The results of their experiment were a fit rate of 0.68, a recall rate of 0.59, and an F-value of 0.63.

B. Morphological analysis

Methods such as splitting a sentence into words, generating a vector based on these words ,and using it as input for machine learning is often used in NLP(Natural Language Processing). Japanese is not divided into words like English. So it needs to be divided to the word level, and this is done by a morphological analyzer.

MeCab is an open source morphological analyzer developed through a joint research unit project between the Graduate School of Informatics, Kyoto University and the Communication Science Laboratories of Nippon Telegraph and Telephone Corporation. For example, the morphological analysis of" 当社グループにとって過去最高の結果となった "(The results were the best for our group.) by MeCab is shown in Figure 1.

C. Engagement analysis

Engagement analysis (syntactic analysis), which is the process of analyzing modification relationships at the word level and in clauses, is the process of analyzing the structure of a sentence. In this study, we used CaboCha, a Japanese clause analyzer. CaboCha is based on SVM.

For example, Figure 2 below shows the result of using CaboCha to analyze the phrase "当社グループにとって過去最高の結果となった" (The results were the best ever for our group.")

Using CaboCha, the sentences are listed by clause with a set of clause IDs that indicate the clauses to be engaged. This method is used to obtain the relationships between sentences and clauses, which are used as part of the input to SVM.

To make the list, we used the tree structure obtained by analysing sentences with CaboCha.The tree structure is shown in Figure 3. From the chunk and its link in the tree structure, it is possible to obtain information on Japanese clauses and their destinations.

An example of a list obtained by the above method is shown in Figure 4. The "c" represents a clause, and the "to" indicates the ID of the destination. A value of -1 indicates that there is no target.

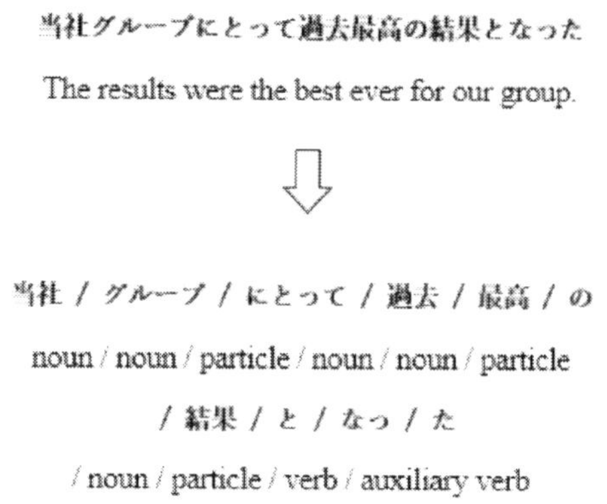

Figure 1. Examples of Morphological Analysis

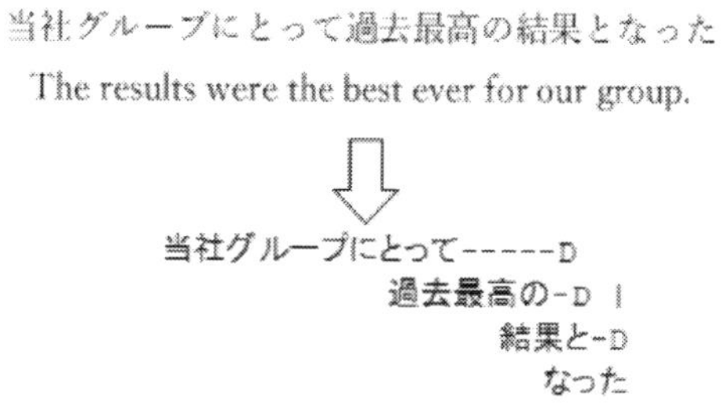

Figure 2. Example of Engagement Analysis

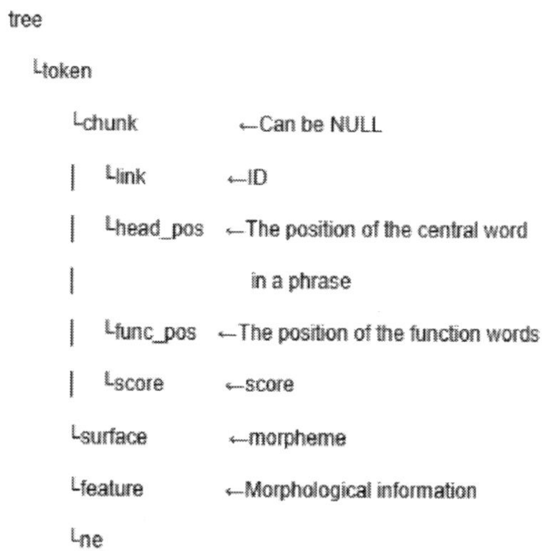

Figure 3. The tree structure of Cabocha

当社グループにとって過去最高の結果となった

The results were the best ever for our group.

⇩

[{'c':'当社グループにとって(for out group)','to':3},

{'c':'過去最高の(the best ever)','to':2},

{'c':'結果と(The results)','to':3},

{'c':'なった(were)','to':-1}]

Figure 4. Example of list that can be retrieved.

The list obtained by this method is used to extract syntactic features of sentences.

III. EXTRACTION OF CAUSAL RELATIONSHIPS USING CLUE EXPRESSIONS

In this paper, after extracting candidate causal sentences from securities reports issued by three companies (Nissan, Honda, and Toyota) using clue expressions, we propose a causal relationship extraction method that adds inter-sentence similarity as a feature and common usage as a new feature to the features used in existing research and uses them as input to SVM. In addition, we show the data used in this study.

A. Overview of the Proposed Method

The rough execution sequence of the proposed method in this study is shown in Figure 5 below.

The first step is to extract the items "業績等の概要" (Summary of business performance), "対処すべき課題" (Issues to be addressed), and "事業等のリスク" (Business risks) from the securities reports issued by three companies (Nissan, Honda, and Toyota), which contain sentences related to business performance, and then to extract candidate causal sentences containing clue expressions and the sentences immediately preceding them.

In the related study shown in Section 2, the clue expressions for extracting single sentence causal relationship candidates were determined, so they cannot be used directly. The clue expressions used in this study are those that were determined to be possible clue expressions in the case of a causal relationship spanning two sentences from the securities reports of the three companies mentioned above. Next, the obtained candidate causal sentences and the sentences immediately before them are assigned positive labels if they are causal relationships spanning two sentences, and negative labels if they are not. Finally, we obtain particle pairs, included clue expressions, morphological unigrams, and morphological bigrams from the sentences containing the clue expressions, and when all the obtained features are arranged, we assign 1 to the features included in the sentence and 0 to the features not included. The inter-sentence similarity with the immediately preceding sentence and the features of common usage are also added to the features and input to SVM.

By comparing the above method with the existing methods, we verify the effectiveness of the method for extracting causal relations across two sentences from the target securities report.

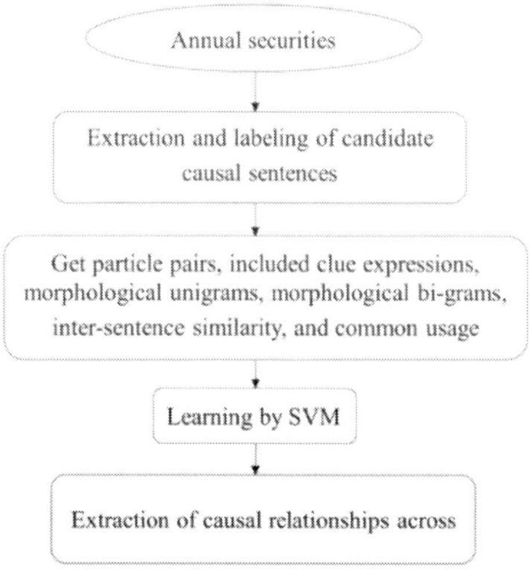

Figure 5. Flow of the proposed method

B. The data used in this study

The data used in this study are Nissan's securities reports for fiscal years 2000, 2004, 2005, 2007~2019, Honda's securities reports for fiscal years 2007~2019, and Toyota's securities reports for fiscal years 2003~2020. From these reports, the following items were included "業績等の概要 "(Summary of business performance), " 対処すべき課題 "(Issues to be addressed), and " 事業等のリスク "(Business risks) including text that specifically discusses business results. The wording and structure of the securities reports of the same company do not change significantly from one year to the next. Therefore, the extraction of cause-and-effect expressions describing factors and results using clues is easier than in news articles.

C. Extraction of causal expression candidates

It is necessary to appropriately extract causal candidate sentences securities reports. Considering that clue expressions appear especially at the beginning and end of sentences in the case of causal candidate sentences that span two sentences, we surveyed securities reports and selected many expressions that appear at the beginning and end of sentences, referring to the clue expressions in the study by Sakaji et al.[2]

Figure 6 below shows the original clue expressions selected in this study.Based on these clue expressions, causal candidate sentences are extracted from the target part of the securities report.

Specifically, if a sentence contains a clue expression, the sentence and the immediately preceding sentence are extracted as causal candidates spanning two sentences.

このようななか (in this situation)	この結果、 (as a result)	その結果、 (as a result)
このような (such as this)	したがって (therefore)	従って (therefore)
これらの要因 (These factors)	要因は (The factor is)	要因に (The factor is)
主な (mainly)	主な成果として (The main results are)	によるものです (due to)
そのため (for the reason)	その為 (for the reason)	ためである (due to)
可能性がある (may be affected)	貢献して (contributing to)	が響いた (take its toll)
これらの (These)	これは主に (This is mainly because)	可能性があります (may be affected)
それらの要因 (Those factors)	によるものである (due to)	を反映 (reflect)

Figure 6. Selected clue expressions

D. Features used

In this study, we used particle pairs as syntactic features, and cue expressions in sentences, morphological unigrams, morphological bigrams, inter-sentence similarity, and common usage as other features.To obtain particle pairs, we used CaboCha to group morphemes into clauses, and extracted particle pairs based on the clause id of the target sentence.For morphological unigrams and morphological bigrams, those with a frequency of 100 or more were used at the stage of arranging the overall features.

The inter-sentence similarity is the value calculated for the similarity between two sentences. The calculation method was based on Yamamoto et al's study [3]. In the case of cause-and-effect sentences that span two sentences, the content (result or cause) of the immediately preceding sentence tends to be supplementary to the content of the following sentence. Therefore, the similarity between the two sentences was calculated by focusing on the nouns, adjectives, and verbs that appeared in the previous sentence, without considering the sentence structure such as particle pairs.

Common usage are phrases (nouns, adjectives, verbs) that are common to the previous sentence. The feature of the common usage to be input to the SVM is 1 if the causal candidate sentence has that usage as a common usage, and 0 if it does not.

For the extraction of nouns, adjectives, and verbs in the sentences, we used the part-of-speech information from the MeCab analysis results.

Table 1 below shows an overview of the features.

TABLE I. OVERVIEW OF FEATURES

Feature name	Overview
Pairs of particles	All pairs of particles (excluding redundancies), with the particle in the phrase containing the clue expression (the core phrase) as the front particle and the particle in the phrase pertaining to the phrase to which the core phrase is applied (the base phrase) as the back particle.
Clue expressions in a sentence	Clue expressions contained in the target sentence
Morphologic al uni-gram	A unigram obtained by decomposing candidate sentences containing causal relations with a morphological analyzer.
Morphologic al bi-gram	A bigram obtained by decomposing candidate sentences containing causal relations with a morphological analyzer.
Inter-sentence similarity	The sentence immediately before the sentence containing the clue expression is S_i .the sentence containing the clue expression is S_j.There is a high possibility that S_i and S_j have a common word in the cohesion by use. Therefore, the value expressed in the following equation is the inter-document similarity. $sim\left(T(S_i),T(S_j)\right) = \frac{\lvert T(S_i) \cap T(S_j) \rvert}{\sqrt{\lvert T(S_i)T(S_j) \rvert}}$ $T(S_i)$: Word sets of nouns, verbs, and adjectives in sentence S_i.
Common usage	As with inter-sentence similarity, it is a feature related to the usage (noun, adjective, verb) that is common to the previous sentence. Unlike inter-sentence similarity, it extracts the usage itself that is common to the previous sentence.

E. Input to SVM

For each candidate causal sentence extracted based on the clue expressions, the features can be obtained.

For the input to the SVM, the features were arranged without overlap, except for the inter-sentence similarity, and a vector was created with 1 if the feature obtained from each candidate causal sentence was included and 0 if it was not.

IV. EXPERIMENTS

The experimental procedure based on the proposed method is shown.

A. Data Set

The data used in this study are Nissan's annual securities reports for fiscal years 2000, 2004, 2005, 2007~2019, Honda's annual securities reports for fiscal years 2007~2019, and Toyota's securities reports for fiscal years 2003~2020.

B. Settings

The candidate causal sentences were extracted using the clue expressions shown in Figure 6. The extracted text was extracted line by line and saved in csv format as sentence1 for the sentence immediately before the clue expression if it was included, and sentence2 for the sentence including the cue expression. After that, we manually assigned labels to the saved csv files: 1 if there was a causal relationship between sentence1 and sentence2, and 0 if there was not.

As a result of the extraction, we were able to extract 3879 sentences from the target securities reports as candidate sentences for causal relationships spanning two sentences, of which 989 sentences were assigned positive labels and 2890 sentences were assigned negative labels. The features shown in the proposed method 3.4 were used as the features of each sentence.

We used train_testsplit to split the training data and test data, and test size was set to 0.3. To avoid data bias, we used the stratify parameter. In addition, cross validation was used to reduce overtraining. The kernel of the SVM model was linear, and the value of the regularization C was 10.

V. RESULTS

The results of an experiment conducted based on the experimental method are shown below.

A. Results of existing methods

In order to make comparisons, we also conducted experiments without the addition of the features we devised in this study, and experiments with only one of the two new features.The results are shown below in tabular form.

Table 2 shows the result of existing methods.

TABLE II. RESULTS OF EXISTING METHODS

Count	Accuracy	Precision	Recall	F-measure
1	0.925	0.860	0.843	0.851
2	0.925	0.855	0.851	0.852
3	0.931	0.865	0.867	0.865
4	0.914	0.832	0.833	0.832
5	0.921	0.849	0.842	0.845
Ave	0.923	0.852	0.847	0.849

B. Results of the proposal method

Table 3 below shows the result of our proposal methods.

TABLE III. RESULTS OF THE PROPOSAL METHODS

Count	Accuracy	Precision	Recall	F-measure
1	0.934	0.875	0.864	0.869
2	0.941	0.888	0.880	0.883
3	0.931	0.862	0.872	0.867
4	0.931	0.868	0.864	0.866
5	0.926	0.855	0.856	0.856
Ave	0.933	0.87	0.867	0.868

C. Results of the proposal methods (using only common Ftausage as new feature)

TABLE IV. RESULTS OF THE PROPOSAL METHODS (USING ONLY COMMON USAGE AS NEW FEATURE)

Count	Accuracy	Precision	Recall	F-measure
1	0.932	0.871	0.862	0.866
2	0.931	0.864	0.869	0.866
3	0.925	0.850	0.858	0.853
4	0.926	0.846	0.869	0.857
5	0.931	0.866	0.866	0.866
Ave	0.929	0.859	0.865	0.862

D. Results of the proposal methods (using only inter-sentence similarity as new feature)

TABLE V. RESULTS OF THE PROPOSAL METHODS (USING ONLY INTER-SENTENCE SIMILARITY AS NEW FEATURE)

Count	Accuracy	Precision	Recall	F-measure
1	0.926	0.858	0.854	0.855
2	0.927	0.864	0.846	0.855
3	0.928	0.859	0.861	0.860
4	0.931	0.873	0.855	0.863
5	0.930	0.868	0.858	0.862
Ave	0.928	0.864	0.855	0.859

The tables from II to V shows the results of five-times classifications and their average values by the proposed method.

VI. DISCUSSIONS

In this section, we discuss the experimental results and show the effectiveness and problems of newly devised features.

A. Comparison with conventional methods

As can be seen from Table 2 and 3, Accuracy increased by 1%, and Precision increased by 1.8%, Recall increased by 2%, and F-score increased by 1.9% for the proposed method. In addition, as can be seen from Table 2 and Table 4, Accuracy increased by 0.6%, Precision increased by 0.7%, Recall increased by 1.8%, and the F-measure increased by 1.3% for the proposed method when only the features of common words were added to the existing method. Furthermore, as can be seen from Table 2 and Table 5, Accuracy increased by 0.5%, Precision increased by 1.2%, Recall increased by 0.8%, and the F-measure increased by 1% for the method that only added the feature of inter-sentence similarity to the existing method.

In the above comparisons, the proposed method for extracting causal relationships across multiple sentences has certain results, as it produces better results than the conventional method. However, as shown in Table 2 and Table 3, the proposed method is not always better than the conventional method in the third and fifth comparisons, respectively. The proposed method must be improved by increasing the amount of target data, dividing the training data, and appropriately adjusting each parameter of SVM.

B. Inter-sentential similarity and its validity as a feature of common speech and its problems

The comparison between the proposed method and the existing method with the addition of inter-sentence similarity and common usage as features is confirmed that all the evaluation indices increased even when each of them was added by itself. Therefore, we believe that these two features are effective as features for extracting causal relations across two sentences.

As a result, we were able to obtain a better evaluation value compared to the existing methods, and we were able to prove the effectiveness of the inter-sentence similarity and common terms.

Future work includes increasing the number of target data, re-examining the cue expressions used to extract causal candidate sentences spanning two sentences, adjusting the data partitioning method and each parameter of machine learning, and examining the extraction method when a causal sentence exists before the previous sentence.

The increase in the evaluation index value with the addition of these new features was between 0.5 and 1.0, which does not necessarily mean that the effectiveness of this study on other companies' securities reports data is guaranteed, since the learning and evaluation was conducted using a limited amount of securities report data. As a countermeasure to this problem, an increase in the number of securities reports can be considered.

In addition, when we look at the average of the absolute value of the difference from the mean for each evaluation value of the proposed method, we can see that the Accuracy is 0.4, Precision is 0.9, Recall is 0.7, and the F-score is 0.6. This is thought to be due to the influence of the data used for training, but to have a stable two-sentence causal relationship extraction method, it is necessary to reduce this blur by using appropriate training data that reflects the characteristics of all data from among all data.

VII. CONCLUSION

In this study, we used clue expressions that can be used as clues for causal sentences spanning two sentences selected independently from the "業績の概要"(Summary of Business Results), "対処すべき課題"(Issues to Be Addressed), and "業績等のリスク"(Business Risks) where text data can be obtained from the securities reports of Nissan, Honda, and Toyota, especially for the contents related to business results. We then created a model for extracting causal relations spanning two sentences using SVM with the features of particle pairs, included clue expressions, morphological unigrams, and morphological bigrams used in existing research, plus inter-sentence similarity and common usage.

In future research, we aim to extract sentences containing causal relationships from a wide range of text data, not limited to securities reports. For this purpose, it is necessary to consider the extraction of candidate sentences other than clue expressions. In addition, we aim to extract the causal part and the resultant part from the extracted sentences.

REFERENCES

[1] Fumihiro Sato, Hiroaki Sakuma, and Shunya Kodera, "Extraciton of Causal Knowledge from Annual Securities Report",The 32nd Annual Conference of the Japanese Society for Artificial Intelligence, 4pp. (2018)

[2] H. Sakaji and M. Sigeru(Toyohashi University of Technology), "Extraction of Causal Knowledge by Using Text Mining", 第54回自動制御連合講演会, 4pp. (2011)

[3] Yuji Yamamoto, Shigeru Masuyama, and Hiroyuki Sakai, "小説自動要約のための隣接文間の結束判定手法", 言語処理学会年次大会発表論文集 (Proceedings of the Annual Meeting of the Association for Natural Language Processing), pp.1083-1086 (2006)

Optimizing Statistical Distance Measures in Multivariate SVM for Sentiment Quantification

Kevin Labille
University of Arkansas
Computer Science and Computer Engineering
Fayetteville, Arkansas, USA
Email: kclabill@uark.edu

Susan Gauch
University of Arkansas
Computer Science and Computer Engineering
Fayetteville, Arkansas, USA
Email: sgauch@uark.edu

***Abstract*—Twitter sentiment classification has been widely investigated in recent years and it is today possible to accurately determine the class label of a single tweet through various approaches. Although it could open new horizons for business or research, Twitter sentiment quantification, which aims to predict the prevalence of the positive class and the negative class within a set of tweets, has drawn much less attention. This paper presents our research on improving lexicon-based Twitter sentiment quantification. We first introduce a new approach to building a paired-score sentiment lexicon that is better suited for sentiment quantification. We then propose a novel feature vector representation for tweets that incorporates a collection of sentiment features. Finally, we investigate and compare several statistical distance kernels in multivariate Support Vector Machine for sentiment quantification. Results suggest that optimizing the Hellinger Distance with a multivariate SVM using our new sentiment lexicon outperforms current sentiment quantification approaches, including neural network approaches.**

***Keywords*—sentiment quantification, sentiment lexicon, multivariate SVM, statistical distances**

I. Introduction

The amount of user feedback available online has increased tremendously and it is now possible to read the opinions of millions of people all over the Internet on movies, restaurants, hotels, books, products, and professionals. This wealth of information allows researchers to study the ways in which individuals express opinions and to mine collections of opinions to identify trends and consensus. Two new research area have arisen from this phenomenon: sentiment analysis and sentiment quantification. Namely, sentiment analysis is the computational analysis of opinions in text; its goal is to identify the semantic orientation, or polarity, of such textual data. In contrast, sentiment quantification aims to estimate the distribution of documents that belong to each polarity class. Sentiment analysis is widely applicable in various areas, for example, politics and retail. For example, Wang et al. [1] applied real-time sentiment analysis to Twitter data to analyze public sentiment toward presidential candidates in the U.S elections of 2012. The most prominent and perhaps the most prevalent utilization of sentiment analysis and sentiment quantification, however, is in business intelligence, since customer's feedback directly reflects their opinion about a product or service. Sentiment analysis and sentiment quantification can be used as a concept testing tool when a new product, campaign, or logo is launched. It can be used to improve a company's own performances by analyzing competitor's sentiment data and gain competitive advantage. It can also be applied to gain insight from the opinions of customers to diagnose possible problems and make improvement. Additionally, sentiment analysis and sentiment quantification can be used to track customer sentiment over time. Although a lot of work has been conducted in sentiment analysis, we believe that the last application aforementioned can be further exploited through sentiment quantification to open new horizons for businesses and for research. In this paper, we focus on sentiment quantification over a set of tweets wherein the goal is to accurately predict the proportion of tweets that are positive and the proportion of tweets that are negative. This paper offers three contributions. In particular, (1) we propose a new statistical method for building sentiment lexicons from tweets that maps each word to a pair of **positive** and **negative** sentiment scores rather than the usual single sentiment score. (2) We investigate using this sentiment lexicon to derive sentiment features that capture tweets' positive aspects and negative aspects. These feature vectors include a combination of word sentiment features and additional features that summarize the positive and negative word distributions within the dataset. (3) Finally, through a multivariate Support Vector Machine (SVM) we optimize and compare numerous statistical distance kernels to evaluate which one performs best in a sentiment quantification task. Our results show that sentiment features derived from the pair of sentiment scores improve the performances of the quantifier. Finally, we show that a multivariate SVM that optimizes the Hellinger Distance outperform several other statistical distance measures such as the widely used Kullback-Leibler divergence (KLD), and therefore is a better approach for sentiment quantification. Our results outperform recent approaches to sentiment quantification, including neural network-based approaches. The paper is organized as follows, Section 2 will describe research works that are closely related to ours, Section 3 will detail the methodology of our approach to extract sentiment from text and to perform sentiment quantification, Section 4 will present our experimental evaluation, followed by the results in Section 5. Section 6 will end with a conclusion.

II. Related Work

With over 500 million tweets shared every day (6,000 tweets per second), Twitter has become the fastest growing source of information. Users generally tweet about their feelings or opinions about what's happening around the world. This makes Twitter a valuable source of data for sentiment analysis. However, tweets differ from regular text in many ways: the length of a tweets is restricted to 280 characters and, because they are often posted from cellphones, the language used contains many spelling mistakes, abbreviations, and slang words. These characteristics make traditional Natural Language Processing techniques, language models, and traditional sentiment analysis tasks trickier to apply. Despite these challenges, numerous projects have investigated Twitter sentiment classification ([2]–[6]. One of the pioneer works is that of Go et al. [7] wherein they compared a SVM classifier (with feature vectors composed of unigrams, bigrams, or unigrams+bigrams), a Maximum Entropy (MaxEnt) classifier, and a Naive Bayes classifier. Their results suggest that Part Of Speech (POS) tags are not useful in Twitter sentiment classification. They achieved their best accuracy with the MaxEnt classifier and the lowest accuracy with the Naive Bayes classifier. Mohammad et al. [8] and [9] tackled the same problem using a SVM classifier that uses sentiment lexicons as part of the feature vector. They showed that lexicons-related features were valuable features that improved the accuracy of the SVM classifier by more than 8.5%. More recently, a new research focus has emerged from automated classification: quantification. In contrast to classification that aims to estimate the class label of individual instances, the purpose of quantification is to evaluate the population or prevalence of the different classes within the dataset. Although the tasks are related, a method with a high accuracy on the individual level can be biased and achieve poor performance when estimating the proportion of the different classes, requiring new approaches. Esuli and Sebastiani [10] focused on text quantification using multivariate SVM, i.e., SVM_{perf}, that uses the Kullback-Leibler divergence as a loss function (KLD is a measure of the divergence between two probability distributions). They found that SVM(KLD) outperforms all other linear SVM approaches and other quantification methods and is therefore a more appropriate choice for text quantification. Gao and Sebastiani [11] apply the approach from [10] to Twitter data. They concluded that $SVM(KLD)$ outperforms the traditional $SVM(HL)$. In 2016 and 2017, the high-impact conference "International Workshop on Semantic Evaluation", i.e., SemEval, held a track on sentiment quantification. The best approach from SemEval 2016 was by Stojanovski et al. [12]. They used a combination of a Convolutional Neural Network (CNN) and a Gated Neural Network (GNN), which was then fed into a softmax layer. They concluded that the combination of the two neural network is well suited for quantification. In the 2017 edition Mathieu Cliche [13] achieved first place on the sentiment quantification task. He used a deep-learning method that uses both a Convolutional Neural Network (CNN) and a LSTM (Long Short-Term Memory) neural networks that uses word embedding. Our work is similar to [10] and [9] but differs from theirs in several key ways. In particular, we propose a new statistical method for building sentiment lexicons on tweets that maps each word to a pair of **positive** and **negative** sentiment score rather than the usual single sentiment score. Furthermore, although [9] also represents a tweet as a feature vector that uses a sentiment lexicon, we investigate using our newly built sentiment lexicon to derive sentiment features that reflect the words' positive distribution and negative distribution of the tweet. In addition, although [10] optimize the Kullback-Leibler Divergence (KLD) with the multivariate SVM, their choice of that particular statistical distance is not clearly motivated. We believe that mathematically stronger statistical distances could be a better choice in place of KLD. We therefore extend their approach and compare several other statistical distances measures and evaluate how they perform in the sentiment quantification task.

III. Quantifying Tweets

Our approach to quantify tweets is the following. We first represent a tweet in the Vector Space Model (VSM) through a feature vector that captures the sentiment of the tweet. The feature vectors use the Bag-Of-Words (BOW) representation augmented with sentiment features that we compute from a sentiment lexicon. The sentiment lexicon employs a new format and is built through a new statistical approach that we describe in this document. We then use a multivariate Support Vector Machine (SVM) to classify each tweet and count the number of positively classified instances as well as the number of negatively classified instances.

A. Paired-score Sentiment Lexicon

From a collection of tweets, we first build a sentiment lexicon, that is, a list of words with associated sentiment scores. The sentiment scores are calculated using a probabilistic approach. We define the positivity of a word w as $pos(w)$, and its negativity as $neg(w)$. While a single sentiment score gives us information about the polarity strength (its score) and the polarity orientation (its sign) of a word, it does not capture the word's distribution across positive and negative occurrences. Indeed, let's assume that we define the score of a word to be the difference between its positivity and its negativity. Then, if two words have the same sentiment scores does not necessarily mean that they have the same positivity and negativity. For instance, if two words have a score of -0.6, they could be the results of $0.11 - 0.71$ or $0.3 - 0.9$. In other words, we are losing information about the word's distribution across the dataset. We believe that using positivity and negativity values of words separately could improve the effectiveness of the feature vector in catching the sentiment of the tweet, since it embeds more information on the distribution of the words across the different classes. While single-score lexicons perform well for sentiment analysis, it is our intuition that paired-score lexicons are more suitable for sentiment quantification. In addition, such lexicons allows us to compute distributional statistics such as the average negativity score or the average positivity score of a tweet, which could be useful information in sentiment quantification tasks. We therefore propose a new type of sentiment lexicon that maps each word to a pair of scores $< pos, neg >$, i.e., its positivity and its negativity.

The positivity of a word is calculated by dividing the positive document frequency of the word with the aggregated positive document frequency of every word. To account for potential unbalanced data, it is then normalized by the overall frequency of the word. The same calculation is done on the negative aspect as well. The positivity and negativity scores of a word are therefore calculated as follows:

$$\begin{aligned} Pos(w) &= \frac{pdf(w)}{N_{pos}} \times \frac{1}{df(w)} \\ Neg(w) &= \frac{ndf(w)}{N_{neg}} \times \frac{1}{df(w)} \end{aligned} \tag{1}$$

and:

$$pdf(w) = \sum_{t \in T_{pos}} x \begin{cases} x = \frac{1}{|tweet|} & \text{if } w \in t \\ x = 0 & \text{otherwise} \end{cases}$$

$$ndf(w) = \sum_{t \in T_{neg}} x \begin{cases} x = \frac{1}{|tweet|} & \text{if } w \in t \\ x = 0 & \text{otherwise} \end{cases}$$

$$df(w) = pdf(w) + ndf(w)$$

$$N_{pos} = \sum_{w \in vocab} pdf(w)$$

$$N_{neg} = \sum_{w \in vocab} ndf(w)$$

We first define three terms: $pdf(w)$, $ndf(w)$, and $df(w)$ where $pdf(w)$ is the positive document frequency of w, i.e., the number of time w occurs in positive tweets from the tweet collection T; $ndf(w)$ is the negative document frequency of w, i.e., the number of time w occurs in negative tweets from the tweets collection T; and $df(w)$ is the total number of occurrences of w in the tweet collection T. The positive document frequency . Furthermore, N_{pos} is the proportion of positive words in the collection of tweets, i.e., it is the sum of the the positive document frequency pdf of every word in the dictionary; Likewise, N_{neg} is the proportion of negative words in the collection of tweets, i.e., the sum of the negative document frequency $ndf(w)$ of every word in the dictionary. Pre-processing is performed similarly on all datasets, that is, URL, emojis, Tweet mentions, Tweet hashtags, and smileys are removed. Punctuations and number are further removed and the remaining is lower-cased. After pre-processing the tweets from our training dataset, each unique word is extracted from the remaining text in order to build a dictionary. Using the above formula, we compute each word's positive score and negative score as real values in the range [0, 1].

B. Building a Sentiment Feature Vector

A common way of representing documents in the Vector Space Model is using the Bag-Of-Words (BOW). In this approach, each document is represented by a vector wherein each feature is a word from the dictionary. Therefore, the size of the vector is equal to the size of the vocabulary. For the BOW features, we will use the tf-idf (term-frequency inverse document frequency) value of the word within the tweet. We do not take into consideration the Part-Of-Speech (POS) of the words based on results from Go et al. [7] that demonstrated that POS is not helpful in Twitter data. We further derive additional numerical features that catch several sentiment aspects of the tweet using each word's sentiment scores extracted from the paired-score lexicons. Our intuition is that adding sentiment features to the basic tf-idf BOW could improve the performance by providing crucial sentiment information. The sentiment features we consider are described below.

- *token found*: the number of words in the tweet that were found in the lexicon
- *token total*: the number of words in the tweet
- *max pos*: the maximum positive score in the tweet
- *min pos*: the minimum positive score in the tweet
- *max neg*: the maximum negative score in the tweet
- *min neg*: the minimum negative score in the tweet
- *ratio*: the ratio of *avg pos* over *avg neg*

C. Sentiment Quantifier

A traditional SVM optimizes an univariate loss function, it classifies each item one by one, independently of each other, i.e., an item does not impact how another item is classified. A traditional SVM machine can therefore be used to quantify by classifying each unlabeled documents and by then counting how many documents belong to the positive class and how many documents belong to the negative class.

However, even if the classifier correctly quantifies the positive and negative class proportions in the training set, there is no guarantee that the proportion of positive documents and negative documents will be the same in the test set. In fact, we are expecting a change in the proportion of the positive class and negative class ratios in the test set. Thus, such a quantifier will most likely suffer from statistical bias.

To overcome this problem, we will use a Support Vector Machine (SVM) for multivariate performance measures. The key here is that the multivariate SVM allows the optimization of multivariate performance measures, and particularly all that can be computed from a contingency table. It works by considering hypotheses $\bar{h}$ that maps a set of n feature vectors $\bar{x} = (x_1, x_2, ..., x_n) \in \bar{X}$ where $\bar{X} = X \times ... \times X$ to a set of n labels $\bar{y} \in \bar{Y}$ where $\bar{Y} \subseteq \{-1, +1\}^n$, i.e., $\bar{h} : \bar{X} \longrightarrow \bar{Y}$, as opposed to considering hypotheses h that maps one single feature vector $x \in X$ to one single label $y \in Y$, i.e., $h : X \longrightarrow Y$ [14]. Since statistical distance measures are used to evaluate how similar two probability distributions are, and since they are computable with the contingency table, it makes perfect sense to optimize them through a multivariate SVM to perform quantification. Thorsten Joachims [14] developed such an SVM machine called SVM^{perf} which was originally developed to optimize the F1-Score, Prec/Rec Breakeven, Prec@k, Prec@k, and ROCArea metrics. We perform quantification using SVM^{perf} similarly to our baseline, that is, by classifying each unlabeled documents and then counting how many documents belong to the positive class and how many documents belong to the negative class. Specifically, we use SVM^{perf} with several statistical distance metrics and compare them to our baseline univariate SVM. Our results should confirm that of [10] wherein they concluded that a multivariate SVM outperforms a univariate SVM in the quantification task. The Kullback-Leibler Divergence (KLD) is a loss function that measures how one probability distribution p diverges from a second predicted distribution q. It is defined as follows:

$$KLD(p,q) = \sum_{c_i \in C} p(c_i) \cdot log\frac{p(c_i)}{q(c_i)}$$

SVM^{perf} was extended to optimize KLD in [10]. We compare it to our own approaches described below. The goal is to compare various measures of statistical distance that have different mathematical properties and compare their performance in a sentiment quantification task. Our first sentiment quantification machine is a SVM^{perf} that optimizes the Hellinger Distance instead of KLD. The Hellinger Distance is a statistical distance used to measure the similarity between two probability distributions. HD is defined as follows:

$$HD(p,q) = \frac{1}{\sqrt{(2)}} \cdot \|\sqrt{(p)} - \sqrt{q}\|_2 \tag{5}$$

The second SVM^{perf} optimizes the Bhattacharyya distance. The Bhattacharyya distance is another statistical distance that measures how similar two probability distributions are. It is defined as follows:

$$D_B(p,q) = -\ln(BC(p,q)) \tag{6}$$

where:

$$BC(p,q) = \sum_{x \in X} \sqrt{p(x)q(x)}$$

is the Bhattacharyya coefficient.

The third statistical distance that we optimize through SVM^{perf} is the Jensen Shannon Divergence. The Jensen Shannon Divergence is a smoothed and symmetrized version of the Kullback-Leibler Divergence. It is defined as follows:

$$JSD(p,q) = \frac{1}{2}KLD(p,m) + \frac{1}{2}KLD(q,m) \tag{7}$$

where:

$$m = \frac{1}{2}(p+q)$$

The next statistical distance that we use in the multivariate SVM machine is the Total Variation Distance. It is yet another metric used to measure the distance between two probability distributions and is defined as follows:

$$TVD(p,q) = \frac{1}{2}\sum_{x \in X} \|p(x) - q(x)\|$$

The last statistical distance that we use is another symmetrized version of KLD called Resistor-Average Distance introduced by Johnson and Sinanović [15]. It is equal to the harmonic mean of both Kullback-Leibler distances $KLD(p,q)$ and $KLD(q,p)$ and is formally defined as follows:

$$RAD(p,q) = \left[\frac{1}{KLD(p,q)} + \frac{1}{KLD(q,p)}\right]^{-1}$$

We call these SVM $SVM^{perf}(KLD)$, $SVM^{perf}(HD)$, $SVM^{perf}(BD)$, $SVM^{perf}(JSD)$, $SVM^{perf}(TVD)$, and $SVM^{perf}(RAD)$ respectively.

D. Notes on Statistical Distances

From a pure mathematical perspective, a function d in a space χ is said to be a **distance** if for any $x, y, z \in \chi$ the following three axioms are satisfied:

(i) $d(x,y) > 0$ when $x \neq y$ and $d(x,y) = 0$ if and only if $x = y$
(ii) $d(x,y) = d(y,x)$
(iii) $d(x,y) + d(x,z) \geq d(y,z)$

The axiom (i) implies that the distance must be non-negative and respect the identity of indiscernible, axiom (ii) implies that the distance must be symmetric, i.e., $d(x,y) = d(y,x)$, and axiom (iii) implies that the distance satisfies the triangular inequality, i.e., $d(x,y)+d(y,z) \geq d(x,z)$ (for any $x,y,z \in \chi$, the distance $d(x,z)$ is the shortest distance from x to z in the space) [16]. We now discuss a few properties of all 6 statistical measures mentioned in the previous section.

1) Kullback-Leibler Divergence:
The Kullback-Leibler Divergence does not satisfy axiom (ii) and (iii), KLD is therefore not a distance but a pseudo-distance or directed divergence measure. It is considered a measure of divergence because of its ratio $\frac{p(x)}{q(x)}$, that is, the difference in the probability distributions is large when the ratio is far from 1. $KLD(p,q)$ is undefined if there exists a $q(x) = 0$ for which $p(x) \neq 0$. $KLD(p,q)$ has no upper bound, that is, KLD's limit goes to $+\infty$ when $q(x)$ is infinitely small.

2) Hellinger Distance:
The Hellinger Distance satisfies all three axioms,and is therefore a true distance. $HD(p,q)$ is bounded, it has a lower bound of 0 and an upper bound of 1 (due to the $1/\sqrt{2}$ term in the formula). $HD(p,q)$ is also well defined.

3) Bhattacharrya Distance:
The Bhattacharyya Distance does not satisfy axiom (iii), BD is therefore not a distance in the proper sense but a non-directional divergence measure. As per its definition that employs the natural logarithm, BD is undefined is there exists a $q(x) = 0$ for which $p(x) = 0$. BD has an upper bound.

4) Jensen-Shannon Divergence:
The Jensen-Shannon Divergence does not satisfy axiom (iii), JSD is therefore not a distance in the proper sense but a non-directional divergence measure. JSD is a smoothed and symmetrized version of the Kullback-Leibler Divergence. $JSD(p, q)$ is bounded, it has a lower bound of 0 and an upper bound of $\ln(2)$. Because it uses the KLD, $JSD(p, q)$ is undefined if there exists a $p(x) = 0$ or $q(x) = 0$.

5) Total Variation Distance:
The Total Variation Distance satisfies all three axioms and is therefore a true distance. $TVD(p, q)$ is bounded, it has a lower bound of 0 and an upper bound of 1. Furthermore, $TVD(p, q)$ is well defined.

6) Resistor-Average Distance:
The Resistor-Average Distance does not satisfy axiom (iii), and is therefore not a distance in the proper sense but a non-directional divergence measure. RAD is another symmetrized version of KLD. It is equal to the harmonic mean of both $KLD(p, q)$ and $KLD(q, p)$. $RAD(p, q)$ is not defined when either $KLD(p, q)$ or $KLD(q, p)$ is equal to 0.
Although there exists numerous statistical distance measures and divergence measures available, for no apparent reason, the Kullback-Leibler Divergence has become the *de facto* standard measure for evaluating the distance between two statistical distributions. Our intuition is that statistical distances that are mathematically stronger might be a better choice in place of KLD. Our work aims at comparing several statistical distance measures to see which is best for sentiment quantification.

IV. Experimental Evaluation

A. Datasets

We evaluate our approach over several widely used datasets. The datasets include collections of tweets annotated with a class label chosen from *positive, negative, neutral*. Because we are dealing with 2-class sentiment quantification, we ignore tweets that are labeled *neutral* for both training and testing. The datasets are publicly available on the Internet and the tweets contained in each of them were annotated manually to ensure accurate class labels:

- International Workshop on Semantic Evaluation Task 2 A: Sentiment Analysis in Twitter 2013 [17]
- International Workshop on Semantic Evaluation Task 9 A: Sentiment Analysis in Twitter 2014 [18]
- International Workshop on Semantic Evaluation Task 10 A: Sentiment Analysis in Twitter 2015 [19]
- International Workshop on Semantic Evaluation Task 4 D: Tweet quantification 2016 [20]
- International Workshop on Semantic Evaluation Task 4 D: Tweet quantification 2017 [21]
- Sentiment Strength Twitter (SST) dataset created by [22] and modified by [23] to have the *positive, negative*, or *neutral* classes
- Sanders

The SemEval2016 datasets is split into 4 subsets: train, dev, devtest, and test. We combine the train, dev, and devtest subsets for training and use the remaining test subset for testing. In addition, both the SemEval2016 and SemEval2017 datasest are composed of tweets that belong to a particular topic (the Twitter query). The topic is ignored during training, i.e., all tweets are combined and used for training. However, during testing, we use each topic from the test set as a separate test subset. Table I details the size and contents of each of these two datasets.

TABLE I
TWEET QUANTIFICATION DATASETS

Dataset	Topics	Pos	Neg	**Total**
SemEval2016-train	60	2,841	582	3,423
SemEval2016-dev	20	778	279	1,057
SemEval2016-devtest	20	893	216	1,109
SemEval2016-test	100	8,212	2,339	10,551
SemEval2017-train	100	8,212	2,339	10,551
SemEval2017-test	125	2,463	3,722	6,185

TABLE II
SENTIMENT ANALYSIS DATASETS

Dataset	Train(+dev)			Test		
	# pos	# neg	Total	# pos	# neg	Total
SemEval2013	4,215	1,798	6,013	1,475	559	2,034
SemEval2014	4,215	1,798	6,013	982	202	1,184
SemEval2015	4,215	1,798	6,013	1,038	365	1,403
SST	989	842	1,831	263	195	458
Sanders	418	54	872	101	118	219

Unlike the aforementioned datasets, the sentiment analysis datasets (Table II) are not split into topics. We therefore consider the whole dataset as a single topic. Furthermore, the SemEval-task_A (2013-2015) datasets are partitioned into three subsets (training, dev, test), while the Sanders and the SST datasets are not. We therefore split those into two subsets with 80% used for the training set and 20% reserved for the testing set. The training and dev subsets will be combined and used for training while the test sets will be used for testing.

B. Metrics

Commonly used metrics used to evaluate quantification will be used throughout our experiments: the Kullback-Leibler Divergence (KLD), the Mean Absolute Error (MAE), and the Relative Absolute Error (RAE). The Kullback-Leibler Divergence measures how one probability distribution p diverges from a second predicted distribution $\hat{p}$ and is defined as follows:

$$KLD(\hat{p}, p) = \sum_{c_i \in C} p(c_i) \cdot log\frac{p(c_i)}{\hat{p}(c_i)}$$

The Mean Absolute Error and the Relative Absolute Error are the absolute error between the class prevalence of two quantities and are defined as follows:

$$MAE(\hat{p}, p) = \frac{1}{|C|} \sum_{c \in C} |\hat{p}(c) - p(c)|$$

$$RAE(\hat{p}, p) = \frac{1}{|C|} \sum_{c \in C} \frac{|\hat{p}(c) - p(c)|}{p(c)}$$

TABLE III
RESULTS OF THE QUANTIFICATION USING UNIVARIATE SVM VS MULTIVARIATE SVM

	Metrics	univariate SVM	SVM(perf)	SVM(KLD)	SVM(HD)	SVM(BD)	SVM(JSD)	SVM(TVD)	SVM(RAD)
SST	KLD	0.031	0.011	0.036	0.005	0.044	0.046	**0.000**	0.030
	AE	0.124	0.148	0.266	0.100	0.295	0.301	0.028	0.245
	RAE	0.254	0.149	0.268	0.101	0.296	0.303	0.029	0.246
Sanders	KLD	0.000	0.004	0.010	0.001	0.007	0.028	**0.000**	0.007
	AE	0.005	0.088	0.138	0.037	0.115	0.230	0.005	0.115
	RAE	0.010	0.088	0.138	0.037	0.115	0.231	0.005	0.115
SemEval 2013	KLD	0.003	0.046	0.019	**0.000**	0.018	0.024	0.003	0.019
	AE	0.032	0.275	0.194	0.006	0.191	0.219	0.080	0.194
	RAE	0.081	0.290	0.204	0.006	0.201	0.230	0.084	0.204
SemEval 2014	KLD	0.011	0.018	0.022	**0.001**	0.020	0.026	0.001	0.022
	AE	0.059	0.171	0.204	0.040	0.197	0.222	0.045	0.204
	RAE	0.208	0.191	0.228	0.045	0.221	0.249	0.050	0.228
SemEval 2015	KLD	0.017	0.041	0.032	**0.001**	0.030	0.036	0.002	0.031
	AE	0.085	0.260	0.251	0.047	0.244	0.267	0.058	0.248
	RAE	0.220	0.276	0.266	0.050	0.259	0.283	0.061	0.263
SemEval 2016	KLD	0.090	0.069	**0.010**	0.013	0.014	0.011	0.018	0.014
	AE	0.130	0.242	0.098	0.111	0.108	0.098	0.136	0.106
	RAE	1.378	0.266	0.111	0.125	0.121	0.111	0.156	0.119
SemEval 2017	KLD	0.138	0.254	**0.024**	0.028	0.034	0.025	0.031	0.033
	AE	0.188	0.577	0.171	0.182	0.207	0.176	0.192	0.203
	RAE	2.559	0.676	0.200	0.213	0.241	0.205	0.225	0.237
Average	KLD	0.041	0.063	0.022	**0.007**	0.024	0.028	0.008	0.022
	AE	0.089	0.252	0.189	**0.075**	0.194	0.216	0.078	0.188
	RAE	0.673	0.276	0.202	**0.082**	0.208	0.230	0.087	0.202

We calculate the macro average KLD, MAE, and RAE, which is the harmonic mean of each metric. For instance, the macro average KLD will be defined as follows:

$$\text{Macro Average KLD} = \frac{\sum_{i=1}^{n} KLD_i}{n}$$

where n is the number of instances, i.e., the number of datasets in our case.

KLD is not defined in some special cases, namely when the predicted prevalence $\hat{p}$ is zero. To circumvent this problem we smooth both prevalence p and $\hat{p}$ through additive smoothing similarly to [20], [21], that is, $p(c_i)$ becomes:

$$p^s(c_i) = \frac{p(c_i) + \epsilon}{1 + \epsilon * 2}$$

where ϵ is the smoothing factor and is defined as follows:

$$\epsilon = \frac{1}{2 * |dataset|}$$

$\hat{p}$ is be smoothed similarly. We use smoothed KLD throughout the rest of the paper. The metrics are computed for each run and then averaged to yield the final score. Similar to [20], [21], we report three metrics to evaluate the quantification machines but we mainly focus on the smoothed KLD.

C. Experimental Protocol

Quantification can be performed through univariate SVM by classifying each unlabeled documents and by then counting how many documents belong to the positive class and how many documents belong to the negative class. We use this approach as our baseline using a univariate SVM [24] with a linear kernel [8] since it is known to be effective on text classification.

D. Single score vs paired score lexicons

To support our intuition that paired score sentiment lexicon are better suited for sentiment quantification than single score lexicons, we compare their performances using the aforementioned baseline on the datasets described in Table I and report our results in Table IV. The (single) score of a word is defined as the difference between its positivity $Pos(w)$ and negativity $Neg(w)$ as calculated in Section III-A. We derive sentiment features that are similar so the features derived from the paired score lexicon :

- *token found*: the number of words in the tweet that were found in the lexicon
- *token total*: the number of words in the tweet
- *max*: the maximum score in the tweet
- *min*: the minimum score in the tweet
- *avg*: the average of the scores in the tweet
- *nb pos*: the number of positive words in the tweet
- *nb neg*: the number of negative words in the tweet

TABLE IV
SINGLE SCORE VS PAIRED SCORE LEXICONS ON SENTIMENT QUANTIFICATION USING UNIVARIATE SVM

	Metrics	single score lexicon	paired score lexicon
SemEval 2016	KLD	0.094	**0.090**
	AE	0.132	**0.130**
	RAE	**1.269**	1.378
SemEval 2017	KLD	0.174	**0.138**
	AE	0.216	**0.188**
	RAE	2.972	**2.559**
Average	KLD	0.134	**0.114**
	AE	0.174	**0.159**
	RAE	2.121	**1.969**

TABLE V
KLD OF OUR SVM VS OTHER APPROACHES

	SST	Sanders	SemEval 2013	SemEval 2014	SemEval 2015	SemEval 2016	SemEval 2017
SVM(HD)	**0.005**	**0.001**	**0.000**	**0.001**	**0.000**	0.013	0.028
SVM(KLD)	0.036	0.010	0.019	0.022	0.032	**0.010**	**0.024**
SVM(KLD) [11]	0.011	**0.001**	0.029	0.033	0.076	-	-
Stojanovski et al	-	-	-	-	-	0.034	-
Mathieu Cliche	-	-	-	-	-	-	0.036

E. Sentiment quantification

We train the various multivariate SVM using the training subsets and evaluate on the test subsets. Additionally, when using both SemEval2016 and SemEval2017- datasets we will train each quantifier on each individual topic (that is a total of 100 topics when combining train, dev, devtest) and evaluate each quantifier on each of the 100 topics for SemEval2016-test, and each of the 215 topics for SemEval2017-test. We compare the baseline univariate SVM to the various multivariate SVM approaches described in Section III-C, and report our findings in Table III.

V. RESULTS

A. Single score vs paired score lexicons

Table IV shows that the paired score lexicons outperform the single score lexicon on both datasets. Although the performances of the single score lexicons are close to that of the paired score lexicons on the SemEval 2016 dataset, the paired score lexicons achieve a much better KLD on the SemEval 2017 dataset, yielding an average KLD difference of 0.020. It demonstrates using both the negativity and the positivity of the words help to derive sentiment features that help to more accurately catch the distribution of the positive class and negative class in the dataset.

B. Sentiment quantification

Table III shows that all but one multivariate SVM outperforms the univariate SVM. Precisely, the multivariate SVM(perf) (which is the original multivariate SVM) did not perform better than our baseline univariate SVM. However, this is not surprising since SVM(perf) optimizes the error rate which is not a statistical distance and therefore may not be suitable to perform sentiment quantification. We further compare our best approach, e.g. SVM(HD), to other published results. Specifically, we compare our SVM(HD) with the results published by go et al. [11] whom are the originators of SVM(KLD). In addition, we compare our feature vectors to theirs in the SVM(KLD) setting. We also compare with the work of Stojanovski et al. [12] and Mathieu Cliche [13]. The approach from Stojanovski et al. ranked first on the SemEval2016 competition, while the approach of Mathieu Cliche ranked first on the SemEval2017 competition. We report our results in Table V, due to length constraints, we only report the KLD.

Our SVM(HD) outperform the SVM(KLD) from Go et al. [11] on all datasets but the Sanders dataset on which both approaches perform equivalently. In addition, the feature vector that we use with SVM(KLD) outperforms the feature vector used by Go et al. Likewise, our approach outperform both best approaches from SemEval 2016 and SemEval 2017 competitions. Our results suggest that (1) our feature vector that uses sentiment features derived from our paired-score lexicon is a strong model to represent Tweet sentiment in the VSM, and (2) the multivariate SVM machine that minimizes the Hellinger Distance is a very strong approach to the sentiment quantification problem.

Our experimental results show that the best performance is achieved with our SVM(HD), which outperforms all other multivariate SVM. We believe that the mathematical properties of the distances could explain why one would outperform another. Unlike KLD, BD, JSD, and RAD, both the HD and the TVD are true distance metrics, which means that they perfectly capture the notion of distance within a space and satisfy all three axioms. While property (i) is satisfied by all six metrics that we compared, property (ii) and (iii) are not always satisfied. JSD and RAD are both symmetrized version of KLD and yet provide no improvement upon KLD. Hence, we can not positively assert that the symmetrical property (axiom ii) plays a key role in our task. If the triangular inequality (property iii) is not met, then the distance measured by a function d between two points is not guaranteed to be the shortest in that space. This property is one key difference between a true distance metric. KLD, BD, JSD, and RAD do not satisfy axiom iii and are therefore pseudo-distance measure (or divergence measure), whilst both the HD and the TVD do and are therefore true distance metrics, meaning that they perfectly capture the notion of distance within a space. When optimizing a divergence measure through SVM we are minimizing a distance that is not guaranteed to be the minimal distance between both points. Our results indicate that HD and TVD both yield the best results. Therefore, we believe that a true distance metric is more effective for the sentiment quantification task.

VI. CONCLUSION

In this paper, we have presented a statistical approach to build a sentiment lexicon that computes and maps each word to a pair of score, i.e., its positive weight and its negative weight rather than a single sentiment score. Such sentiment values can then be used in a feature vector to represent tweets in the Vector Space Model. We further confirm previous results that showed that a Support Vector Machine for multivariate performance measures performs better than a traditional univariate SVM when dealing with the sentiment quantification problem. Our experiments compare and optimize several statistical distance measures through a multivariate SVM machine and our results suggest that the choice of the statistical distance to employ when performing sentiment quantification is crucial and heavily impacts the accuracy. Our experiments show that the Hellinger Distance outperforms all other statistical distances that we explored. Finally, we argue that, since it is a true statistical distance measures, the Hellinger Distance is an ideal candidate for performing sentiment quantification with a multivariate SVM.

References

[1] H. Wang, D. Can, A. Kazemzadeh, F. Bar, and S. Narayanan, "A system for real-time twitter sentiment analysis of 2012 us presidential election cycle," in *Proceedings of the ACL 2012 System Demonstrations*. Association for Computational Linguistics, 2012, pp. 115–120.

[2] A. Pak and P. Paroubek, "Twitter as a corpus for sentiment analysis and opinion mining." in *LREc*, vol. 10, no. 2010, 2010, pp. 1320–1326.

[3] D. Davidov, O. Tsur, and A. Rappoport, "Enhanced sentiment learning using twitter hashtags and smileys," in *Proceedings of the 23rd international conference on computational linguistics: posters*. Association for Computational Linguistics, 2010, pp. 241–249.

[4] L. Barbosa and J. Feng, "Robust sentiment detection on twitter from biased and noisy data," in *Proceedings of the 23rd international conference on computational linguistics: posters*. Association for Computational Linguistics, 2010, pp. 36–44.

[5] E. Kouloumpis, T. Wilson, and J. Moore, "Twitter sentiment analysis: The good the bad and the omg!" in *Fifth International AAAI conference on weblogs and social media*, 2011.

[6] J. Zhao, L. Dong, J. Wu, and K. Xu, "Moodlens: an emoticon-based sentiment analysis system for chinese tweets," in *Proceedings of the 18th ACM SIGKDD international conference on Knowledge discovery and data mining*. ACM, 2012, pp. 1528–1531.

[7] A. Go, R. Bhayani, and L. Huang, "Twitter sentiment classification using distant supervision," *CS224N Project Report, Stanford*, vol. 1, no. 12, p. 2009, 2009.

[8] S. M. Mohammad, S. Kiritchenko, and X. Zhu, "Nrc-canada: Building the state-of-the-art in sentiment analysis of tweets," *arXiv preprint arXiv:1308.6242*, 2013.

[9] S. Kiritchenko, X. Zhu, and S. M. Mohammad, "Sentiment analysis of short informal texts," *Journal of Artificial Intelligence Research*, vol. 50, pp. 723–762, 2014.

[10] A. Esuli and F. Sebastiani, "Optimizing text quantifiers for multivariate loss functions," *ACM Transactions on Knowledge Discovery from Data (TKDD)*, vol. 9, no. 4, p. 27, 2015.

[11] W. Gao and F. Sebastiani, "Tweet sentiment: From classification to quantification," in *Proceedings of the 2015 IEEE/ACM International Conference on Advances in Social Networks Analysis and Mining 2015*. ACM, 2015, pp. 97–104.

[12] D. Stojanovski, G. Strezoski, G. Madjarov, and I. Dimitrovski, "Finki at semeval-2016 task 4: Deep learning architecture for twitter sentiment analysis," in *Proceedings of the 10th International workshop on semantic evaluation (SemEval-2016)*, 2016, pp. 149–154.

[13] M. Cliche, "Bb_twtr at semeval-2017 task 4: twitter sentiment analysis with cnns and lstms," *arXiv preprint arXiv:1704.06125*, 2017.

[14] T. Joachims, "A support vector method for multivariate performance measures," in *Proceedings of the 22nd international conference on Machine learning*. ACM, 2005, pp. 377–384.

[15] D. Johnson and S. Sinanovic, "Symmetrizing the kullback-leibler distance," *IEEE Transactions on Information Theory*, 2001.

[16] A. Ullah, "Entropy, divergence and distance measures with econometric applications," *Journal of Statistical Planning and Inference*, vol. 49, no. 1, pp. 137–162, 1996.

[17] P. Nakov, Z. Kozareva, A. Ritter, S. Rosenthal, V. Stoyanov, and T. Wilson, "Semeval-2013 task 2: Sentiment analysis in twitter," 2019.

[18] S. Rosenthal, P. Nakov, A. Ritter, and V. Stoyanov, "Semeval-2014 task 9: Sentiment analysis in twitter," 2019.

[19] S. Rosenthal, S. M. Mohammad, P. Nakov, A. Ritter, S. Kiritchenko, and V. Stoyanov, "Semeval-2015 task 10: Sentiment analysis in twitter," 2019.

[20] P. Nakov, A. Ritter, S. Rosenthal, F. Sebastiani, and V. Stoyanov, "Semeval-2016 task 4: Sentiment analysis in twitter," in *Proceedings of the 10th international workshop on semantic evaluation (semeval-2016)*, 2016, pp. 1–18.

[21] S. Rosenthal, N. Farra, and P. Nakov, "Semeval-2017 task 4: Sentiment analysis in twitter," in *Proceedings of the 11th international workshop on semantic evaluation (SemEval-2017)*, 2017, pp. 502–518.

[22] M. Thelwall, K. Buckley, G. Paltoglou, D. Cai, and A. Kappas, "Sentiment strength detection in short informal text," *Journal of the American Society for Information Science and Technology*, vol. 61, no. 12, pp. 2544–2558, 2010.

[23] H. Saif, M. Fernandez, Y. He, and H. Alani, "Evaluation datasets for twitter sentiment analysis: a survey and a new dataset, the sts-gold," 2013.

[24] T. Joachims, "Text categorization with support vector machines: Learning with many relevant features," in *European conference on machine learning*. Springer, 1998, pp. 137–142.

Detecting Fake News Through Emotion Analysis

Andrew L. Mackey
Computer Science and Engineering
University of Arkansas
Fayetteville, Arkansas, USA
almackey@uark.edu

Susan Gauch
Computer Science and Engineering
University of Arkansas
Fayetteville, Arkansas, USA
sgauch@uark.edu

Kevin Labille
Computer Science and Engineering
University of Arkansas
Fayetteville, Arkansas, USA
kclabill@uark.edu

***Abstract*—Automating the detection of fake news is a challenging problem for the research community due to the various degrees of falsified information and ways in which it can be classified. In this work, we present a Bidirectional Encoder Representations (BERT)-based machine learning model that captures linguistic and emotional features of a document to improve the task of classifying misinformation. The different types of psychological emotions are presented along with the methods used to capture the emotions of words. We investigate how different emotional features can augment existing data to facilitate the detection of fake news and improve upon existing baseline results. Our work demonstrates the ability for emotional features, when combined with other word-embedding models, such as BERT, to improve the performance benchmarks of fake news detection tasks.**

***Index Terms*—Fake news classification; misinformation; emotion analysis natural language processing**

I. Introduction

Social media providers and other distributors of online content are facing increasing pressure to find ways to curtail the spread of falsified information with the intention to deceive users, while also balancing the legalities and potential repercussions from actions taken. Furthermore, journalists who author publications that run contrary to the primary views held by certain groups find themselves being labeled as fake or misleading, even in situations where content was authored solely for the purpose of entertainment. This compels organizations responsible for managing content to differentiate between information as being factually true, misleading, factually untrue for the purpose of entertainment, or blatantly false with the intent to deceive others, often for malicious purposes.

Organizations have been established with the purpose of investigating content and measuring the accuracy of various claims. In recent years, the number of companies dedicated to this task has increased [27]. For example, PolitiFact analyzes comments that were made and ranks them on a scale with values between between true and false, rather than strictly true or false. Small claims are analyzed for the degree of their truthfulness. The task of evaluating the degree of truthfulness is challenging as individuals can easily misidentify claims as being true despite small discrepancies in the way a claim was worded.

Fake news detection using emotion analysis is a classification problem, either binary or multi-class, involving the creation of emotion vectors to augment lexical features and machine learning algorithms to effectively identify content that contains misinformation. Emotion analysis involves the utilization of techniques, mostly derived from lexicons and machine learning algorithms, to extract the psychological associations between words and emotions. Research experiments have been conducted using artificial intelligence and machine learning algorithms to identify and detect falsified content [27]. While there have been significant advancements in the fields of machine learning and natural language processing to tackle and identify fake news articles, additional work is necessary to improve our ability to handle different types of fake news effectively [33]. The identification of smaller text claims, such as social media posts, have not received the same amount of coverage as other forms of fake news (i.e. propaganda, falsified news articles, etc.). Similarly, different types of fake information, such as satirical publications, may receive incorrect classifications in spite of the fact that no malicious intent was assumed.

In this paper, we present an analytic study covering the emotional content contained within varying types of news articles. A model is introduced for incorporating emotion analysis in fake news detection tasks to mitigate the spread of misinformation intending to deceive users. In doing so, the efficiency of emotion vectors are demonstrated as a way to improve existing models. Furthermore, we propose a neural network model for incorporating emotion analysis with word embedding vectors produced by through the Bidirectional Encoder Representations (BERT) model.

II. Related Work

In the following sections, we consider previous work in the areas of emotion analysis and fake news detection.

A. Emotion Analysis

Numerous fields addressing affective computing [16] have demonstrated an interest in the study of emotions and the implications it has for human-computer interaction. The emotion analysis of text allows for the latent emotions and sentiment of words, phrases, and sentences to be extracted. Emotion analysis is often analogous to applications of opinion mining and sentiment analysis [14] and the study of affective lexicons from the field of pyscholinguistics, which evaluates the relationship between psychological processes and linguistic behaviors [4]. In contrast to opinion mining and sentiment analysis where polarity is often measured, emotion analysis aims to associate text with a predefined set of psychological models as determined by the dimensions of valence, activation, and control [19] [22] [23].

Prior studies in the field of psychology focused on the universality of emotions [7] [9] [10]. Six emotions were originally emphasized as being *universal*: ANGER, DISGUST, FEAR, JOY, SADNESS, and SURPRISE [11]. In general, these emotions are represented in models as a discrete set of possibilities or as a domain-general scale (valence, arousal, etc.). Debate over the topic of emotion models still persists in research literature with some researchers proposing categories that are highly dimensional [6] and others suggesting emotions are organized along affective dimensions [2]. Studies questioned the qualitative differences between emotions [26] and the possibility of an existence of overlapping affective features between emotion categories [2].

Emotion classification is typically categorized as being 1) rule-based or 2) machine learning. In earlier implementations of rule-based techniques, authors build or expand existing lexicons of varying emotional characteristics to identify words in data sets evoking emotional features. Techniques for annotating these lexicons involve either crowdsourcing or curation by experts. One study was conducted to model the independent, neurophysiological systems of valence and arousal of social media posts to produce a data set and model that measures the affective norms of subjective social media postings [17]; this served as a departure from prior work that focused predominantly on valence or sentiment [24] [25]. The model proposed utilized the circumplex model of affect with emotions being projected into a vector space of valence, arousal, and dominance [19]. Another study evaluated the concreteness and abstractness of social networking data while measuring emotional intensity [12].

Several advancements in the fields of machine learning and natural language processing have paved the way for new methods of learning semantic relationships between words and emotions. The goal these algorithms is to improve upon dictionary techniques by utilizing supervised machine learning algorithms over lexical features, such as n-grams, word embeddings, and affect lexicons [1]. Machine learning techniques are then able to categorize and predict the appropriate emotion category for text. Many state-of-the-art methods utilize pre-trained word embeddings to extract features using unsupervised machine learning [1] [5] [13] [15] . Through these embeddings, words can be projected into a space such that they are represented as function of their context words.

B. Fake News Detection

Fake news is defined broadly as being news articles that demonstrate the intention of being verifiably false to mislead consumers of this information for entertainment or deceptive purposes. Fake news, while not necessarily a new topic, is one that has received considerable attention from both the public and academic research communities. Similar to other terms that are loosely defined, fake news has many varying definitions between authors and publications. Consider the situation of satirical publications. Whereas some authors include these types of articles as fake news, other authors narrow the definition to news articles as fabrications, hoaxes, or news that is, otherwise, deliberately false with negative intentions, despite attempts to convey the entertainment goal of the articles.

As the aim of each type of fake news differs, we define each of the following as the distinct categories used for the classification of fake news: satire, hoax, propaganda, and clickbait. *Satire* represents a collection of articles where the author of the article intends to entertain the reader through misinformation, sarcasm, or fabrications [27]. It is important to note that an author of satirical work does not intend to mislead the reader. Unlike satire, *hoaxes* are false articles passed as truth, often with the intent of humorous deception. *Propaganda* are articles that are false and meant to deliberately harm a specific party. *Clickbait* is a type of article where the goal is to obtain a reader's attention through misleading headlines, images, etc. that do not align with the perceived goal of the article. It is important to stress that the underlying motivation of the work to deceive, as demonstrated in satire, is a component used in distinguishing the type of fake news a document is classified as being.

The advent of social media, accompanied by the widespread adoption of these services, has proven to be problematic for news consumption by users. Information is able to flow through these social networks rapidly in a manner that is cheap and easy to access. With few limitations in place, it enables the dissemination of fake, misleading, or erroneous news through these same networks, often unabated [28]. Consequently, deceptive practices of misleading or shifting public opinion in a particular direction could adversely influence groups of individuals in social networks based on false pretenses. Fake news increases the mistrust individuals have in real news as users express more skepticism in all information.

In general, there are three characteristics demonstrated in prior work for fake news detection [18]: the content of the article, response from users as a result of posting the article, and the source of the article. Automating the detection of fake news is challenging for several reasons. A number of studies demonstrate the difficulty users have in discerning whether or not an article is fake [3] [8] . The intentionally misleading nature of fake news curtails attempts to categorize documents as being real and fake by the content alone [21]. This presents numerous challenges unique to this task [20] [21]. Variations of the original content is often spread through social media, thus exacerbating the problem of classifying fake news while adding additional complexity due to the additional noise. Prior work has demonstrated that auxiliary information is needed to facilitate the classification of news.

C. Dataset

The data used for this was the publicly available dataset from [27], which is comprised of news articles obtained from crawling seven different unreliable news sites, including The Onion, The Borowitz Report, Clickhole, American News, DC Gazette, The Natural News, and Activist Report.. The types of news were defined as being *satire*, *hoax*, *propaganda*, or *trusted*. For the trusted news source, we include data from [29] where the authors constructed an approach to building a supervised reading comprehension dataset with news articles obtained from convolutional neural networks ($n = 90,266$). We limited the number of documents from the CNN dataset to a randomly extracted sample of $n = 10,000$ documents to limit the overrepresentation of any specific class.

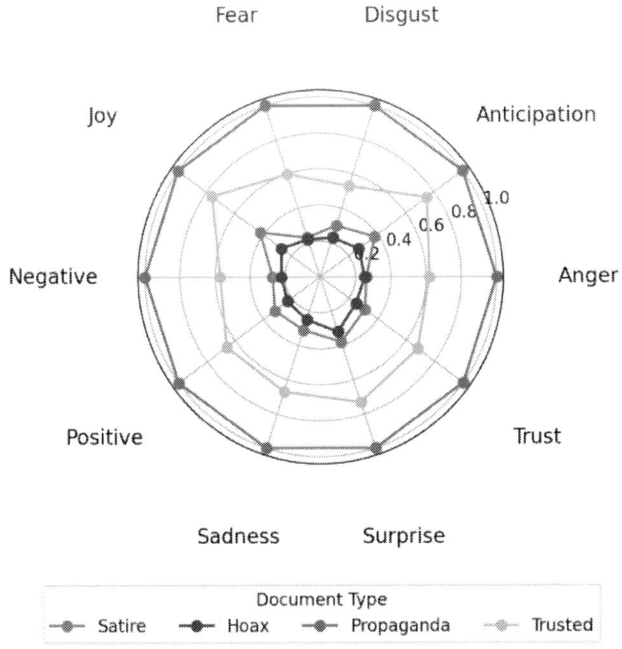

Fig. 1. The emotion feature frequency is shown for each document type, normalized by the maximum of each category.

Table II summarizes the type of news articles, document frequencies, mean document lengths and standard deviations, and median document lengths. Figure 1 visually represents this data normalized by the maximum for each category. New articles from the propaganda class have a higher average number of tokens than other classes. When considering the robustness of the statistical measures to control for outliers, the median of the propaganda class is marginally higher than the trusted class. All data is preprocessed using standard natural language preprocessing techniques, including downcasing, stopword removal, tokenization, etc. We utilize the NLTK toolkit for computational linguistic analysis. The overall distribution of the data can be seen in Figure 2.

III. Fake News Detection

The representation of sentiment as a set of psycholinguistic features has been of interest in prior literature in the field of natural language processing. We augment this work by conducting several experiments to determine which combinations of feature sets yield the best predictive capabilities for the classification of fake news. Our goal is to demonstrate the efficiency of emotion vectors and prove the efficacy of augmenting existing feature sets with emotion features to facilitate classification tasks. To this end, we construct three baseline models for automated fake news detection and compare several models that leverage these emotion vectors. The models, parameters, and configurations are described in the following sections. The models are evaluated using the datasets as described below.

A. Overview

In our experimentation tasks, we evaluated multiple classification algorithms – support vector machines, logistic regression, etc. – and found neural network models to perform the best with a word embedding features. Each document is represented in the training set as a vector of size $n = |V|$ where V is the lexicon derived from the training data. The second baseline model constructed uses the word embeddings formed by extracting fixed-length feature representations from the words in a variable-length documents [30].

B. Emotion Vectors

Our model $E = \{E_1, E_2, E_3\}$ leverages emotions from the discrete and continuous sets of the following emotions and sentiment. We define the set of emotions E with the following ($|E| = 12$):

$$E_1 = \{\ \textit{anger, anticipation, disgust, fear, joy, sadness, surprise, trust}\ \}$$
$$E_2 = \{\ \textit{positive, negative}\ \}$$
$$E_3 = \{\ \textit{valence, arousal}\}$$

For each document, an emotion vector is generated the aggregation of tagged words in the EmoLex emotional resource [31]. We investigated variations of the vector as seen in Table 2. The first approach, EMO$_{SUM}$, is an emotion vector produced by aggregating the sum of each emotion for each word tagged in the document. EMO$_{ZS}$ represents the vector of z-scores for each emotion, such that every emotion e_i is calculated as:

$$z_i = \frac{e_i - \bar{e}_i}{\sigma_{e_i}}$$

Finally, we consider normalizing the vectors using a relative maximum EMO$_{RM}$ for each emotion feature e_i as:

$$RM(e_i) = \frac{e_i}{\underset{d \in D}{\arg\max}(e_i)}$$

Our next task was to determine how to incorporate the number of matching tokens with the emotion scores produced. EMO$_{RM1}$ represents relative maximum of the emotion scores multiplied by the number of matching tokens, whereas EMO$_{RM2}$ is the relative maximum of the emotion scores divided by the number of matching tokens. After testing

TABLE I
NEWS ARTICLES AND MEAN EMOTION TOKENS PER DOCUMENT AND STANDARD DEVIATION

Type	Anger	Anticipation	Disgust	Fear	Joy	Negative	Positive	Sadness	Surprise	Trust
Satire	5.3 ± 6.8	8.8 ± 8.5	3.5 ± 4.6	7.2 ± 9.3	6.4 ± 7.0	11.6 ± 12.5	18.5 ± 17.2	5.5 ± 6.6	3.8 ± 4.2	12.0 ± 11.8
Hoax	5.1 ± 5.4	6.2 ± 5.8	2.7 ± 3.2	6.9 ± 7.6	4.1 ± 4.8	9.5 ± 9.0	13.2 ± 12.1	4.4 ± 5.0	3.2 ± 3.3	9.6 ± 8.7
Prop.	20.5 ± 33.5	23.1 ± 31.3	12.0 ± 23.7	31.1 ± 48.6	15.2 ± 22.3	44.0 ± 71.8	57.0 ± 74.7	18.0 ± 31.4	10.0 ± 15.7	38.9 ± 50.0
Trusted	12.7 ± 11.0	17.3 ± 11.2	6.3 ± 6.2	19.0 ± 15.1	11.5 ± 9.4	25.1 ± 17.4	37.6 ± 22.0	12.1 ± 9.6	7.3 ± 5.5	26.3 ± 16.0

TABLE II
NEWS ARTICLES WITH NUMBER OF DOCUMENTS, AVERAGE DOCUMENT LENGTHS, AND MEDIAN DOCUMENT LENGTHS

Doc. Type	# of Docs	Avg. Tokens	Med. Tokens
Satire	13,942	206 ± 177	105
Hoax	6,892	141 ± 122	109
Propaganda	15,061	587 ± 808	458
Trusted	9,681	428 ± 205	401

both techniques, we constructed each emotion vector for its corresponding document using word frequencies normalized by the number of matching tokens (EMO_{RM2}).

C. Baseline Models

We investigate the impact of both the emotion and extended emotion feature vectors due to their efficiency for the fake news detection task . The first model is constructed by utilizing emotion features obtained from the input documents. We construct a feed forward neural network architecture with two fully connected layers with 512 neurons using the rectified linear unit (ReLU) activation function. Following each fully connected layer, we implement a Dropout layer with dropout rates of 0.5 and 0.3, respectively. We add a final dense layer as the output using the softmax activation function with the number of units corresponding to the number of $\hat{\mathbf{y}}$ target classes. In previous sections, we introduced the methods by which we encode news articles and construct emotion vectors for each article. We define $\hat{\mathbf{y}}$ as the predicted probability of the target class being fake or real news. The procedure would be similar in a multi-class classification problem for detecting hoaxes, propganda, clickbait, satire, or legitimate news. We define $\mathbf{d}$ and $\mathbf{e}$ as the learned features for news documents and emotion vectors, respectively. Furthermore, $\mathbf{b}$ is defined as the bias term and $\mathbf{W}$ represents the learned weights.

$$\hat{\mathbf{y}} = \text{softmax}([\hat{\mathbf{d}}, \hat{\mathbf{e}}]\mathbf{W} + \mathbf{b})$$

The batch size was set to 64 and we implemented early stopping criteria to limit potential overfitting. We utilize the Adam optimization algorithm and a categorical cross-entropy loss function for this multi-class classification task. A learning rate of 0.001 was used.

The second model is constructed by forming document-level word embeddings from BERT for each of the input documents [32]. The BERT embeddings were formed from $L = 12$ hidden layers (transformer blocks), with a hidden size of $H = 128$ and $A = 2$ attention heads. After the BERT layers, we implement the same feed forward network architecture as described above. The final model architecture was formed by using bag of words feature vectors using TF-IDF weights. To measure the impact and effectiveness of emotion vectors, we consider the top k features for the BOW model. We established $k = 128$ for comparison to the BERT model. The feature vectors were normalized using min-max scale.

All documents containing a low number of tokens or convey no emotional content such that the magnitude of the vector $||\mathbf{e}|| = 0$ were removed from the document corpus. Each experiment was conducted from training, testing, and validation splits of sizes 0.7, 0.2, and 0.1, respectively. The mean performance metric from each experiment conducted 10 times from random shuffles of the data is reported.

IV. EVALUATION

Having presented models for the task of identifying fake news, we evaluate the models using the data described in earlier sections. Our hypothesis is that emotion vectors can improve the detection of fake news detection by augmenting existing models with additional information. Given the complexity of fake news detection, we expect that emotion analysis alone may not be suitable to compress the information needed correctly identify falsified information. The experiments are therefore designed to evaluate the effectiveness of emotion analysis in the classification of fake news. First, we want to establish whether or not emotion features can be used in fake news detection. Second, we compare our baseline models to those where features have been augmented with emotions. Third, we want to measure the efficiency of emotion features by evaluating the gains achieved through adding emotional

TABLE III
FAKE NEWS CLASSIFICATION METHODS WITH EACH OF THE PROPOSED MODELS

Type	Method	Accuracy	Precision	Recall	F1
BASELINE	EMO+NN	0.569	0.692	0.308	0.423
	BERT+NN	0.763	0.798	0.721	0.757
WORD EMBED	EMOEX+NN	0.593	0.704	0.369	0.482
	EMO+BERT+NN	0.792	0.824	0.753	0.786
	EMOEX+BERT+NN	0.794	0.823	0.754	0.786
BAG OF WORDS	BOW+NN	0.793	0.795	0.792	0.794
	BOWEX+NN	0.798	0.799	0.797	0.798
	EMO+BOW+NN	0.861	0.863	0.857	0.861

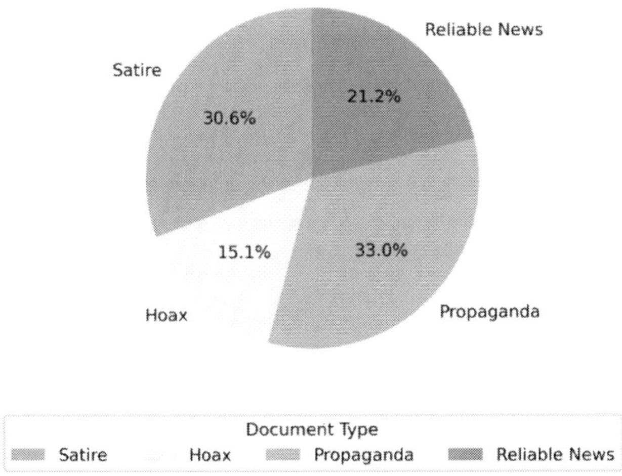

Fig. 2. The distribution of the dataset used for classification is presented by the news article type.

context to existing models in comparison to other lexical feature additions.

TABLE IV
BASELINE MODEL EVALUATION

Method	Accuracy	Precision	Recall	F1
EMO+NN	0.569	0.692	0.308	0.423
EMOEX+NN	0.593	0.704	0.369	0.482
BERT+NN	0.763	0.798	0.721	0.757

The results presented in Table III demonstrate that emotional features can enhance existing models to improve the classification of fake news. For our baseline models as seen in Table IV, we consider the emotional features baseline EMO+NN or word embeddings baseline BERT+NN produced from BERT to use for training. The EMO+NN model using emotion vectors reported a baseline accuracy of 0.569, whereas the BERT+NN word embeddings model produced 0.763 for the same task. For our experimental models, we augment the existing feature vectors with our emotion vectors EMO+BERT+NN or the extended emotion vector EMOEX+BERT+NN for the document. The concatenation of emotion vectors and BERT word embeddings for neural network classifier improved the accuracy and F1 metrics by 2.9%. This can be observed in Table V. Similarly, the extended emotion vectors EMOEX+BERT+NN improved the accuracy performance by 3.1% and the F1 score by 2.9%. When considered individually, EMOEX+BERT+NN had an overall accuracy improvement over the baseline EMO+BERT+NN by 2.4% and 5.9% for the F1 score.

TABLE V
EVALUATION OF WORD EMBEDDINGS AND EMOTION FEATURE MODELS

Method	Accuracy	Precision	Recall	F1
BERT+NN	0.763	0.798	0.721	0.757
EMO+BERT+NN	0.792	**0.824**	0.753	0.785
EMOEX+BERT+NN	**0.794**	0.823	**0.754**	**0.786**

To demonstrate the application of emotion vectors to other tasks, we consider a model trained with TF-IDF weighted bag of words feature vectors BOW with $k = 128$ features. The model achieves an accuracy performance of 0.793 and F1 score of 0.794. The impact from adding the emotion vectors to the model is demonstrated in EMO+BOW+NN. The model achieves an accuracy and F1 score of 0.861, which is a 6.8% improvement over the BOW model for comparison. Similarly, we consider the impact of adding $|EMO| = 18$ features to the $k = 128$ top features selected for the BOW model. An additional 18 features are added to the top k features to produce an expanded bag of words feature vector of length $k = 146$ to produce model BOWEX+NN. By increasing the

BOW model by the same number of features as the emotion lexicon, we obtain an accuracy of 0.798, which is a marginal improvement of 0.5%. The improvements from increasing the feature vectors with additional word features did not have the same measurable impact as adding the same number of emotion features as seen in Table VI.

TABLE VI
COMPARISON OF BAG OF WORDS MODELS AND EMOTION FEATURES

Method	Accuracy	Precision	Recall	F1
BOW+NN	0.793	0.795	0.792	0.794
BOWEX+NN	0.798	0.799	0.797	0.798
EMO+BOW+NN	0.861	0.863	0.857	0.861

The experiments presented here demonstrate the ability of emotion features to facilitate the classification of fake news in a multiclass environment. The stronger improvements to bag of words models over word embedding models suggests that word embeddings capture additional semantics in lexical meanings that are otherwise not present in bag of words models. Gains were similarly observed in word embedding models, and subsequently demonstrating the ability for emotion features to improve existing models.

V. CONCLUSION

The utilization of emotion analysis and features for improving existing machine learning tasks in the detection of fake news provides a promising track for building systems capable of understanding the patterns of information with intentions of deceiving the user. The effectiveness of applying emotion features to fake news detection and existing frameworks or models was demonstrated. The incorporation of other sources of data into models may be necessary to expand beyond the tasks described here. Given the ability of emotions to distinguish between targets in a multiclass setting, further experimentation will need to be conducted to better understand how to improve upon existing techniques for extracting emotional context through a combination of lexicon and machine-learning based techniques.

REFERENCES

[1] Jeremy Barnes, Roman Klinger, and Sabine Schulte im Walde. Assessing state-of-the-art sentiment models on state-of-the-art sentiment datasets. *arXiv preprint arXiv:1709.04219*, 2017.

[2] Lisa Feldman Barrett, Zulqarnain Khan, Jennifer Dy, and Dana Brooks. Nature of emotion categories: Comment on cowen and keltner. *Trends in cognitive sciences*, 22(2):97–99, 2018.

[3] Michael Barthel, Amy Mitchel, and Jesse Holcomb. Many americans believe fake news is sowing confusion. *Pew Research Center*, 2016.

[4] Gerald L Clore, Andrew Ortony, and Mark A Foss. The psychological foundations of the affective lexicon. *Journal of personality and social psychology*, 53(4):751, 1987.

[5] Ronan Collobert, Jason Weston, Léon Bottou, Michael Karlen, Koray Kavukcuoglu, and Pavel Kuksa. Natural language processing (almost) from scratch. *Journal of machine learning research*, 12(ARTICLE):2493–2537, 2011.

[6] Alan S Cowen and Dacher Keltner. Clarifying the conceptualization, dimensionality, and structure of emotion: Response to barrett and colleagues. *Trends in cognitive sciences*, 22(4):274–276, 2018.

[7] Charles Darwin. *The expression of the emotions in man and animals*. Oxford University Press, USA, 1872.

[8] Camila Domonoske. Students have 'dismaying' inability to tell fake news from real, study finds. *National Public Radio*, 23, 2016.

[9] Paul Eckman. Universal and cultural differences in facial expression of emotion. In *Nebraska symposium on motivation*, volume 19, pages 207–284, 1972.

[10] Paul Ekman. *Darwin and facial expression: A century of research in review*. Ishk, 1973.

[11] Paul Ekman. Facial expression and emotion. *American psychologist*, 48(4):384, 1993.

[12] Maximilian Köper, Evgeny Kim, and Roman Klinger. IMS at EmoInt-2017: Emotion intensity prediction with affective norms, automatically extended resources and deep learning. In *Proceedings of the 8th Workshop on Computational Approaches to Subjectivity, Sentiment and Social Media Analysis*, pages 50–57, Copenhagen, Denmark, September 2017. Association for Computational Linguistics.

[13] Tomas Mikolov, Kai Chen, Greg Corrado, and Jeffrey Dean. Efficient estimation of word representations in vector space. *arXiv preprint arXiv:1301.3781*, 2013.

[14] Bo Pang and Lillian Lee. Opinion mining and sentiment analysis. *Found. Trends Inf. Retr.*, 2(1–2):1–135, January 2008.

[15] Jeffrey Pennington, Richard Socher, and Christopher D Manning. Glove: Global vectors for word representation. In *Proceedings of the 2014 conference on empirical methods in natural language processing (EMNLP)*, pages 1532–1543, 2014.

[16] Rosalind W Picard. *Affective computing*. MIT press, 2000.

[17] Daniel Preoţiuc-Pietro, H Andrew Schwartz, Gregory Park, Johannes Eichstaedt, Margaret Kern, Lyle Ungar, and Elisabeth Shulman. Modelling valence and arousal in facebook posts. In *Proceedings of the 7th workshop on computational approaches to subjectivity, sentiment and social media analysis*, pages 9–15, 2016.

[18] Natali Ruchansky, Sungyong Seo, and Yan Liu. Csi: A hybrid deep model for fake news detection. In *Proceedings of the 2017 ACM on Conference on Information and Knowledge Management*, pages 797–806, 2017.

[19] James A Russell. A circumplex model of affect. *Journal of personality and social psychology*, 39(6):1161, 1980.

[20] Kai Shu, Limeng Cui, Suhang Wang, Dongwon Lee, and Huan Liu. defend: Explainable fake news detection. In *Proceedings of the 25th ACM SIGKDD International Conference on Knowledge Discovery & Data Mining*, pages 395–405, 2019.

[21] Kai Shu, Amy Sliva, Suhang Wang, Jiliang Tang, and Huan Liu. Fake news detection on social media: A data mining perspective. *ACM SIGKDD explorations newsletter*, 19(1):22–36, 2017.

[22] Carlo Strapparava and Rada Mihalcea. Learning to identify emotions in text. In *Proceedings of the 2008 ACM symposium on Applied computing*, pages 1556–1560, 2008.

[23] Mike Thelwall, Kevan Buckley, and Georgios Paltoglou. Sentiment strength detection for the social web. *Journal of the American Society for Information Science and Technology*, 63(1):163–173, 2012.

[24] Mike Thelwall, Kevan Buckley, Georgios Paltoglou, Di Cai, and Arvid Kappas. Sentiment strength detection in short informal text. *Journal of the American society for information science and technology*, 61(12):2544–2558, 2010.

[25] Theresa Wilson, Janyce Wiebe, and Paul Hoffmann. Recognizing contextual polarity in phrase-level sentiment analysis. In *Proceedings of human language technology conference and conference on empirical methods in natural language processing*, pages 347–354, 2005.

[26] Christine D Wilson-Mendenhall, Lisa Feldman Barrett, and Lawrence W Barsalou. Variety in emotional life: within-category typicality of emotional experiences is associated with neural activity in large-scale brain networks. *Social cognitive and affective neuroscience*, 10(1):62–71, 2015.

[27] Hannah Rashkin, Eunsol Choi, Jin Yea Jang, Svitlana Volkova, and Yejin Choi. Truth of varying shades: analyzing language in fake news and political fact-checking. *Proceedings of the 2017 Conference on Empirical Methods in Natural Language Processing*, pages 2931–2937, 2017.

[28] Castillo, Carlos and Mendoza, Marcelo and Poblete, Barbara Information credibility on twitter *Proceedings of the 20th international conference on World wide web*, pages 675–684, 2011.
[29] Karl Moritz Hermann, Tomáš Kocisky, Edward Grefenstette, Lasse Espeholt, Will Kay, Mustafa Suleyman, and Phil Blunsom. Teaching machines to read and comprehend. 2015.
[30] Quoc V. Le and Tomas Mikolov Distributed representations of sentences and documents. 2014.
[31] Mohammad, Saif M. and Turney, Peter D. Crowdsourcing a word-emotion association lexicon. *Computational Intelligence* 2013.
[32] Jacob Devlin, Ming-Wei Chang, Kenton Lee, and Kristina Toutanova. Bert: Pre-training of deep bidirectional transformers for language understanding. *arXiv preprint* 2018.
[33] Xinyi Zhou and Reza Zafarani A survey of fake news: fundamental theories, detection methods, and opportunities *ACM Comput. Surv* 2020.

Usage of Blockchain Technology for the Improvement of Industry and The Training of Future Talents

Fadhila Djouggane, Samia Aitouche, Karima Aksa, Hanane Zermane
Laboratory of Automation and manufacturing, Industrial engineering department, University Batna 2, Batna, Algeria
e-mail: djougganefadila@yahoo.fr, s.aitouche@univ-batna2.dz, k.aksa@univ-batna2.dz

Abstract— **This study presents a systematic review using the Kitchenham method, to analyze recent research works related to blockchain technology and its application in training. The problems of exchanging data safely and rapidly with transparency and centralization, led to the emergence of this technology that has revolutionized the world and in almost all areas. Different articles are devoted to show the various approaches, equipped, methods, skills, knowledge, etc., necessary to the application of the blockchain. The main objective of this study is to reveal the importance of this technology for the development of industrial and educational world showing different skills, competencies, talents required to implement a blockchain, and use it for management and education.**

Keywords- blockchain; training; skills; competencies.

I. INTRODUCTION

The lack of confidence and dissatisfaction with third parties and traditional mediators, institutions, banks and states, led to the creation of many research challenges in different fields such as: technology, economy, politics and sociology [23]. To face this problem, researches are directed towards blockchain technology i.e. a technology for storing and transmitting information, allowing the constitution of replicated and distributed registers, without a central controlling institution, with a high degree of security, thanks to encryption methods and transmission protocols [16]. It is structured by blocks linked to each other, at regular time intervals [24]. Researchers consider the blockchain as a double-edged sword technology; it has been considered the safest peer-to-peer system [15]. Schematically, the necessary environment for the implementation of a blockchain can resemble to a 4 layers structure (Fig.1) [19].

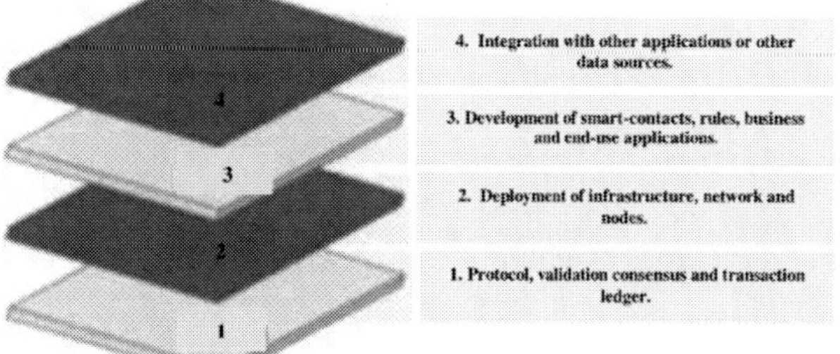

Figure 1. The blockchain structure [19]

Nowadays, researchers are very interested by blockchain technology, with its integration in all fields (Fig. 2) [17]. In order to catch up the fast-paced development of industrial technologies, which requires adaptation to the evolution of the world and the development of interaction with other disciplines and new approaches, therefore it is essential to align the supply of skills with the fast changing of economic needs. This requires sound education policies as well as transformation of education and training systems, as there are signs that educational institutions are not keeping pace with technological advancement, leading to skills shortages [18].

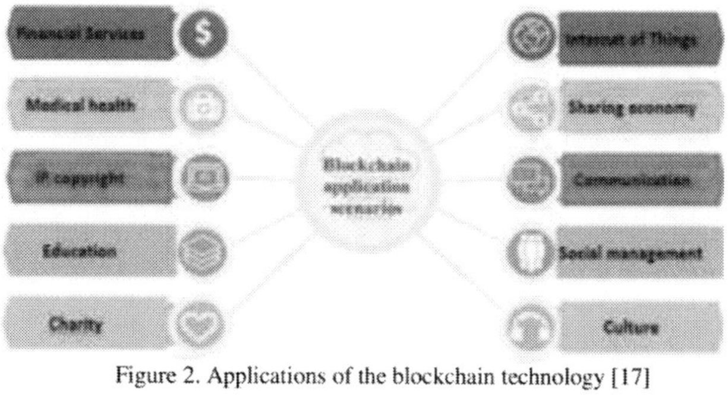

Figure 2. Applications of the blockchain technology [17]

Fifteen articles are used, through a systematic review, using the Kitchenham method [21], a manual division of the articles throughout the reading presented in the diagram (Fig. 3). We choose as criteria: the field of application (education, industry) and application methods (analytical, practical). Section 2 of this article is devoted to detailing the 15 articles, where we will provide an overview of the use of blockchain technology, to improve teaching process, and ensure mastery of the technology and training talent. Section 3 concerns the digitizing the human resources area in industry thanks to blockchain technology. We will finish by a conclusion.

II. EDUCATION AND TRAINING FACE THE BLOCKCHAIN TECHNOLOGY

According to reports published recently through web sites, the blockchain will be the most demanded skill by employers and these profiles are highly demanded [25]. To meet the needs of employers and understand the challenges of this technology, universities have adopted special blockchain training techniques to attract the attention of students, and to achieve the desired skills to master the difficulties of this technology to improve the teaching process. Table 2 presents research that highlight the importance of blockchain technology at the training level (training of future talents, adapting new training techniques) of technology.

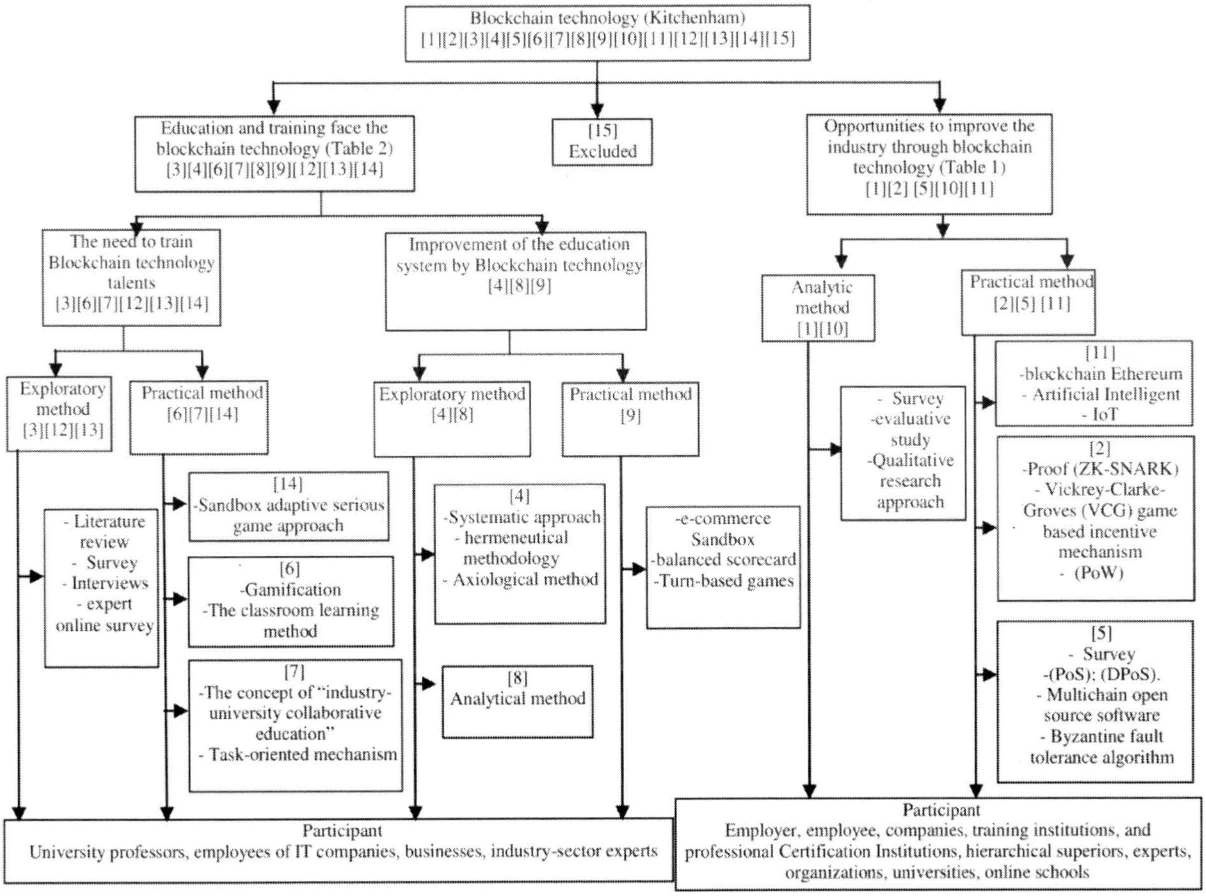

Figure 3. The architecture of the systematic review

TABLE I. BLOCKCHAIN TECHNOLOGY AND HUMAN RESOURCES MANAGEMENT

citation	Aim	technic or method	participant	findings	prospects
[1] N. Pokrovskaia et al.	The article serves to digitize the space of the assessment of qualifications and competences for an optimization and increase of the management of human resources.	A survey off line	employer , employee	results show a general hierarchy of the importance of knowledge and skills of highly qualified employees and their line managers.	
[11] O.Fachrunnisaet al.	The aim of this research is to develop a BC-based HR framework to meet the needs of the business and the skills of the workforce. This framework will help the Corporate Training Center to standardize the skills.	-Ethereum Blockchain –IoT - AI	companies, training institutions, Professional Certification Institutions.	-the blockchain is able to generate information on the skills required by the industry. This information will be used by the training center of the company to organize the procedure concerning the competence standards of the workforce.	
[10] D.Darius z et al.	developed a conceptual model which integrates the description of the Competences and the aptitudes, documents and all the other forms of confirmation of the acquisition of competences	-survey -evaluative study	employer , employee organizations	The proposed model ensures the unification of the way in which documents confirming the qualifications possessed are represented and can thus form the basis for the construction of a system intended to verify their credibility.	Introduce the proposed system first in Poland. However, they will only use universal solutions that can be easily accepted by other EU members as well as third countries.
[2] L.Liu et al.	the item is used for Employee background check (candidate qualifications, such as employment, education and skills) for recruitment with blockchain	- (VCG) game based incentive mechanism - (PoW) - C++, Data Analytics			
[5] H.Onik et al.	Proposed a blockchain-based recruitment management system (BcRMS) as well as a blockchain-based human resources management system (BcHRMS) algorithm.	- survey - (PoS)(DPoS). - Multichain open source - Byzantine fault tolerance algorithm	employer , employee organizations	The proposed system offers empowered users, higher quality and reliable recruitment and management, inter-process integrity, faster transaction and decision with lower cost	

TABLE II. BLOCKCHAIN TECHNOLOGY AND TRAINING

citation	Aim	technics or methods	participant	fadings	prospects
[3] N.Miloslavskaya et al.	the state of current training for BCT technologies around the world, paying particular attention to security issues.	global survey on BCT training	- Univer -sities busines ses	42% of the top 50 universities offer at least one BC or cryptocurrency course, and 22% offer more than one.	- preparation of a course with the proposed structure - the development of all the necessary educational and methodical material - website teacher-student interaction
[4] G.N. Takigawa et al.	The article analyzes the innovative possibilities of using new social media technologies blockchain, big date, collective intelligence technologies, artificial intelligence in higher education in Russia	-systematic approach -hermeneutic methodology-axiological method.	universities	- The use of crowdsourcing, blockchain, big data, collective intelligence, AI, meets the needs of higher professional education - creation of reliable guarantees for the protection of the intellectual property of students and teachers,	
[6] K.C. Benson et al.	- the article serves to combine the conceptual theories of active learning and gamification to use them as a pedagogy for the Blockchain - encourages instructors to use their creative talents to produce gamification for Blockchain pedagogy	- triangular game - symmetric key in cryptography - safe gamification, -role-playing game -(asynchronous learning method)	- Instructor - students	- the application of the theories of interactive learning and gamification, coupled with the asynchronous learning system, can be applied to bring similar advantages in the pedagogy of other disciplines	- a quantitative study aimed at determining the amount of knowledge acquired active learning process would be enlightening in future teaching.
[7] C.Chen et al.	-This paper investigates on the technical requirements of a local company in the city of Weifang and proposes a strategy to train blockchain talents in application-oriented universities.	-the concept of "industry-university collaborative education" - a task-oriented mechanism -Hyperleger Fabric	- training enterprise engineers – students - tutors.	- students learning motivation and reorganize educational elements - the implementation of the strategy successfully in training courses	
[8] Peter Williams	This article considers that universities need to outsource part of their course delivery and assessment in order to remain competitive. It examines a potentially sustainable mission strategy: to move away from narrow academic disciplines to an authentic learning program focused on developing students as full people with rounded education.			-Pilot projects and sharing of expertise between institutions would also be useful at this early stage - universities must be proactive in meeting this last challenge and adapt their missions, structures and practices to maintain viability and sustainability for an uncertain future	
[9] B.Wu et al.	this article proposes a competition mode of application of blockchain technology based on the E-commerce Sandbox of digital education operation	- the balanced scorecard - Fuzzy AHP - Trusted Cloud - Softmax -alliance chain. - e-commerce sandbox	teachers and students .	The correlation coefficient obtained is greater than 0.8, which validates the accuracy of the evaluation model. On the system side, by simulating teacher and student scenarios, user operations and data communication with the blockchain system are tested, which validates the technical feasibility of the prototype system.	The author plans to use machine learning to train the evaluation model and continuously optimize the model in the process of increasing the amount of data.
[12] M.M. Milovanova . et al.	The purpose of the article is to analyze the possibilities of business education in teaching and using blockchain technology for business development (blockchain business training)	- analysis of monographs, articles, and specialized literature - an expert online survey		- the state commitment to the formation of a digital society. - the growing demand for qualified specialists in the application of blockchain technologies requires the development of a commercial training course in this field of activity.	
[13] F.Prager. et al.	the study seeks to apply the fundamentals, identify likely trends and provide BCT education and training programs	-Interviews - literature review -open-ended, semi-structured approach	industry -sector experts	the majority of industrial sectors see the potential of blockchain, either by increasing operational efficiency, reducing transaction costs and creating new growth opportunities.	- the impacts of blockchain on business practices - explore the effectiveness of blockchain training and education
[14] A.Mittal . et al.	The authors offer one of the first such educational tools for blockchain training using an adversarial adaptive sandbox serious game approach for students and tech professionals.	-AI - game experience quiz - adaptive NPC algorithm heuristic techniques -firebase, - chatbox - edutainment -sandbox adaptive serious game	students technology professionals -general public	the introduction of the first serious online game, can increase blockchain technology educational skills for students and industry professionals.	The authors plan to use a subjective questionnaire to determine the effectiveness of their games in terms of user experience

A. *The need to train Blockchain technology talents*

Over time, the challenges of training around the blockchain technology (BCT) multiply, and the question asked is: How to get real "relevant skills" of blockchain projects if there is no comprehensive and practical training on the subject? To solve the issue and identify the challenges and training needs for the mastery of technology, authors of [3] analyze an inventory of current training in the BCT around the world, through a global survey, where they paid particular attention to security issues. They offered training divided into two groups where the first is designed for distance education only and the second for full-time face-to-face training (not online), with a list of standards and books that can support this training and specify the skills sought after mastering a full-time BCT course with exemplary course structure. [12] has analyzed the possibilities of business education in teaching the use of blockchain technology for business development. Based on an expert survey, the main provisions of the business training course "Blockchain: Basic Principles and Application Examples" have been developed, the skills and learning outcomes for this course have been determined, and the sample business program "Blockchain: Fundamentals and Application Examples" were presented.

In order to contribute to the economic development of South Bay, authors of [13] relied on a case study informed by interviews with experts in the fields of BCT and the workforce of the industrial sector, as well as through a literature review and analysis of labor force trends for the region, to inform public officials and policy makers working on issues of new technologies, regional economic development, and investment in the workforce. According to this study, answers suggest that those in the majority of industrial sectors see the potential of blockchain as a disruptive and positive force in their workplace. Many answers highlight the potential of blockchain investments to expand their workplaces, whether by increasing operational efficiency, reducing transaction costs, or creating new growth opportunities.

Other researchers find that BCT involves a lot of theoretical knowledge, which can easily discourage students' enthusiasm for learning. To bridge the gap between theoretical and practical knowledge, the authors have tried to make learning easier. This is the case with [7] where the authors analyzed the technical requirements of a local company in the city of Weifang, they came up with a task-oriented strategy, to train blockchain talents in application-oriented universities. They adopt the concept of "collaborative industry-university education", a strategy that takes into account the real knowledge levels of students in applied universities and sets a reasonable degree of learning difficulty. The strategy has been applied to the School of Computer Engineering of Weifang University and some positive effects have been achieved.

For their part, the authors of [6] and [14] have integrated experiential learning theories using game concepts to engage, motivate and attract student interest to acquire more knowledge. In [14], the authors suggest one of the first educational tools for blockchain training using an adversarial adaptive sandbox serious game approach for students and tech professionals, which can improve cybersecurity in management systems information where blockchain technology impregnates the corresponding disciplines. They further suggested the use of artificial intelligence (AI) to improve the interactivity of NPCs (Non-Player Character) based on player responses. This research is essential for the introduction of the first serious online game, which can increase educational skills in blockchain technology for students and industry professionals. The authors plan to rate this serious game on a subjective scale based on the Game Experience Survey. In the same context, the authors in [6] chose to use the mid-sized college classroom in the United States to apply the principles of active learning (a process to involve students in the co-creation of the learning experience by sharing leadership and course design, students will be responsible for their own learning), and gamification leading to blockchain education. The used classroom learning method was the asynchronous learning method, in which concepts were categorically divided into blocks. These elementary principles were built on top of each other, which led to the synergistic knowledge and definition of blockchain for the student. The instructor performed these exercises in Introductory Information Technology (IT) courses, as well as higher level ethics and professionalism courses, with the aim of discerning different levels of knowledge regarding the subject of the blockchain. The content of the article encourages instructors to use their creative talents to produce gamification for blockchain pedagogy.

B. *Improvement of the education system by Blockchain technology*

In a world full of transformation that faces the acceleration of innovation and new technologies, the formal educational systems can quickly become obsolete. Educational systems are increasingly called upon to correspond to the realities and needs of societies. To improve the higher educational system in Russia, [4] explores the new needs of their system in the context of the global digitization of society and it analyzes the innovative possibilities of merging new social media technologies, blockchain, big data, artificial intelligence, with each other. At the end, all available knowledge and its supports will be brought together in a single system called collective intelligence and most importantly the guarantee of intellectual property of the latest curricula and educational resources. Authors consider Russian projects for their use in practical activities of teachers, on the basis of systems analysis methods, new directions in training of specialists have been identified and characterized: the development of forms of collective creativity the participation in complex projects based on blockchain technologies, the involvement of young initiative in the framework of crowdsourcing technologies, the development of individualized training based on artificial intelligence technologies. As the acquisition of qualifications became more decoupled from the academy, universities would lose the virtual monopoly they currently enjoy on degrees and would have to reinvent themselves as graduate educators in a broader sense, to that the university always remains competitive. The article [8] describes the changing nature of graduate occupations and examines the possible impacts of developments in knowledge-intensive work and AI. It examines the analysis of learning and blockchain technologies to assess their potential to automate the secure recognition of student activities and achievements. It makes an original and timely contribution to higher education literature by considering how a convergence of three technologies (learning analytics, (AI) and blockchain) could lead to radical changes.

To go further than the current mode of application of the blockchain which is limited to recording the educational experience of students, the author of [9] offers a competition mode of application of blockchain technology based on the e-commerce sandbox of digital education operation, to help teachers to test students' knowledge and their ability to use the knowledge. This mode applies blockchain technology to effectively simplify the competition process and improve competition efficiency. At the same time, the credibility of the competition is resolved by the characteristics of system transparency and non-disruption of data. To provide traceability information for digital education products, the authors propose to combine with Trusted Cloud.

III. Digitizing the Human Resources Area in Industry Thanks to Blockchain Technology

Authenticating credentials can be a real headache for corporate recruiters. Fraud with false diplomas and approximations during interviews still represent an important part of applications today. In an increasingly competitive job market, the blockchain is one of the strengths of technology that comes from its total transparency particularly in the verification of candidate profiles, verification of diplomas, experiences, their duration, etc. Table 1 presents the research that focused on finding solutions to these problems.

In the same context, [5] proposed a blockchain-based on the recruitment management system (BcRMS) as well as a blockchain-based human resources management system (BcHRMS) algorithm. It is a fast efficient and transparent system using blockchain to reduce the risk to the human resources authority. The proposed system thus provides authentic and effective decision support information for the management of the human resources of an organization. This research reveals that the proposed models can be more efficient than the existing HRM systems in terms of safety, cost, time and quality of work. Thus, the proposed system will have significant effects on the construction of smart cities as well as smart industries in the era of existing industry 4.0 and future industry 5.0.

For the researches [1][10], the authors relied on analytical methods. In [1], it uses blockchain technology to build a global register of certificates of qualification and evaluation of skills, to face the central issue of research in the field of training and professional integration of highly qualified specialties. The register content includes two main characteristics which are requested by the employer and offered by an individual as a potential employee:

• Qualifying characteristics are reflected, as a rule, in educational documents and in professional standards of an industry;

• Competency parameters are presented in the functional description of the vacant positions of the company and in the resumes and portfolios of candidates listing the functional tasks that have been performed in their previous jobs, qualifying characteristics of a person are reflected in a variety of certificates.

For their part, the authors of [10] carry out an in-depth analysis of laws, professional regulations and government reports, a conceptual model has been developed which integrates the description of competences and aptitudes, documents and all other forms of confirmation of skills acquisition. The application of blockchain technology allows all data to be integrated into an autonomous system while using existing skills registers. The computer conceptual model developed by a qualitative research approach meets the requirements of all interested parties: employees, employers and organizations issuing such documents. Based on the model developed for document representation, as an integrator of personal skills, the authors propose an Integrated Personal Competence Ledger (IPeCoL) to collect and provide access to information certifying the possession of specific skills. The proposed model ensures the unification of the way in which documents confirming the qualifications possessed are represented and can thus form the basis for the construction of a system intended to verify their credibility.

To help the Corporate Training Center to standardize the skills then to use them by the human resources department to develop the training material, [11] developed a blockchain-based Human Resources (HR) framework to meet the needs of the business and the skills of the workforce. In order to obtain information on the skills required by the industry, the authors use technological applications: in particular AI and blockchain. By integrating the above two technologies, the blockchain - IoT application is formulated to meet practical skills gap mitigation needs. For proof of concept and validation, the authors are developing a prototype system using the Ethereum blockchain to meet the needs of industry and education as a competent source of skilled labor. The proposed system not only enables holistic HR training content, but also dynamic workforce skills according to business needs. The result of the validation with the prototyping blockchain shows that the blockchain is able to generate information on the skills required by the industry. This information will be used by the Corporate Training Center to organize the procedure relating to the competence standard of the personnel. Accordingly, this information will be used by the training provider to organize the program.

IV. Conclusion

Blockchain has been considered as an innovative technology with a strong potential for transformation [19], it is not easy to say whether or not it will revolutionize industrial or educational processes, because most of the challenges facing companies in this area of process management are less technological than organizational and human. Like any new technology, blockchain is an idea that initially disrupts; it is a double-edged sword on one side, a tool for individual liberation or emancipation; a means of promoting collaboration between different actors, through distributed coordination and consensus mechanisms. On the other hand, a technology that can be used primarily by criminals, eager to evade the rule of law by relying on infrastructures that operate beyond the control of any sovereign authority. And since this technology is still in the research and development stage, most of the studies presented in this article are exploratory in nature and seek to apply basic principles, identify likely trends, and provide education and training programs adequate training for mastery. Education and training in blockchain technology therefore have a key role to play in understanding its mass adoption.

Education is undoubtedly one of the first factors that will ensure that the technological transformation of the 21st century is not missed, given the various future trends in this technology represented in the following, [22]:

- The trend of coding research and development will focus more on the ability to process big data fast.
- Hardware blockchain technology will spread the big data market by improving data speed and security.
- Technologies related to future applications will be developed in close collaboration with encryption techniques, which are an essential part of artificial intelligence and the Internet of Things.
- Exchange-related technologies will focus on solving problems in cryptocurrency transactions.
- Other sections of digital transaction technologies will focus on big data processing.

Each technology has limits in its use, concerning the blockchain there are limits in terms of privacy, the environment, inclusion, its threat to democracy and citizenship, [17].

Finally, the most important factor in the promotion of blockchain technology and their legalization is the commitment of the state in the formation of digital societies.

REFERENCES

[1] N. Pokrovskaia, A. Spivak and O. Snisarenko, "Developing Global Qualification-Competencies, Ledger on Blockchain Platform," Conference: 2018 XVII Russian Scientific and Practical Conference on Planning and Teaching Engineering Staff for the Industrial and Economic Complex of the Region (PTES), doi:10.1109/PTES.2018.8604177.

[2] L.Liu, M.Han, Y. Zhou, and M. Parizi, "E2C-Chain: A Two-stage Incentive Education, Employment and Skill Certification Blockchain," 2019 IEEE International Conference on Blockchain (Blockchain), doi :10.1109/Blockchain. 2019.00027 Corpus ID: 209854554.

[3] N.Miloslavskaya and A.Tolstoy, "Blockchain and Its Security: Ignore or Insert into Academic Training?," IFIP International Federation for Information Processing 2019, pp. 102–113, 2019. Published by Springer Nature Switzerland AG 2019, doi.org/10.1007/978-3-030-23451-5_8.

[4] G.N.Takigawa, O.B. Skorodumova, and I.M. Melikov, "application of blockchain technologies, crowdsourcing and artificial intelligence in student training review," compusoft, An international journal of advanced computer technology, 9(10),October-2020, https://ijact.in/index.php/ijact/article/view/1251.

[5] H.Onik, H. Miraz, and C.Kim, "A Recruitment and Human Resource Management Technique Using Blockchain Technology for Industry 4.0," in Proceeding of Smart Cities Symposium (SCS-2018), Manama, Bahrain, 2018, pp. 11-16.IET. doi: 10.1049/cp.2018.1371.

[6] K.C. Benson, B.Tran, and L.Jonassen, "Pedagogy of Blockchain: Training College Students on the Basics of Blockchain," International Journal of Engineering Research & Technology (IJERT), ISSN: 2278-0181, Vol. 7 Issue 05, May-2018, pp. 11-16.IET.

[7] C.Chen et al. "Strategy of Training Blockchain Talents in Application-oriented Universities: A Case Study," 2019 9th International Conference on Education, Management, and Computer (ICEMC 2019), Francis Academic Press, UK, doi:10.25236/icemc.2019.087.

[8] P.Williams, "Does competency-based education with blockchain signal a new mission for universities?," Journal of Higher Education Policy and Management, ISSN: 1360-080X (2018), doi:10.1080/1360080X.2018.1520491.

[9] B.Wu and Y.Li, "Design of Evaluation System for Digital Education Operational Skill Competition Based on Blockchain," 2018 IEEE 15th International Conference on e-Business Engineering. 978-1-5386-7992-0/18/$31.00, doi:10.1109/ICEBE.2018.00025.

[10] D.Dariusz, K.Paweł, P.Dariusz, S.Janusz, and T.Jan, "Conceptual Model of Personal Competence Integrator Based on Blockchain Technology," Americas Conference on Information Systems (AMCIS) 2020 at AIS Electronic Library, https://aisel.aisnet.org/amcis2020

[11] O.Fachrunnisa and F.K. Hussain, "Blockchain-based human resource management practices for mitigating skills and competencies gap in workforce," International Journal of Engineering Business Management, Volume 12: 1–112020, journals.sagepub.com/home/enb, doi:10.1177/1847979020966400.

[12] M.M.Milovanova, T.S.Markova, V.A.Mushrub, M.E.Ordynskaya, and J. V.Plaksa, "Business education: training in the use of blockchain technology for business development," ISSN 0719-4706 volumen 7 – número especial – julio/septiembre 2020, pp. 408-420.

[13] F.Prager, J.Martinez, and C.Cagle, " Blockchain and Regional Workforce Development: Identifying Opportunities and Training Needs," ISSN 2512-1812, Public Administration and Information Technology, ISBN 978-3-030-55745-4, Springer Nature Switzerland AG 2021, doi:org/10.1007/978-3-030-55746-1.

[14] A.Mittal, M.P. Gupta , M.Chaturvedi , S.R. Chansarkar, and S.Gupta, "Cybersecurity Enhancement through Blockchain Training (CEBT) –A serious game approach," International Journal of Information Management Data Insights 1 (2021), doi:org/10.1016/j.jjimei.2020.100001. http://creativecommons.org/licenses/by-nc-nd/4.0/.

[15] I.Alarab, S.Prakoonwit, and M.I.Nacer, "Competence of Graph Convolutional Networks for Anti-Money Laundering in Bitcoin Blockchain," Conference Paper June 2020, doi: 10.1145/3409073.3409080, https://www.researchgate.net/publication/343301363.

[16] J.Toledano and L.Janin" The challenges of blockchains," france stratégie, juin 2018, www.strategie.gouv.fr.

[17] M.Pignel and D.Stokkink, " Blockchain technology An opportunity for the social economy?," Notes d'analyse, juin 19 Économie sociale.

[18] Rapport sur la technologie et l'innovation 2018 " Cutting-edge technologies for sustainable development, " , Publication des Nations Unies établie par la Conférence des Nations Unies sur le commerce et le développement.

[19] P.Coëtlogon et al. "Les technologies blockchain au service du secteur public," HAL Id: hal-03232816, https://hal.archives-ouvertes.fr/hal-03232816, Preprint submitted on 22 May 2021.

[20] https://www.sciencedirect.com/science/article/abs/pii/S1574013720300241.

[21] Kitchenham B. et al. , 2007, Guidelines for performing Systematic Literature Reviews in Software Engineering, Version 2.3, EBSE Technical Report, Software Engineering Group School of Computer Science and Mathematics, Keele University, UK, and Department of Computer Science, University of Durham, UK.

[22] S. Kim, S. Yoon, N. Raghavan, N. -T. Le and H. Park, "Developmental Trajectories in Blockchain Technology Using Patent-Based Knowledge Network Analysis," in IEEE Access, vol. 9, pp. 44704-44717, 2021, doi: 10.1109/ACCESS.2021.3066573.

[23] A. M.J. Skulimowski, " Future Trends of Intelligent Decision Support Systems and Models," June 2011, Communications in Computer and Information Science Vol.2.:pp.11-20, doi:10.1007/978-3-642-22333-4_2.

[24] V. Faure-muntian, M. Claude, and M. Ronan, "Issues of Technological Blockchains (Chain Block)," Parliamentary Office for Evaluation of Scientific and Technological, n° 584 (2017-2018) - 20 juin 2018.

[25] https://cryptoast.fr/etude-linkedin-la-blockchain-est-la-competence-la-plus-demandee-par-les-employeurs-en-2020/